The works of Lucian, translated from the Greek, by several eminent hands. ... With the life of Lucian, a discourse on his writings, and a character of some of the present translators. Written by John Dryden, ... Volume 2 of 4

of Samosata Lucian

PRINT EDITIONS

The works of Lucian, translated from the Greek, by several eminent hands. ... With the life of Lucian, a discourse on his writings, and a character of some of the present translators. Written by John Dryden, ... Volume 2 of 4

Lucian, of Samosata
ESTCID: T112839

The imprint to 'The second volume of the works of Lucian' reads: "printed for Samuel Briscoe, and sold by James Woodward", 1710; the imprint to 'The third volume of the works of Lucian' reads: "printed for, and sold by James Woodward", 1711; the imprint t
London : printed for Sam. Briscoe, and sold by J. Woodward, and J. Morphew, 1710-11.
4v.,plate : port. ; 8°

Eighteenth Century
Collections Online
Print Editions

Gale ECCO Print Editions

Relive history with *Eighteenth Century Collections Online*, now available in print for the independent historian and collector. This series includes the most significant English-language and foreign-language works printed in Great Britain during the eighteenth century, and is organized in seven different subject areas including literature and language; medicine, science, and technology; and religion and philosophy. The collection also includes thousands of important works from the Americas.

The eighteenth century has been called "The Age of Enlightenment." It was a period of rapid advance in print culture and publishing, in world exploration, and in the rapid growth of science and technology – all of which had a profound impact on the political and cultural landscape. At the end of the century the American Revolution, French Revolution and Industrial Revolution, perhaps three of the most significant events in modern history, set in motion developments that eventually dominated world political, economic, and social life.

In a groundbreaking effort, Gale initiated a revolution of its own: digitization of epic proportions to preserve these invaluable works in the largest online archive of its kind. Contributions from major world libraries constitute over 175,000 original printed works. Scanned images of the actual pages, rather than transcriptions, recreate the works *as they first appeared.*

Now for the first time, these high-quality digital scans of original works are available via print-on-demand, making them readily accessible to libraries, students, independent scholars, and readers of all ages.

For our initial release we have created seven robust collections to form one the world's most comprehensive catalogs of 18th century works.

Initial Gale ECCO Print Editions collections include:

History and Geography
Rich in titles on English life and social history, this collection spans the world as it was known to eighteenth-century historians and explorers. Titles include a wealth of travel accounts and diaries, histories of nations from throughout the world, and maps and charts of a world that was still being discovered. Students of the War of American Independence will find fascinating accounts from the British side of conflict.

Social Science

Delve into what it was like to live during the eighteenth century by reading the first-hand accounts of everyday people, including city dwellers and farmers, businessmen and bankers, artisans and merchants, artists and their patrons, politicians and their constituents. Original texts make the American, French, and Industrial revolutions vividly contemporary.

Medicine, Science and Technology

Medical theory and practice of the 1700s developed rapidly, as is evidenced by the extensive collection, which includes descriptions of diseases, their conditions, and treatments. Books on science and technology, agriculture, military technology, natural philosophy, even cookbooks, are all contained here.

Literature and Language

Western literary study flows out of eighteenth-century works by Alexander Pope, Daniel Defoe, Henry Fielding, Frances Burney, Denis Diderot, Johann Gottfried Herder, Johann Wolfgang von Goethe, and others. Experience the birth of the modern novel, or compare the development of language using dictionaries and grammar discourses.

Religion and Philosophy

The Age of Enlightenment profoundly enriched religious and philosophical understanding and continues to influence present-day thinking. Works collected here include masterpieces by David Hume, Immanuel Kant, and Jean-Jacques Rousseau, as well as religious sermons and moral debates on the issues of the day, such as the slave trade. The Age of Reason saw conflict between Protestantism and Catholicism transformed into one between faith and logic -- a debate that continues in the twenty-first century.

Law and Reference

This collection reveals the history of English common law and Empire law in a vastly changing world of British expansion. Dominating the legal field is the *Commentaries of the Law of England* by Sir William Blackstone, which first appeared in 1765. Reference works such as almanacs and catalogues continue to educate us by revealing the day-to-day workings of society.

Fine Arts

The eighteenth-century fascination with Greek and Roman antiquity followed the systematic excavation of the ruins at Pompeii and Herculaneum in southern Italy; and after 1750 a neoclassical style dominated all artistic fields. The titles here trace developments in mostly English-language works on painting, sculpture, architecture, music, theater, and other disciplines. Instructional works on musical instruments, catalogs of art objects, comic operas, and more are also included.

The BiblioLife Network

This project was made possible in part by the BiblioLife Network (BLN), a project aimed at addressing some of the huge challenges facing book preservationists around the world. The BLN includes libraries, library networks, archives, subject matter experts, online communities and library service providers. We believe every book ever published should be available as a high-quality print reproduction; printed on-demand anywhere in the world. This insures the ongoing accessibility of the content and helps generate sustainable revenue for the libraries and organizations that work to preserve these important materials.

The following book is in the "public domain" and represents an authentic reproduction of the text as printed by the original publisher. While we have attempted to accurately maintain the integrity of the original work, there are sometimes problems with the original work or the micro-film from which the books were digitized. This can result in minor errors in reproduction. Possible imperfections include missing and blurred pages, poor pictures, markings and other reproduction issues beyond our control. Because this work is culturally important, we have made it available as part of our commitment to protecting, preserving, and promoting the world's literature.

GUIDE TO FOLD-OUTS MAPS and OVERSIZED IMAGES

The book you are reading was digitized from microfilm captured over the past thirty to forty years. Years after the creation of the original microfilm, the book was converted to digital files and made available in an online database.

In an online database, page images do not need to conform to the size restrictions found in a printed book. When converting these images back into a printed bound book, the page sizes are standardized in ways that maintain the detail of the original. For large images, such as fold-out maps, the original page image is split into two or more pages

Guidelines used to determine how to split the page image follows:

• Some images are split vertically; large images require vertical and horizontal splits.
• For horizontal splits, the content is split left to right.
• For vertical splits, the content is split from top to bottom.
• For both vertical and horizontal splits, the image is processed from top left to bottom right.

THE
Second Volume
OF THE
WORKS
OF
LUCIAN.

Tranflated from the GREEK

BY

Several Eminent Hands.

LONDON,

Printed for SAMUEL BRISCOE, and Sold by
JAMES WOODWARD, in St. *Chriftopher's*
Church-Yard, near the *Royal Exchange,* 1710.

TO THE

Right HONOURABLE

Sir Thomas Manfel,

of Margam *Bar.*

One of the Lords Com-
miffioners, *of Her Ma-*
jefties Treafury.

S I R,

THE Honour I have had of
knowing you fo long, and
the Publick Teftimonies you have
given of thofe Admirable Accomplifhments, which have engag'd
Her *Majefties* eminent Care of
the Publick good, to place you in
a Poft of fuch Confequence to
the Service of the Nation, wou'd
nor

not permit me to lose this Occasion of paying my Acknow-
ledgments to you by this Present,
which I presume worthy of the
Acceptation of a Person, of Sir *Thomas* *Kensels* Wit, and Penetration.

I need say little of an Author,
whose Merit is so well known, and
less of a Patron, whose daily Actions Witness how worthy he is
of such an Author.

The Learned and the Ingenious of every Age, and Nation
are Vouchers of the first, and we
are all Living Witnesses of the
later. As he was the brightest
Spirit of his time, so it is but just
that the bright Spirits of our's
should affor'd him a Protection,
when he visits us in a Language
that was unknown to him. Whatever Disadvantage he may have
in an *English Garb*, I do not doubt
but

but that the Gentlemen concern'd in this Translation, have taken care to make it up by maintaining the Wit, and Vigour of his Sense.

A Learn'd Gentleman of my Acquaintance, has observ'd that it may reasonably be suppos'd, that the Popular Scene of the Grave-maker in *Shakespear*, was borrow'd from *Lucian's Dialogues of the Dead*; at least that a hint of that was taken from them. This is certain, that the *Timon* of the same *Poet*, is visibly borrow'd from the *Timon* of *Lucian*. How those Gentlemen will Solve this difficulty, who allow *Shakespear* no manner of Learning, I know not; but the Author of the Notes on that *Poets* Plays, has proved this beyond Controversie.

Sir,

The Epistle Dedicatory.

Sir, I know very well that the Business of Dedications is the Praise of the Gentlemen, to whom we address, but I am too Conscious of my own Inabilitie of saying Things worthy of Sir *Thomas Mansel*, to attempt a Task, which, if never so well discharg'd, wou'd offend my Patrons Modesty, all the while, it pleased the rest of the World. I shall therefore say nothing of your Judgment, Generosity, Sense, and Zeal, for the Publick Good, and those other Qualities, which brighten your Character, but only beg leave to Shelter this Second Volume of *Lucian*, under your Protection, and assure you, Sir, that I am proud to Subscribe my self.

S I R,

Your most humble,

and Obedient Servant,

SAM. BRISCOE.

The Contents of the Second Volume of LUCIAN's Works, translated from the Greek by several Hands.

The Contents.

The Contents.

Hermo-

The Contents.

THE
PREFACE
TO THE
Second Volume
OF
Lucian's Works

THERE can be nothing of Consequence added to what Mr.
Dryden has said of *Lucian* and his
Works. I shall therefore only prefix to this
Second Volume something about the Rise,
Progress and Excellence of Translation,
by which the Reader may be able to
form a Judgement of a Performance
of this Nature. The *Greeks*, whether
instructed Originally by the *Ægyptians* or
Phænicians, were the Fathers of Politeness
and Learning in *Europe*; and I doubt
not but the great Progress they made in

all

all forts of Literature was in fome Meafure owing to their Writing on them in
their own Mother-Tongue. For tho'
we Read of many of their Sages, as
well as *Pythagoras, Plato, Plutarch,* &c. who
travell'd into *Ægypt* for Enquiry into the
Myfteries of their Doctrines, yet we
find no Record of any Tranflations
from them or the *Chaldeans,* to whofe
Country the Defire of an Infight into
the Abftrufer Knowledge invited fome
Greeks to Travel. For their Doctrines
feem to have been Conveyed, like thofe
of the *Druids* of *Gaul,* and *Britain,* by a
Traditional Delivery without Writing.
And this feems to have been followed by
Pythagoras. Befides the *Ægyptians* had
the ufe of Letters late, (in regard to
their Antiquity) all in their earlier Days
being expreffed by the *Hieroglyphics.*

Thus a Native of *Greece* was not
oblig'd to the ftudy of a Foreign, or
dead Language for ten Years, before
he cou'd come to apply himfelf to
Things and Arts; and that Pedantique
Pretence to Learning, now in fuch
Efteem, the Knowledge of a Speech
they had no ufe for, was then not
known. The young Student being
fufficiently Inftructed by Nature and

a

The PREFACE.

a little Infight into the Propriety of his own Tongue, apply'd himfelf immediately to the Study of Art; and as that made its early Impreffion on their Minds, their Progrefs in it was Greater and more Swift, than now a-days.

When the *Roman* Power had fubdu'd moft part of *Europe*, *Afia* and *Africa*, *Greece* fell into her Subjection. But by the Force of her Learning, and the Glory of her Arts fhe Vanquifhed the Minds of her Conquerors fo far, as to become the Miftrefs of the *Romans* in Knowledge. *Philofophy* was by the *Grecians* taught the *Romans* in *Greek*, and Ignorance was the Portion of thofe who apply'd not themfelves to the Study of that Language.

Cicero was the firft who endeavoured to free his Countrymen from that Yoke, and began to Write of Phylofophy in *Latin*, he and others tranflating not only the Books but the Terms of Art, that *Philofophy* might be Learned without the previous Study of the Terms of a Foreign and Conquer'd Nation. But *Livius Andronicus*, a *Greek* by Birth, and *Terence* (to fay nothing of *Plautus*) Tranflated the Plays of the *Greek* Poets
with

with Applaufe; and one of the fineft
Pieces of *Catullus* is a Tranflation of
that Ode of *Sappho*, which is ftill Extant.
The later Ages of the *Romans* produced
many Tranflations of the *Greek* Authors,
tho' the People ran fo much in Love
with *Greek*, that they chofe rather to
Write in that Tongue, than in their
own; for then the Vanity of Writing
in a Language not commonly known
prevail'd.

After the Reftoration of Learning
by *Cofmo* and *Lorenzo di Medici*, (who
had fav'd many *Greek* Manufcripts from
the Inundation of the *Turks*, when they
took *Conftantinople* and over-run that
part of *Europe*,) feveral of the *Greeks*
who fled into *Italy* fet up for Mafters
and Inftructors of thofe, who defired to
be capable of reading thefe Authors in
their own Native Drefs. And then began not only many Eminent *Comments*
but feveral Tranflations of *Plutarch*, *Homer*,
Thucydides and others. This was fuc-
ceeded by a Review of the Celebrated
Latins, who now began to appear in
the feveral Modern Tongues.

Among all Nations, who have made
a Progrefs in this Art, none have done

it with greater Application, than the *French*. They have translated almost all the Books of any Consequence in *History*, *Poetry*, *Philosophy*, that are to be found among the Ancients, nay, and the most Valuable of the Moderns. Some of them have made it the Business of their Lives to give a good Version of some one Author. But in *England* we have gon upon a very Wrong Foot. For tho' our Translations from all Languages are perhaps more Numerous, than of any other Nation, yet the Performances for the most part are inferiour to them all. The Reason is very Plain. The Bookfellers are here the Undertakers, and (their Vent being so very small) are oblig'd to Employ those to translate, who will do it for the least Money. And this has made many apply themselves to this Work, who scarce know the Parts of Speech in any Language. For the Bookfellers Market depending upon Titles, they value little the Performance, provided a Plausible Title carries off the Impression, for they little expect a Second Edition. How few Men translate for Fame? Reputation is the fartheft of their Thoughts, a servile Price of their Scrible is the Heighth of their Ambition.   The

The PREFACE.

This being the Source of our Ill Tranflations, I fee no end of the Scandal,
unlefs a Juft Encouragement of Men of
Judgement were fixt, by which only
thofe, who are Mafters not only of the
Language they tranflate from, and the
Language they tranflate into, but alfo
of the Subject each Author they attempt
difcourfes of. For I have known Gentlemen tranflate Books of Chyrurgery,
Mathematicks, Phyfick and the like,
who knew no more of the Terms of
the Art when they fet to their Woik
than a *Laplander*, and trufted to the
help of their Dictionaries in fo nice a
Part of their Performance.

But this can only be remedy'd by the
Eftablifhment of an Academy of Sciences upon fuch a Fund, that all Valuable Books may be made to Speak Eng-
lifh with the utmoft Accuracy, by Men,
who may apply their whole Study to
render their Authors, having a Comfor
table Support while they are labour
ing for the Publick Service.

By this means our People might arrive at all manner of Sciences in their
Mother-Tongue, and Knowledge the
                              Pi efei ve:

The PREFACE.

Preferver of Liberty fpread Wide among the People.

Having faid this of the Rule, Progrefs and prefent State of Tranflation, I muft repeat a Hint or Two, that has been touch'd on in the Life about forming a true Judgement of the Performances of this kind.

Every Language has its peculiar Beauty that is not Communicable with another Tongue; befides fome *Idioms* which cannot be tranflated without Abfurdity. The Tranflator ought therefore chiefly to mind the Senfe of the Author, and endeavour to Exprefs that with Beauty and Energy in the Speech he tranflates into, which he cannot mifs if he be Mafter of his Subject, and of both the Languages, and ufe a Juft Application. And he is but a very fuperficial Hypercritic, who will cavil at the Interpretation of a Word, as not fully Exprefled, provided the Senfe of the Author be fo. For a Verbatim Tranflation muft always be a Wretched Performance.

This is the Meafure of Judgement the Reader ought to obferve in the prefent, as well, as in all other Tranflations, and ought to pafs his cenfure in thefe Particulars after a Juft Weighing of every Point in both Languages. For he that cannot do this is no proper Judge of this Caufe, becaufe he cannot hear both Sides; and that is an Injuftice, taken notice of by our Author in his Oration againft Calumny, and will hold as ftrongly in the particular under our Confideration. 'Tis true, the Fate of an Author is harder, than that of the greateft Criminal, he is not only often Condemned without being heard, but even by thofe, who do not underftand the Merits, or Demerits of his Caufe; yet knowing what he has to expect when he Launches out, he has no Reafon to Complain of the Storm.

I muft advertife the Reader that the Life of *Lucian* was Writ by Mr. *Dryden* near fifteen Years ago, for fo long has this Book been doing; and if any one doubt the Truth, he may convince himfelf by a View of the Copy at the Publifhers.

The

THE
SECOND VOLUME
OF THE
WORKS
OF
LUCIAN.

Tranflated by feveral Hands.

CHARIDEMUS:

OR

Of BEAUTY.

By J. Drake, *M. D. F. R. S*

The Argument.

This D.alogue contains the Praife of Beauty, di-
vided into Three Orations, as handled by three
diftinct Perfons at a Feaft ; the two firft that
fpeak extol the Excellence and Dignity of Beau-

B   *ty,*

ty, by the Examples of many Gods and Men.
The last shews the Force and Effect of it from a
mutual Collation of it, with the other Virtues,
and those other Things which are commonly
reckoned among G O O D S.

Interlocutors.

Hermippus and *Charidemus*.

Hermippus. I Happen'd Yesterday, *Charidemus*, to take a Walk into
the Suburbs, and out parts
of the City, both for the
sake of breathing the fresh Air of the Fields,
and of the Quiet and Retreat of the Place
from the Noise and Hurry of the Town, because I was then ingag'd in Reflection and
Study. I there met *Proxemus*, the Son of *Epi-
crates* Saluting him, as I used to do, and
asking him the usual Questions of *Whence
come you?* and, *Whither go you?* he replied, that
he came to that place to refresh, and delight
himself according to his Custom, with the
Sight and Air of the Country. But that he
came from a Feast, that was set out in the
most elegant Order imaginable in the *Piraum*,
at the House of *Androcles*, the Son of *Epicha-
ris*, who had sacrificed to *Mercury*, in Ac-
knowledgment of the Victory he had obtained
on the reading a Book of his in the *Diasi*, or
Festivals of *Melichian Jove*. Among many
Polite Entertainments, which he describ'd,
he told me the praise of Beauty was celebrated by some of the Company; but accusing
the treachery of his Memory, now extreamly
fr ll

frail by Old Age; and his never having us'd it much to Difcourfes, he affur'd me he cou'd not tell me the Particulars, but referr'd me to you, who not only had a particular Regard to all that was faid the whole Night, but who alfo fpoke your felf in the Encomium I mentioned.

Charidemus. What you fay (*Hermippus*) is true, there was fuch a Difcourfe; yet it wou'd not be a little difficult for me to give you an exact and particular Account of all that was faid. For confidering the noife of the Servitors, and Guefts, it was not poffible for me to hear every Word, or to remember and carry away every thing that is faid at a Feaft. For the Confufion, the Company, and the Entertainment make thofe forget Particulars who are furnifh'd with the beft Memories. However to gratify your Curiofity, I fhall tell you all that I can remember, defrauding you of no part, that is in my Power to give you.

Hermip. I thank you for this Favour; but to make it the more compleat, if you'l inform me what that Book of *Androcles* was, and whom he overcame on the Recital of it, and laftly, Who were the Guefts he invited to the Feaft, you will double the Obligation and my Thanks.

Char. The Book was the Encomium or Praife of *Hercules*, compofed by him, as he faid, out of a Dream which he had, the Perfon he overcame was *Dietimus* of *Megara*, with whom he ftrugled hard for Glory.

Herm. But what was the Book which *Dio-timus* recited.

Char.

Char. The Praise of *Castor* and *Pollux*; This he said was defign'd as a grateful Return for feveral Deliverances, he avow'd to have received from thofe Gods, particularly for faving him at Sea, when they appear'd to him on the Sails of the Ship, when it was in the laft Danger. As for the Guefts they were numerous, and confifted partly of his Relations, and partly of his Friends and Acquaintance: But thofe who are worthy to be nam'd, and honour'd the whole Company, and who celebrated the praife of Beauty, was *Philo* the Son of *Denias*, and *Ariftippus* the Son of *Agafthenes*, and my felf: there was at the Table with us *Cleonymus*, the beautiful *Nephew* of *Androcles*, a Youth of a tender and delicate Compofition, who even then feem'd to have a ripe Underftanding and Genius, for he liftned with the utmoft Attention to all that was faid. *Philo* was the firft that began to fpeak of Beauty, with this Exordium.

Herm. Hold, my Dear Friend, before you begin your Encomium, pray let us know what was the occafion that gave Rife to this Difcourfe.

Cha. Indeed, my good Friend, your Queftions are a little out of the way, and delay my Account, which elfe might by this time have been finifhed, and we returning to the City, but allowances muft be made to the oportunity of a Friend, for whom a Man of Honour ought to do and fuffer any thing. The Origin of this Argument which you feek, and the Caufe which threw us upon it then was, Beauteous Youth *Cleonymus*. For, he

fitting

fitting betwixt me and *Androcles*, whose Nephew he was, the Vulgar and Unlearned at
the Feast turning all their Eyes with amazement on his Beauty, made it the important
Subject of their whole Discourse; nothing almost coming from their Mouths but Praises
and Encomiums on the Youth. Surpriz'd and
pleas'd with their zeal and love of Beauty,
and giving them their just Commendation
for it, it seem'd a sort of sloathful Ignominy
to be, as it were, vanquished and outdone
in Words by the Illiterate and Vulgar, especially on a Subject so agreeable as Beauty,
since we value our selves above them in our
Ability and faculty of Speaking. We did not
therefore think it proper to descend to the
particular Praises of this Youth by Name;
(for that had not been quite so Honourable
for our Beards, and it had been to raise him
to a greater Pride and Influence) but neither
yet shou'd our Discourse be so Disordered
and Irregular, and the rude Suggestions of
every Man's mind on that Head, with the
common interruption of Company and Conversation, but every one was in his turn to
say what ever he cou'd on the Subject, without Interruption. *Philo* therefore first began
in this manner:

It seems to my Conduct something Scandalous, that we close our Lips and sit Silent
on the Subject of Beauty it self, as if we were
really afraid to let fall the least word out of
our Mouths for the very things for which
we employ so much Labour; since there is
nothing which takes up the care and industry
of all our Days, but has something in it

which

which we esteem agreeable, and in some sense
Beautiful, as having Charms to engage our
pursuit. But what just Use do we make of
such, when we contend so mightily for things
of little Value, and say not a Syllable for that
which is the most Beauteous thing in the
World? Or how can that which is beautiful
in Words, be better preserved than all other
things, if we pass in Silence the end and
aim of those things which are daily done?
But lest I should seem to insinuate that I
know what regard we ought to have, and
how we ought to be affected to Beauty, but
can say nothing upon it my self, I shall endeavour, in as few words as I can, to deliver
my sentiments of the Matter: For Beauty
is what all Men are desirous of enjoying, tho'
they are very few who have perfectly obtain'd
it. Those who have been so lucky to possess
this admirable Gift, have been esteem'd the most
Happy of all, and have been Honoured both
by Gods and Men. These shall be the Proofs of
this Assertion. *Hercules, Castor,* and *Pollux,*
and *Helena,* and *Jupiter*; *Hercules* indeed is
said to have received this favour in consideration of his Valour and Fortitude; but after
Helena, when by the influence of her Beauty
she had chang'd her self into a Goddess, she
was the Cause and Motive of her Brother's
ascending into Heaven before her, being
freed from those things which other Mortals
are oblig'd to pass through under the Earth,
after their Death. Nor shall we be able to
find any one Example of any Mortal that
was thought worthy the familiarity of the
Gods, but such as were distinguished by Beauty

ty. For this was the Merit that rais'd *Pelops* to share with the Gods in their *Ambrosia*;
and this was the Reason that bore the *Trojan
Ganymed* aloft to mingle *Nectar* for the chief
of all the Gods; and for this cause *Jupiter* let
any other of the Gods share with them in
this sort of Chace, that is, his Amours, but
thought only fit for him to fly down to *Mount
Idea*, and thence Steal and Convey the Boy
lov'd, to that place where he shou'd enjoy
him time without end. But *Jupiter's* cue of
Beauty was always so great, and so conspicuous, that he has not only exalted the Pos-
sessours of it up to Heaven, but has himself
frequently, and whereever Beauty was to be
found, Descended to Earth to enjoy this Beloved in every Place. For the sake of this
he enjoy'd *Leda* in the shape of a Swan, and
Europa in the Form of a Bull; and transform-
ing himself into the shape and likeness of *Am-
phitryon*, he begot *Hercules*. But every body
can tell the various other Disguises *Jupiter*
put on, to come to the Embraces of those
he had a mind to possess. But what is the
greatest wonder of all, and most worthy of
Admiration-is, that when he convers'd and
had many Affairs with the Gods, (nor did he
ever converse with any Mortal but the Beautiful) and as often as he harangu'd them, *Homer*
makes them so Austere, that in his first Speech
he so terrified *Juno*, who used always to
plague him with her Tongue at other times,
and in all places, that she seem'd well pleas'd
that he kept his Anger within the Bounds of
Words. In the second Speech he no less affects all the Gods with Terrour at what he

said, threatning to lift up aloft the Earth, and Sea, and Men   But whenever he was to Encounter the Fair and Beautiful, he was Gentle, Tender and Kind, and render'd himself Equal to all : That he might not be Terrible, Troublesome, or Disagreeable to those he Lov'd, he laid aside that Majesty by which *he was *Jupiter*, and put on another Form, and that the most Beautiful, and which he thought the most Engaging to the Person that beheld him : So great is the Honour and Deference which he pays to Beauty.   But that what is said may not rather seem an Accusation of *Jupiter*'s singularity,   than a just Praise of Beauty, *Jove* was not the only God who was so captivated to it, for whoever will reflect and recollect the Accounts of those Matters, will easily find that the same Things have happen'd to all the other Gods; thus for Example, *Neptune* was in Love with the Beauteous Form of *Pelops*;   *Apollo* with *Hyacinthus*, and *Mercury* with *Cadmus*.

Nay, the very Goddesses themselves, have not been ashamed to avow their Subjection to Beauty, and own themselves Captive to it, but esteem it a Point of Honour and Emulation among themselves , as suppose she who had to do with some Handsome Fellow, shou'd tell that she had surrendred herself to Men.

Again, we do not find that the Goddesses ever fall out about the Functions and Particularities of their Offices on which each presides; but *Minerva* leads the Warriours to the Field, nor has the least Contest with *Diana* about her Province of Hunting; nor does

Diana meddle or make with *Minerva*'s Ranks and Files, and other Warlike Affairs, thus *Juno* yields the Nuptial Affairs to *Venus*, without any Regret, she having other Affairs to look after, o're which she presides.   But on the other hand, when Beauty is the Question, they are all out of Temper, and every one will needs excell the other, as each does in her own Opinion, as when *Eris* the Goddess of Quarrels had a mind to set them together by the Ears, all the Instrument she made use of was Beauty, being sufficiently assur'd that there was no surer way in the World to the end she proposed.   And her Invention was very Prudent and Judicious, and may demonstrate to any one the power and force of Beauty   For no sooner had they got the Golden Apple, and read the Inscription, that it shou'd be given to the most Beautiful, but every one wou'd needs have it her Due, nor being able to suffer any Suffrages against them to render one less considerable for Beauty than the other, they Appeal to *Jupiter* the Father of two of them, and the Husband of the third, to decide the Dispute   But he, tho' he might have pass'd Sentence himself of which was the most Beautiful of the Three, or might have refer'd it to many Stout, Wise, and Prudent Men, both in *Greece*, and among the *Barbarians*, he Delegates the Controversy to *Paris*, the Son of *Priam*, by that giving a clear Decision that Beauty surpasses Strength, Prudence, and Wisdom · Nay, they are always so fond of the Epithete of Beauty, and seek it with such Contention, that they prevailed with *Homer*, who Celebrates the Gods
and

and Men, to Adress 'em by the Names of Beauty rather than any thing else. Thus *Juno* is better pleas'd with the Title of *Snowy Arms* and *Bosom*, than that of the *Ancient Goddess*, and the Daughter of *Great Saturn*: Nor wou'd *Minerva* rather be call'd *Tritogenia*, or *Head-born*, than *Azure Eyed*, and *Venus* wou'd purchase the Name of *Golden* at the price of the whole Universe. All which Appellations have relation to Beauty.

But all these Instances are not only Arguments, and a manifestation of what regard Beauty is with the more powerful Beings, but bear infallible Witness incapable of Falshood, that Beauty is more excellent than all things else. Thus *Minerva*, who presides over Valour and Prudence, owns Beauty superiour to both, by her Contest for it; and *Juno*, by appealing to *Jove*, and calling *Jupiter* to her assistance, declares its worth the purchase of universal Empire and Power. But if Beauty be a thing so Divine and Adorable, and sought and affected with so Zealous a desire and Ambition by the Gods themselves, how can we act according to the Dignity of our Reason, if we do not in imitation of the Gods, both in Thing and Words defend Beauty to our Power?

Thus *Philo* ended his Discourse of Beauty, adding that it was not for want of more to say on this Suject, that he left off, but because he was sensible that a Feast was not a proper Place for Multiplicity of Words and a long Discourse.

When *Philo* was now silent at the earnest Entreaty of *Androcles*, *Aristippus* began: For he wou'd not at first be prevail'd on, being
afraid

afraid to follow *Philo* immediately. But he at last began in this manner.

Many Men do often (said he) neglect speaking of those things which are best, and to acrew a great deal of benefit and advantage, being drawn away to I know what kind of Arguments; from the handling which they promise themselves Fame and Reputation, but banter and confound their Hearers, with empty Words, without Loss or Profit.

Some accustom themselves to a war of Words, when they Treat of the same Things, Others Amuse themselves with Chimeras, and Things that have no real Existence, or are to be found any where but in the Fancy and Imagination of the Disputants, and Others are for handling Things which are of no Necessity, nor worth the Enquiry: Whereas, they all ought to quit Trifles, and consider how they may advance something of use to Mankind, if they are able to do it.

But since I am of Opinion that these Men know nothing of Things which have any real Existence, and at the same time think it a Folly in him who reprehends the Ignorance of others in the best Things, to fall into the same faults he Condemns, I shall propose the same most useful and beautiful Argument of my Discourse to my Hearers, and I know that every Man will allow that to be the most noble and worthy, which is granted to be the most Beautiful and Elegant.

Were our Enquiry therefore of any Thing but Beauty, it had been sufficient to have heard one Speaker on the same Subject, and quitting that to have call'd a new Cause, but

since the present Argument yields such a
plentiful Matter for Discourse, no Man ought
to imagine that he has miscarried in his Essay,
if he has come short of the Dignity and Co-
piousness of the Subject; but should believe
himself very fortunate to have been able to
add any thing to the former Praise, after the
precious Attempts of so many. For that
which is so manifestly held in perpetual Honour by our Superiours, and esteemed by Men
as a Divine Thing, and word, as our Labours, remains a peculiar Ornament to all
Men Living. Besides, we find that it makes
those who possess it be Lov'd and Courted by
all Men, and those who want it hated, and
unworthy to employ our Eyes. Who therefore is the Master of so great Eloquence, and
blest with such a faculty of speaking, that is
able to raise his Discourse up to the Dignity
of the Subject? But since it requires so many Panegyrists, and so great, that it can scarce
ever be handled equal to its Desert, I hope
it is not at all alien to my Duty, or unworthy
the Attempt for me to endeavour likewise
to say something of it, altho' I do not with
a little dread venture to speak after *Philo.*

Beauty is a Thing so Divine and so worthy
of Veneration above all other Things that
are besides in the World, that if we omit
those Honours paid to it by the Gods, we
shall not want sufficient Matter for its Praise.
In the days of our Forefathers, *Helena* the
Daughter of *Jove*, was so admired by all
Men, that e'er she was yet Ripe for Man,
made such a Conquest of *Theseus*, who came
into the *Peloponesus* on some other Errand,
that

that tho' he poſſeſt a Kingdom in great ſafe-
ty, and was happy in the firſt Rank of Glory,
yet on the firſt ſight of her he cou'd not
think all his good Fortune cou'd give any Re-
liſh to Life if he cou'd not be poſſeſſed of her;
but that having her he ſhou'd by vaſt Degrees
be the Happieſt of Mortal Men.

In the midſt of this Height of Paſſion he
was in the utmoſt Deſpair of obtaining her
of her Father, for he wou'd never give his
Conſent to her Marriage, before ſhe was of
ſufficient Age for that Eſtate. But contemning her Father's Empire, and the Force of
all the other Princes, who then reign'd in the
Peloponeſus, taking only *Perithous* with him, as
the Companion of his Rape, he carries her by
Force away to *Aphidna*, a City of *Arca*.
His love to *Perithous* for this Service, was ſo
great, and continued ſo firm all his Life after,
that the Friendſhip of *Theſeus* and *Perithous* is
left as an Example to all Poſterity. Afterwards, when *Perithous* was in Love with *Pro-
ſerpina*, the Daughter of *Ceres*, and was re-
ſolved to go down into the Kingdom of *Pluto*
in queſt of her, when all his Arguments and
Perſuaſions againſt ſo raſh an Attempt were
in vain, he thought himſelf oblig'd to go
along with him, and venture the greateſt
hazard of his Life for him.

But *Theſeus* being thus gon Abroad from his
own Country, *Helena* return'd to *Argos*, and
ſhe was now become Marriageable, tho' the
Grecian Princes cou'd have got themſelves
Wives enow of ſufficient Beauty, yet they
all came to *Argos* as Suitors to her, contemning all other Women as Vile and Deſpi-
cable.

cable. But knowing that there was no carrying her without the Combat, and fearing that from the fighting of particulars a general War might arise to all *Greece,* they all agreed to enter into this common Oath, that they wou'd all assist him with their Power and Arms who was thought worthy to have her for a Wife, nor to yield or agree with any one who shou'd insult or affront the Happy Man; every one believing he made this Security for himself. All therefore being disappointed of their Hopes by their own Sentence, except *Menelaus.* But they soon after gave Proofs of this common Compact For in a few Years the Contention of the three Goddess about Beauty happening, the Controversy was delegated to the decision of *Paris* the Son of *Priam*; who unable by the Weakness of his Judgment to distinguish between the Bodies of the Goddesses to the Advantage of either, was bribed by the Gifts that were offered to him to exert the Judge. *Juno*, offered him the Empire of all *Asia*; *Pallas*, Strength and Force in War; but *Venus*, this very *Helena* for Wife. Weighing the Bribes in his Mind, he considered that Empire often fell to the Lot of Vile and Contemptible Men, and Courage and Martial Prowess to Fools and Blockheads, but that *Helena* cou'd not be the Prize of any of those who succeeded, he preferr'd the Marriage of her to all other Considerations.

From this Cause afterwards arose that Famous War, and celebrated Expedition against the *Trojans*, and *Europe* being then first provok'd, and stir'd up to War against *Asia*, the *Trojans* might

might by the restoring of *Helena*, have possessed their Country in Peace and Security; and the *Grecians* leaving her to the quiet Possession of *Paris*, might have been free from all those Hazards, Fatigues, and Difficulties which are usually experienced in such Expeditions: But neither Party wou'd consult their own Ease, being persuaded that they cou'd not find out any better and more beautiful Cause of War, for which they might lay down their Lives.

Again, when the Gods knew that several of their Offspring were to perish in this War, were so far from deterring them from going to it, that they of their own accord oblig'd them to take up Arms, being of Opinion that they wou'd not obtain less Glory by dying for *Helena*, than by being Sons of the Gods.

But why shou'd we dwell on the Sons of the Gods, when the Gods themselves had greater Conflicts among themselves in that War, than in the impious Assaults of the Giants against their Heavenly Dwellings? For in the Giants Wars they were all of a side and yielded one another mutual Help and Assistance, but in this they were of contrary Parties, and bore Arms against each other. By what has been urg'd it is sufficiently manifest, and clearer than any thing else can be, that in the Opinion of the Gods themselves, that Beauty is the most excellent of all Human Things? For when they never had for any Human thing beside the least Difference among themselves, yet in the Cause of *Beauty* they have not only offer'd their Children to Death, but have fought with each other, and some of them received Wounds in their

Immortal Bodies· Muſt not all Mens Votes agree from hence that *Beauty* muſt be preferr'd to all other things in the Univerſe?

But leſt by dwelling ſo long on this particular we might ſeem to be confined by a Penury of Matter in the praiſe of Beauty, I ſhall paſs hence to another Topic not of leſs force for the Proof of the Excellence of Beauty, than what has been urg'd, that is, to *Hippodamia*, the Daughter of the *Arcadian Ocnomaus.* For how many has his Decree diſcovered more willing to offer themſelves to death, being vanquiſh'd by her Charms, than to behold the Sun and be depriv'd of her? *Hippodamia* being now arived to the Years of Marriage, her Father was not only ſenſible that her Beauty was far ſuperior to all her Contemporaries, but was himſelf in love with her. For this Perfection was ſo excellent in her as to be able in ſpight of Nature to ſubdue the Heart of her Father who begot her.

Deſirous of keeping her to himſelf, and yet to avoid the cenſure of the World, pretending an Intention to Match her to ſuch a one as ſhew'd himſelf worthy of her; he deviſed a Stratagem much more unjuſt than his Paſſion, by which he hop'd to bring his Deſigns about; for having caus'd a Chariot to be made with the utmoſt Art for Velocity, and procur'd the ſwifteſt Horſes of *Arcadia,* (where then were the fleeteſt in the World,) he would drive a Chariot with the Suiters of his Daughter, on this Condition, that he who vanquiſh'd him in the Race ſhou'd have the Lady, but he who was overcome ſhou'd loſe his Head. At the ſame time he commanded

his

his Daughter to be in the Chariot, that holding the Heart and fixing the Eyes of her Loves on her, they shou'd forget to manage and drive their Chariots.

But when the first who adventured on this unequal Race had been vanquish'd, and so fond to loose both his Mistress and his Life, the Rest, who remained, were not so ready to undertake the Contest, yet thought it little and childish to desist from what they had once resolved, and again detesting the Cruelty of *Oenomaus*, they prevented one another, each anticipating the turn of his Rival in dying, as if they had been afraid left they shou'd be deprived of the Opportunity of perishing for so beautiful a Virgin. This Slaughter reach'd thirteen of the Lovers; but the Gods abominating the Wickedness of the Father, and compassionating both the Daughter and her dead Adorers, these for loosing so great a Blessing, and her because she was deny'd the Enjoyment of her Youth, taking care of him who was next to enter the Race, (who was *Pelops*) they gave him a Chariot beyond all Art, and immortal Horses, by which he was to possess the Lady, and become her Lord, as he was, his Father-in-law, being slain at the Goal or end of the Race. So Divine a thing does Beauty seem to Mankind, and daily meets with the Adoration of all Men, and even of the Gods themselves.

No Man can therefore blame me with any Show of Justice, if I have thought it worth my while to say these things of Beauty.

C   Thus

Thus likewise *Aristippus* made an end of his Discourse.

Herm. You still remain, (O *Charidemus*) let us therefore have what you said on this Head as a Crown on these beautiful disquisitions on Beauty.

Char. I beg you by the Gods not to press me to go any farther, for it is sufficient that I have given you a Specimen of our Conversation, and related what I have already; especially since they owe some Defects to the Badness of my Memory. And a Man remembers with much more ease what another Man says in company, than what he says himself.

Herm. But this was what I from the beginning most desired to hear, not what others, but what you your self had said on this Subject; wherefore if you deprive me of this, assure your self you have spent all your Breath in vain, without affording me the most desired Satisfaction. But I beg you for the sake of *Mercury* himself, to relate to me all your Discourse from the beginning to the End.

Char. It wou'd be more safe and prudent in me to abstain from the most difficult part, and content my self with what is already said: yet since you are so importunate to hear my Speech likewise, I cannot help complying with your Desire. In the manner following, therefore, I delivered my self on this Head.

Had I been the first, who had spoke upon *Beauty*, I shou'd have been perhaps oblig'd to make use of frequent and close *Proemiums.* But since I am to speak after so many, I suppose it will not be foreign to make use of what they have said as a Preface to my following

ing

ing Difcourfe, efpecially fince they have been uttered in the fame day, and at the fame Table, as if no Man had made a private and particular Speech, but every one continued the fame Oration. What each of you have faid of Beauty wou'd really fuffice another to obtain Applaufe; but there is yet fo much behind to celebrate the Praife of Beauty, that thofe who are to come after us will find Matter enough for the Panegyric, without touching on any thing we have faid. For we are furrounded on every fide with Arguments which offer themfelves as firft worthy to be aken notice of, as in a Flowery Mead where the Flower that the Gatherer laft difcovers is yet the moft tempting to his Finger. But, I fhall, to comply with your Defires, and yet not tire you with my Prolixity, take notice with all the Brevity I am able of all thefe chofen Heads, which feem to me worthy of remark.

It is evident thofe who excel in Valour, or any other Virtue, if they do not by honourable Actions daily court the good Opinion of the World, and fo as it were force us to love them, the good Qualities they poffefs rather promote Envy than Good Will, and all things they do proceed with great Difficulty. But we are fo far from enving the Beautiful the Charms they poffefs, that we no fooner behold them but we are taken with them, and even more than love them, and we wou'd as much as in us lies ferve them, as our Superiours. Thus every Man had rather obey the Beauteous, than command the Ugly, and more pleas'd with the frequent Command of the Charmer, than in not being commanded at all, we are not so uneasy in the pursuit, not so insatiate in the Possession of all other Goods that we have occasion for, but in the pursuit of Beauty we are restless, and in the possession uncloy'd. Shou'd we excel the Beauty of *Nereus*, the Son of *Aglaia* who went with the *Grecians* to *Troy*, or the charming *Hyacinthus*, or the *Lacedemonian Narcissus*, we are afraid that Posterity shou'd think us out done by some others. Beauty is set as I may say almost as a certain common Example to Men in all the Actions and Affairs of Life. For the Leaders of Armies do not neglect a sort of Beauty in the Marshaling their Men; to this the Orators have an Eye in their Discourse, and the Painters observe it in their Pictures. But what shou'd we instance those things whose very End is Beauty? Nor are the things necessary for our daily Use, are not to be pass'd over in silence, since even in them we endeavour as much as possible to prepare in the most beautiful Form. For *Menelaus* had not only an Eye to the Use and Convenience of his Palace, but a particular care of the Beauty of it, so that the Front shou'd strike with Amazement the Beholder as they enter'd. That this is true we have the Son of *Ulysses* to witness, whose Admiration of them is celebrated in his search after his Father, as he expresses himself to *Pisistratus* the Son of *Nestor*.

This sure Great Jove's *Etherial Palace shines.*

For this Reason likewise his Father *Ulysses* had his Ships painted when he went with the *Greek* to *Troy*, by that to strike the Beholders

with

with Admiration. Thus let any one examine every Act, and he shall find *Beauty* is aim'd at by each, and that each arrives at Perfection as it obtains *Beauty*.

So great is the Excellence of *Beauty* above all things else, that whereas in all things that are done by Justice, Prudence, Fortitude, you will still find none but what has been or may be excelled by something else, and to which something is wanting to Perfection, and the full satisfaction of the Mind. But it is impossible to find any thing better and more perfect than those which have any Communication with *Beauty*, and on the other side, nothing more dishonourable and unworthy than those things which have no correspondence with *Beauty*. For we call nothing base, but that which is not beautiful, as if all the Qualifications a Man can have were of no manner of Value, tho' he excells others in them, if those Qualifications want their just *Beauty*, and Charms.

Since, therefore, *Beauty* is so venerable a thing, and is so much the aim of all Vows Wishes, and to be able to pay any Service to this is thought a sort of Gain and Advantage How can we avoid Censure, that when we may gain this Advantage we betray it, and not it all foreseeing and fearing the Loss.

Thus much I said of *Beauty*, omitting a great deal which I had to say, finding we had already spent so much time about it.

Herm. Happy were you, *Charidemus*, who enjoy'd such pleasing Discourses, and so happy a Conversation, nay I am not without my share of the Pleasure by the favour you have done me in the Relation. C 3 *PH-*

PHILOPATRIS:

OR, THE

LEARNER.

By the same Hand.

The Argument.

The Design of this Dialogue is a Compliment to Trajan on some Victory in the East. He attempts to Lash the Gods of the Gentiles, and the Christian Religion.

I must, as well as Mycillus, Apologize to the Reader for some part of the Translation, since the Original is extremely Obscure; but whether on Design by the unknown Author, or the Negligence of the Transcribers, I shall not determine.

I might likewise Apologize for Translating it at all, as being thought to Reflect on the primitive Christianity; but first it is not very Evident that it is design'd to Expose that; and next, the Weakness of these Things that seem to Reflect that way, are more for the Advantage than Disservice of Religion.

Interlocutors.

Treiphon, Critias, Cleolaus.

Treiph. WHAT's the matter, *Critias?* you seem to have metamorphosed your self into another Shape, contracting your Eyebrows backward; you seem to be wholy lost in Thought, and retir'd into the inmost Cabinet of your Breast, reeling and tumbling Head over Heels, as if, as the Poet terms it, you were playing *Christmas Gambols*, while a Paleness overspreads your Face. Have you any where seen *Cerberus* himself? or *Hecate* coming among us from Hell below? or have you unexpectedly fall'n on the View of any of the Gods? But indeed you ought not to be affected in this manner, were all this true, or had you seen the World sinking into a Deluge of Water, as it did in the time of *Ducalion.* What hoa! good *Critias!* I speak to you? What the duce do you not hear me when I call so loud, and am so near? What are you Angry with me? or are you Deaf? or do you stay till I give you a good thump on the Back?

Crit. Alas, my good Friend *Treiphon*, I have been hearing such a Discourse so monstrous and so variously handled, and was repeating those Trifles in my Memory, and shutting up my Ears, that I may never again hear such Stuff, but that I may grow stone with too much Madness, and like the *Niobe* of old furnish the Poet with a new Fable. I had fall'n headlong down a Precipe, my Head

C a turn-

turning round with a certain Vertigo, had not you, my Friend, call'd so loudly on me; and so the same Story might be made of me as was of *Cleombrotus's* leap into the Sea, as if he fought to find that Immortality he had read of in *Pluto's* Discourse of the Soul.

Treiph What wonderful Appearances or Narrations are these, that make so strange an Impression on *Critias* ? For how many mad Poets, and jugling Philosophers, have attempted to touch your Mind in vain, while you have thought all their endeavours meer Trifles, not worth minding ?

Crit. I prithee *Treiphon* be quiet a little, and trouble me no farther; for you are not to be contemnd or neglected by me.

Treiph. Nay, I am sensible that what you revolve thus in your Mind is neither a slight Matter, nor easily liable to Contempt, but I must needs say that it is an Arcanum, a mighty Mystery. For your Colour is of a sort of blewish Hue, and not being able to stand on your Leggs, but tumbling Heels over Head, makes you remarkable enough. But I prithee take a little Breath from the Evils that persecute you, and Disembogue those Trifles, that you may free yourself from any Pain in the Stomach.

Critias. But alas! good *Treiphon*, get you speedily at the distance at least of an Acre of Ground from me, least the Spirit should snatch you up on High, and being lifted above the Earth you become an Apparition amongst Men, and then falling down some where or other, you give the name of *Treiphontine* to some Sea, as *Icarus* did to the *Icarian*

of

of old. For what I have heard this day from those thrice execrable Sophists, have damnably turn'd my Stomach.

Treiph. Well, I'll get me back to what distance you please, do you but take some Breath from these Evils.

Critis. Fy, fy, fy, fy, those Trifles! alas! alas! alas! alas! Evil Consultations! Woe! woe! woe! woe! to vain Hope.

Treiph. Good Gods! What an Evaporation was here? what a Swelling? what a Tumour was there conceal'd within? what Tumults, what Strugles, what Agitations have shook thy Bowels? Why you have been all over Ears, that you have taken so much in as a Man wou'd imagine you heard ev'n at your Fingers ends.

Critias. But it is very admirable and surprizing, Oh, *Trephon,* that I shou'd hear at my Fingers ends when you found my Belly a perfect Bag-pipe, and my Head bringing forth; and the Male nature in effect passing into the Female, and then be chang'd from Women into birds. And in short, life it self is a prodigious thing, if we may believe the Poets.

But since I have met you in this place, let us step yonder into that *Plant we* shade, which binishes the Heat of the Sun Beams, and the Blackbirds and Swallows with their loud Notes enliven the Ears, by the Confort of the Birds, and the Waters gently falling are the Pebles, sooth our Minds with pleasing Murmurs.

Treiph. Thither let us go with all my Heart, O *Critias!* But I am afraid least what

you

you have heard be fome fort of Charm or En-
chantment, and that, that which put you into
fucha Confternation fhou'd turn meinto a Peftle,
or the Bar of a Door, or fome other inani-
mate thing.

Critias. As the Heavenly *Jupiter* fhall I ove
me, you fhall have no fuch Thing befal you.

Trieph. Poh, you have now frighted me more
now you have attefted *Jupiter* · For how can
he punifh you, and you not keep your Oath ?
For I fuppofe you are not ignorant of the nature and qualifications of this your *Jupiter* ?

Critis. What fay you Man ? Why can't
Jupiter ftrike me with his Thunder into Hell ?
Don't you know that he threw down all the
Gods from that Celeftial Floor ? And thus
he ftruck *Salmoneus* with a Thunder-Bolt, for
prefuming to mimick his Thunder, and thus
can't he punifh ev'ry one as he's Saucy now ?
Homer, and the reft of the Poets, make him
the Vanquifher of the *Titans,* and flayer of
the Giants, and as fuch, celebrate him in their
Verfes.

Trieph. 'Tis true, *Critias,* you have run
over all thefe Old Tales which you have
heard of the Achievements of *Jupiter,* but if
it be not too difagreeable to you, I defire you
wou'd a little liften to me. Has not his Luft
turn'd him into a Swan, a Satyr and a Bull.
And had not your Thundering, and Thunder-
Bolt darting *Jupiter* fcamper'd away with his
Whore on his Back with Expedition, I
don't know but he might ftill have been drawing the Plough, if he had fall'n into the Hands
of fome of the Farmers of that Country ; and
fo inftead of darting of Thunder-Bolts, he

wou'd

wou'd be himself driven on with a Goad.   Is not the Story of this Jaunt, to the Country of the *Ethiops*, a very Scandalous Thing, when it makes him feasting with those Sooty Fac'd Gentlemen for a matter of twelve Days together soaking his Gills in Sack, especially when so long a Beard betrays him to be at years of Discretion; but I am really asham'd, and blush to repeat his frolick of the Eagle and *Ida*, and that he used to be impregnated all over his Body.

Critus. Well then, shall I attest *Apollo*, who is both a great Prophet, and an admirable Physician.

Trieph. Do you mean that vain and lying Fortuneteller, who by obscure and ambigious Answers impos'd on and ruin'd *Crœsus*, and the *Salamines*, and innumerable others.

Critias. What say you to *Neptune*? who not only carries the *Trident*, but has a Voice so loud and terrible in War, that it exceeds that of a Thousand, nay, of ten Thousand Men; and is besides call'd the shaker of the Earth, or cause of Earthquakes

Trieph. What mean you that Adulterer, who formerly ravish'd and debauch'd *Tyro*, the Daughter of *Salmoneus*, and Whores on still, and is the Defender and Patron of such sort of Vicces? For when *Mars* was by *Vulcan* caught in Charms and Bands which cou'd not be loosed, while all the other Gods had not really so much Brass in their Face as to speak one word for him, *Equestrian Neptune*, spight of his Gravity, got him unty'd and set at Liberty, falling into abundance of sham Tears, like a Child in fear of his Master,

fter, or the old Wives, when they wou'd impose on the little Girls; with these, and earnest Prayers, he press'd the poor Cuckold *Vulcan*, till he yielded to undo the Chains of *Mars*, and set him free. And that limping Deities Bowels yearning at the Sobs of the ancient God, as *Neptune* comply'd with his Prayer, and deliver'd his Cuckold Maker, which is a proof that he is not only a Whoremaster, but a preserver of Whoremasters.

Critis. Well, what think you of *Mercury?*

Trieph. For shame, not a word of that hardned Thief, and Cheat, and the officious Pimp to all *Jupiter's* most salacious Hours; and himself mad in the pursuit of his Libidinous Adulteries.

Critis. At this Rate I find I have but little hopes that you will accept of *Venus*, or *Mars*, since you have already fall'n foul on them. Dismissing therefore these Obnoxious Deities, I shall venture to propose *Minerva*, a Virgin Goddess, and Arm'd, and Terrible, with the *Gorgons* Head affixt to her Bosom, the Giant Killer. I can't imagine that you have any thing to say against her; you can't say black is her Eye.

Trieph. Yes, I have something to say to her too, if you will Answer me a few Questions.

Critis. Speak your mind freely.

Treph. Tell me then, good *Critias*, what is the use of this *Gorgons* Head? and why is this placed on the Goddesses Bosom, for ornament or use?

Critis. As

Critis. As a terrible fight, and a Defence against any evil Thing, besides that, with this she terrifies the Enemy, and drives the doubtful Victory to which side she pleases.

Trieph. Is it then by this Monstrous Head that the azure Ey'd Maid becomes Invincible?

Critis. Certainly.

Trieph. Why then don't we rather chuse to pay our Sacrifices of Bulls and Goats to those which preserve and Defend, than to those who are only preserv'd and Defended, that so they wou'd render us invincible as well as *Minerva?*

Critic. Oh! Sir, you don't consider the Matter well, these Things have not the power to defend one at a distance, as the Gods have, but are only a security to those that bear them about them.

Trieph. But pray what is the very Thing of the *Gorgons* Head? for being intirely Ignorant my self of the Matter, I desire to be inform'd by you who have found out those Things, and are arriv'd to a perfection in your knowledge in them, for I am indeed ignorant of all the Stories which are told about of her.

Critis. Why *Gorgon* was a most beautiful and lovely Maid. But when *Perseus* had by Treachery cut of her Head, as a learned Person, and famous for Art, Magick, conjur'd by certain Verses and Charms this Head, and then the Gods took it to themselves, and preserv'd it as a Buckler, or Defence.

Trieph. This noble Maxime till now was a secret to me, that is, that the Gods stand in need of the assistance of Men out of

which

what ufe was fhe when alive? fhe play'd the
Whore about in Taverns, or in Private, and
then prtended herfelf a Virgin!

Critias. No, by the *unknown God at Athens,*
fhe remain'd a pure Virgin to the very Minute fhe loft her Head.

Trieph. So that if a Man cut off a Virgins
Head it will be a Bugbear to the Multitude?
For when I was in *Crete,* I faw abundance of
Virgins Beheaded, and had I known this Secret before, I cou'd have brought you a whole
Cargoe of *Gorgons,* and fo made you an invincible General. The Poets then and Orators wou'd have given me the preference to
Perfeus, as having found abundance of *Gorgons,* whereas he found but one. But having
accidentially mentioned *Crete,* by the By I
yet remember that there were People, that
fhew'd me the *Sepulchre* of your *Jupiter,* and
the obfcure Vallies which nourifh'd his Mother, where the Shrubs were yet Green.

Critias. But you did not know the Incan-
tation and Sacrifices which were to be made
ufe of

Trieph. If thefe Things had been done by
Incantations, they might perhaps have call'd
her out of the Shades below, to revifit the
cheerful Day; but thefe are Trifles, Follies,
Fables, continued by the Poets to Deceive.
Let us therefore pafs her likewife.

Critias. Well, but will you not admit
Juno, *Joves* Sifter and his Wife.

Trieph. Not a word of her, I befeech you,
that we may not reflect on her abominable
Conjunction with her Brother, fy, fly from
her with our utmoft fpeed.

Crit. Whoa

Critias. Whom then shall I invoke?

Trieph. God reigning on High, Great, E-
therial, Eternal, the Son of his Father, the
Spirit proceeding from the Father, one out
of Three, and Three out of One. This you
must esteem *Jupiter*, this you must look on as
God.

Critias. What you teach me Numeration,
and yours is an Arithmitical Oath. For you
number like *Nicomachus Gerasenus* For I profess I don't understand what you say, ---
Three One, One Three : What do you mean,
that *Pythagoric* Commander of Four, or Eight,
or Thirty?

Trieph. Hold your Peace, for what I have
yet to tell you, are worthy silence. This is
not the way of measuring the Footsteps of
Fleas; for I will teach you what the Universe
is, and who was before all Things, and what
is the Constitution and Body of the World;
for indeed I have met with that *Galilean* with
a Pate Bald behind, and an Aquiline Nose,
who cutting the Liquid Air penetrated into
the very Third Heaven, and there learned
all that was valuable and great, he renewed
us by Water, and made us walk in the Steps
of the Righteous, and redeemed us from the
Regions of the Impious. And assure your
self if you'l listen to me, I will truly make
you a Man.

Critias. Most learned *Treiphon*, go on with
your Discourse, for there is a sort of fear and
dread that has already seiz'd me.

Treiph. Did you ever read the Comedy of
Aristaphanes, call'd the Birds?

Crit. Cer-

Critias. Certainly, good Sir.

Treiph. In that you will find words to this purpose:

E're yet the World assum'd this beauteous Face,
Rude Chaos, night and gloomy shades took place,
And of deep Tartarus th' unbounded space:
For yet was neither Earth nor Air, nor Pole, &c.

Critias. Your quotation is true; but what of that?

Treiph. But there was a Light, Incorruptible, Invisible, and Incomprehensible, which dissolv'd the Darkness, and banish'd by one word that Deformity, as that slow Tongu'd Gentleman has Written: He fixt the Earth on the Waters, and spread the Heavens, form'd the fixt Stars, and order'd the Course of those Planets which you adore as Gods, He adorn'd the Earth with Flowers, and drew Man out of nothing into Being; and is now in Heaven, beholding both the Just and Unjust, and Writing down in a Book the Actions of every Man · And will repay to all on the Day that he has Commanded.

Critias. Do they insert in the Book all that the Fates decree for all Men

Treiph. I pray, good Friend *Critias,* give me an Account of these Fates; I'll listen to them with a very willing Ear.

Critias Does not the celebrated Poet *Homer* say,

Believe me, none their fate shall e're Escape

The same speaking of the great *Hercules,* says,   *Herculis*

Herculean force contends in vain with Fate,
Tho' to the Gods most dear, and Son of Jove,
Vanquish'd by Fate and partial Juno's *Hate,*
On Oeta's *top the Sting of Death did prove.*

Nay, the same Poet insinuates, that our whole Life, and all the Changes of it are form'd and ordain'd by Fate, when he says,

———— *Where he shall undergo*
Whatever God, or the malignant Fates
Have Wove for him in their Eternal Looms,
When first he left his Mothers general Womb.

He is of Opinion too, that Fate orders those delays of Journies in a Foreign Land, as when *Ulysses* said.

As when King Æolus with a gracious smile,
Had to his Country o're the rolling Tide
Convey'd him safe, but yet that Fate deny'd.

The Poet therefore proves, that all things are directed by Fate: and that *Jupiter*, rather than save his Son from Death at *Troy,* chose,

His bloody Tears from lofty Heaven to shower
For his Sons Death, beneath the Walls of Troy,
When him Patroclus *wou'd e're long destroy.*

Wherefore good *Treiphon* being satisfied with what I have said, I believe you wou'd not say a word more of the *fatal Sisters,* no, tho' you had been lifted aloft with your Master, and been initiated in the Misteries.

         D   *Trieph.* But,

Trieph. But, my friend *Critias*, how comes that Poet to assure us of a double and ambiguous Fate ? so that if a Man does such a thing, such shall be his Fate ; if he do another, another shall be his Fate ; as, when speaking of *Achilles*, he says,

> *My Mother* Thetis *for white Feet renound,*
> *A double Fate for me does thus propound :*
> *If here I stay beneath the Walls of* Troy,
> *And with this Arm the* Phrygian *Host annoy,*
> *I to my Country shall no more return,*
> *But after Death my Fame to Heaven be borne*
> *If to my Country I shou'd basely flie,*
> *My Glory, Honour, and my Fame shou'd die ;*
> *But in their place an Old inglorious Age*
> *I shou'd enjoy.* - - - - -

But he says of *Euchenor* ;

> *Who went to Sea not ignorant of Fate,*
> *For* Polidus *had told his future State,*
> *That he at home shou'd of Diseases die,*
> *Or slain by* Trojans *in the* Grecian *Camp shou'd*
>   (lie.

Are not these things written by *Homer?* or are they not ambiguous, and a doubtful Deception ? But if you please, I shall add the Speech of *Jupiter.* Did he not tell *Egisthus,* that if he abstain'd from the Adultery with his Sister, and the Treacherous Murther of his Brother, the Fates had ordain'd him a long and happy Life ; but that if he entertain'd Thoughts of committing those Evils, his Death was unavoidable. After this way of foretelling,

I

I have, my self, often play'd the Prophet,
viz. If you kill your Neighbour you shall
be condemned to Death; but if you no do not
this wickedness you'l live happily,

Nor shou'd you thus incur a speedy Fate.

By this you muſt certainly ſee, how little Cor-
rectneſs and Exactneſs there is in the Poets nay,
how oblique, uncertain, and ambiguous they
are, and fixt on no certain Bottom.　Throw
therefore aſide all thoſe things, that you may
be inſerted into the Celeſtial Books of the
Good.

Critias. You remember and deſcribe all
Things very well, my friend *Triepbon*, but
pray give me leave to ask you one Queſtion:
Are the Affairs and all the Tranſactions
of the *Scythians* writ down in this Book?

Trieph. All, if Chriſt has been in their
Country.

Critias. You make abundance of Scribes
and Clerks in Heaven, to ſet down ſuch a
multiplicity of Things.

Trieph. None of your Jeſts, good *Critias*, nor
ſpeak any thing vile, contemptuous of the
right God, but being a *Catechumen* or *Probatio-
ner*, if you deſire to live for ever, ſuffer me
to influence you with what I ſay.　For if he
ſpread the Heavens like a Hide, and fixt the
Earth and laid its Foundations on the Waters, and made Man out of Nothing, brought
him into Being, and to enjoy this Light, where
is the great Wonder that the Actions of all
Men ſhou'd be Enter'd and Regiſter'd in the
Heavenly Book? For, ſuppoſe you ſhould

　Build

Build a little House, and shou'd get together there a great many Man-Servants, and Maid-Servants, the least and most vile and inconfiderable thing that was done among them cou'd ever escape your Knowledge. How much easier therefore is it for that God who Created all Things, to run them over, and observe the Defigns and Actions of every one? For your Gods are look'd on by all Men of true Knowledge, to be no more than meer found and trifles of a Mechanick make.

Gi. What you say is very true, and in me the Fable of *Niobe* is inverted, for from a Stock and Stone, I'm turn'd into a Man. This God therefore I propose to you and fwear by that you shall not suffer any ill from me.

Tri. If you love me from your Heart, and your Friendfhip be fincere, I believe you will do me no Injury.

Nor will you one thing think another say.

But to the Point, and let us at last hear those wonderful and amazing Things which you had delivered to you, that I may likewife turn Pale, but I will not like *Niobe* become mute and filent, but be metamorphis'd into a Bird like *Philomela,* and chant out in a Tragical Tone in the Green Fields your furprizing Confternation.

Gi. No by the Son out of the Father, that shall not be.

Tri. Speak therefore you that receive from the Spirit the Power and Force of fpeaking, and I will fit here,

Waiting Achilles, *till his Song was done.*

Gr. Walking in the High-street to buy what I had occasion for, I spied a great Mob got together, and whispering something into one anothers Ears; and so greedy of hearing they were, that they seem'd to hang up on the Lips of those that spoke, casting therefore my Eyes about them, and looking carefully among them all to see if I could find any Friend or Acquaintance of mine, I discover'd *Crato* the Politician, one that from a Boy had been my Friend, and Companion, and Intimate Acquaintance.

Tri. I know him well, you mean the Comptroller; but what follow'd

Gr. Having remov'd a good many with my Elbow, I made my way into the Front of them, and after the first salute plac'd my self by him, but there was a little Dwarfish, Old, Lean Scoundrel, whose Name was *Charicenus,* who whistling at his Nose, he cough'd first something inwardly, and then spit out a sort of languid unconcocted matter, more blew and wan than Death, and after this Exordium or Prelude he began in small whining low Voice to speak in this manner. *This Man (as I said before) leaves the Tricks of the Overseers and Comptrollers, and shall pay the Usurers what is due to them, and all Pensions both Private and Publick; and will take any Pretension not Enquiring into any Mans Art*· Nay, he went on in more bitter Trifles than these; but those who were about him were very much delighted with his Words. There was besides, another

D 3　　　　　　　　such

such sort of Fellow, whose Name was *Chevo-chai amus*, whose Cloak was very Polish and Dirty, without any Shoes on his Feet, or Covering to his Head, who spoke betwixt whiles extreamly in his Praise, and grinning his Applause. --- As a certain Man who came out of the Mountains in bad Cloaths, his Head Shaved, show'd me, written in *Hierogliphyck*, that is, Secret and Misterious Letters in the Theatre, that this Man shou'd bring an Inundation of Gold and throw it into the High-way But, said I, according to the Rules of *Aristander*, and *Artimedorus*, these your Dreams will not have so happy an Event; but your Debts will be encreased according to the proportion of your Yearly Receipts; and that Fellow which was so rich and abounding in Gold, will be in very great need of a Farthing. But you seem to be lull'd into a slumber on the Rock *Leucas*, and Coasts of Dreams, and be so full of strange Visions, as if it were Midnight, and you were plac'd and chain'd on the Rock *Leucas*, and the Coast of Dreams. But I had no sooner done, but they all with one accord burst out into a great Laughter, as if they wou'd Choak themselves, and contemning me as Ignorant. But turning to *Crito*, I said, what have I made Enquiry into all Dreams like a Madman, to use the Phrase of the *Comic* Poet, and not according to *Aristander* and *Artimedorus*? Hold your Peace, reply'd he, *Critias*: For if you hold your Tongue, I will inform you in the most excellent of Sacred Rites, and let you know all future Things, These are no Dreams but Realities: And the Event you will find come

come to pass in the Month call'd *Mesori.*

Having heard *Crato* talk at this rate, and known their fickle Mind, I Blush'd, and departed with a Melancholly Countenance, abundantly accusing *Crato.* But one of the Gang looking on me with a fierce and Titanique Phiz, plucking me by the Coat, instigated by that ancient Deity and believing I had made a Covenant with him, he persuades unhappy me with abundance of Words to go to those Deceivers and Juggling Fellows, and incur the Black Day, as the Proverb has it, for he said he had learnt of them all things that related to the Sacred Rites and Misteries. And thus we past the Iron Gates and Brazen Entrance. Having mounted several Stairs, we got into a House, Illustrious for its Golden Roofs, like that of *Menelaus,* mentioned by *Homer,* and I took a view with Admiration of all those things, which surpriz'd the Insular Youth *Telemachus.* In my Entrance I saw not *Helena,* as he did, but a Company of palefac'd Fellows, with their Faces bow'd down to the Ground. When they saw us they were pleas'd, and came from the other side up to us. They ask'd me if I brought them any ill News? for they seem'd to wish for the worst, and were pleas'd with sorrowful and evil Events, as the Furies in the Theatre. Having joyned their Noddles together, and whispered among themselves a little while, they began to ask me these Questions, Who, what, and whence are you? What is your Country? Who were your Parents? for your Habit shows you to be frugal as far as I can find, said I, there are very few

that

that is, frugal, as far as I can find by all my
Obfervation faid I.   But my name is *Gritias*,
I am of the fame City as you.   But when
thofe fublime Fellows, and who walk in the
Air ask'd me what News from the World,
and how the Affairs of the City and the
World went, I anfwer'd very well, and are
very likely fo to continue.   But they with a
denying Brow faid, you are Sir miftaken in
the matter, the City is in Labour with Evil,
and her Birth will be miferable.   Then I reply'd in their way, you who are lifted above
the Earth aloft, and viewing e'ry thing as it
were from on High, have eafily attain'd the
knowledge of thefe things.   But I pray you
what News from above ?   how go Squares in
the Skye ?   will the Sun be Eclipfed, and the
Moon in a perpendicular be interpos'd ?   will
Mars in a Quadrangle have his Afpect to the
Sun ?   and *Saturn* do the fame in a Diameter ?
will *Venus* and *Mercury* be in Conjunction,
and beget more Hermaphrodites, with which
you are pleas'd ?   will they fend down impe-
tuous vehement Rains ?   will they Cloath the
Earth in Snow, and fcatter down Hail and
Blites on the Corn ?   will they fend down the
Plague and Famine ?   is that great Receptacle
of Thunder full ?   But they prefently gave me
for an Anfwer, that there wou'd immediately be a change of Things ; that Turmoils
and Tumults were juft coming to invade the
City , and that our Armies would fuddenly
be overcome by the Enemy. Difturb'd therefore at this Cant, and fwelling like the
Hen fet on Fire, I cry'd out with a loud
Voice, Oh ! ye moft miferable of Men, be

not thus puff'd up with a vain Loquaciouf-
nefs, fharpning and whetting your Teeth
againft Man, who feem to have the Souls of
Lions, breaking nothing but Darts and
Spears, and fhining in their Crefted Helmets;
but let all your falfe Bodings be thrown on
your own Heads, fince in fo vile a manner
you wou'd deprefs and run down your own
Native Country. For you have not heard
thefe Sinifter Events in your Journies into
the Skie, nor are you fuch expert Mafters of
Judicial Aftrology, and the fate of Affairs.
But if Prophecy and *Delufion* have impos'd
on you, you will incur and merit the double
name of Superftition and Ignorance. Thefe
are the foolifh Inventions of Women, and
old doating Haggs. For thefe are the pur-
fuits of Womans Cares and Solicitudes.

Trieph. Well, and what did thefe Wife
Men of *Gotham* fay to this, good *Critias* ?

Critias. They took no manner of notice of
what I faid, but return'd to thefe their
thoughts of their own Invention, and on
which they were throughly exercifed For,
faid they, let us Faft ten Days without Eating a Bit, and Singing Hymns all the Nights
we fhall Dream of thofe things

Trieph. Well, and what Replie made you
to them ? For they feem'd to promife a
thing very furprizing, and of wonderful di-
ficulty.

Critias. You may affure your felf my Anfwer was not poor and fearful, but brisk and
reafonable, I think. For what will be the
common Report of you, faid I, by the People, and when ever you Dream you deliver

such Monstrous Events? But they with a Doggish kind of a Grinn, lifted themselves a little off the place where they lay; but, continued I, if these things are true, O you Etherial Gentlemen, you will never be able with any security to enquire into Fatalities; but won by these Delusions you will trifle your time away with what neither are or ever will be in being. But I know not by what Infatuation bewitch'd you, put your Faith in Dreams, and abominate what is valuable and excellent in reality. You take delight in the misfortune of mankind, and do no manner of good, and reap no advantage from so great an Abomination. Distrust, therefore, those Foreign Imaginations, and those evil and deprav'd Counsels, and Prophaneness, least God delivers you over to Destruction, for devoting your Country to Misfortunes, and speak to it in adulterated and wicked Words.

But they being all of one mind, gave me a long and severe reprimand. I will, if you please, add those things which they utter'd, that almost turn'd me to a silent Stature, till your wholesome Voice restor'd me to my Manhood, when I was now almost become a Stone.

Trieph. Hold, hold *Critias,* not a word more, dwell no longer on such abominable fooleries as these, for you see how my Belly Swells, and I go like a Woman ready to lie in, for the words you have utter'd have bit me like a Mad Dog: And if I take not a Dose of Oblivion for a Salutiferous Medicine, they will dwell in my Memory, and
haunt

haunt me at Home, and produce some Misfortune to me. Let us therefore quit this Difcourfe with a Prayer, beginning from the Father, and end with that celebrated Verfe, as an Antidote againft the Poifon.   But what do I fee, is not that *Cleolaus* that Trips it fo faft along there?   In good earneft it is he that is a coming to us, fhall we call to him?

Critias. With all my Heart

Trieph. What, hoa! *Cleolaus*, pafs not your Friends with your over hafte, but come and let us participate if you bring any good News.

Cleo. Save ye Gentlemen, fave you ye admirable pair of Friends.

Trieph. What is the occafion of your great fpeed, for you feem quite out of Breath? is there any News more?

Cleo.   *That Eye of* Perfia *once is now no mo e.*
Sufa, *that City fam'd, can fall no lower.*
The noble foil of rich Arabia's *Town,*
By mighty force of Warlike Hords o'erthrown.

Critias.   This is a Proof that God does not always neglect the good, but encreafes their welfare, raifing them ftill to a higher pitch of Fortune.   But *Triephon*, we have made a noble Difcovery.   For I was very follicitous what I fhou'd bequeath to my Children at my Death.   For you know my Poverty, as I am througly acquainted with your Affairs. This happy day of our Emperor is a fufficient Legacy for my Children, nor fhall I ever now want Riches, or be frighted by the Peoples Murmurs and Vanity.

Trieph. Yes

Trieph. Yes, *Critias*, and this shall I leave to my Children, that they shall see *Babylon* over-thrown; *Egypt* reduc'd to Servitude; the *Persians* under the *Roman* Yoke; and the Excursions of the *Scythians* repress'd, and I cou'd wish entirely supprefs'd. But let us with our Hands lifted up to Heaven, adore that unknown Deity found at *Athens*, giving him hearty Thanks that he has thought us worthy to be subject to such a Power, and so much Virtue. Let us suffer those Ideots to play the fool, contenting our selves with that Proverb. -- *These things are none of the Cares of* Hippoclides.

On an Illiterate Fellow that Bought all sorts of Books.

By the same Hand.

This is an Invective *against a Person that had some how or other affronted him.*

YOU expect the Character of a great Scholar, because you have purchas'd a-bundance of Books, when, alas, it only makes thy Ignorance so much the more apparent. Books being altogether out of thy Element, you must wholly rely upon the Opinions of others; and as that is not always certain, so you'l find your self a meer Jest to Men of Sense.

Senſe, and a meer Bubble to your Bookſeller.
Prithee, how come you to be a Judge of
Books, unleſs 'tis from their Age? the eſti-
mate you make of them is proportio-
nable to their being Worm-eaten. But admitting you did know 'em, what good cou'd
this do you, ſince they are kept out of your
Depth, and you are as incapable to diſtinguiſh
the ſolid or the glittering Paſſages, as much
as a Blind Man is to diſtinguiſh Colours. You
ſtare indeed upon a Book, with all the Eyes
you have, and turn it over Leaf by Leaf, but
what then, you know not when 'tis faulty
nor when 'tis fine? How ſhou'd you come by
ſuch Knowledge, unleſs the *Muſes* had inſpir'd
you as they did *Heſiod?* But what do I talk
to thee of *Helicon;* thou knowſt not ſo much
as where it is? And ſhou'd you ever climb
that Sacred Hill, the *Muſes* wou'd be ſo far
from making thee a preſent of a *Laurel
Branch,* that they wou'd Stone thee out of
the Gronnds, leaſt thou ſhoud'ſt Muddy their
Streams; and to this, that thy Life has been
too Scandalous, for Virgins converſe with
thee. Tho' you have a very good Stock, yet
you won't ſay that from your very Youth
you have been train'd up in their Miſteries,
or that the Converſation of Learned Men had
made their Secrets familiar to you. This
Blot you think to conceal behind a vaſt quantity of Books, but give me leave to tell you
that if you had all *Demoſthenes's* Manuſcrpits,
who Copied with his own Hand the Hiſtory
of *Thucidides,* no leſs than Eight times, nay,
had you all the Books that *Sylla* carried away
from *Athens,* they wou'd ſtand thee in no
ſtead,

stead, tho' thou hung'st them about thy Neck,
or slept on them every Night; for, as the
old saying is, *An Ape is no more than an Ape,
tho' he be cover'd with Cloth of Gold.* I own
you have always a Book in your Hand, but
you know no more of it than an Ass does of
Musick. If store of Books was capable of
making a Man a Scholar, who wou'd be so
Learned as the Booksellers, who have a Hundred pass thro' their Hands every Day to any
other Persons One: Nay, their Shops too
wou'd be very knowing. Don't bragg then
of thy Study of Books, as an Evidence of
thy Capacity. What say you to this? If you
can't speak make a sign with your Head at
least; shou'd a Person have *Timotheus*'s Pipe,
or the other which *Ismenias* pay'd three Talents for, wou'd that render him an Artist,
no, tho' he had *Olympias*'s and *Marsias*'s besides
He is no *Hercules* that holds his Club, or
wears his Lions Skin; and if you are not
Philoctetes you know not what to do with his
Arrows. He must be a Pilot to carry a Ship
well, and a good Querry to sit the Great
Horse. Prithee then, candidly acknowlege
that what thou hast done in this matter, only
illustrated thy stupidity. It is not long ago
since a rich Man in *Asia* lost his Feet by Travelling through the deep Snows in the
height of Winter: However, to cover this
Imperfection, he was always very nice in his
Shoes, tho' he was forc't to have Two lusty
tall Fellows to support him as he Walk'd.
He might take a Pride indeed in his neat
Shoes, tho' they were but Shackles to him,
so are Books just the same thing to a Blockhead.

head. In the multitude you have *Homer* perhaps; pray then beg fomebody to tell you the
meaning of *Therfites*, when defcribed Haran-
guing; every thing elfe is befides thy purpofe. Can you be fo ridiculous to think that
that little Man that put on *Achilles*'s Armour
wou'd have ftop'd *Soamanders* Currier by
Heaps of Dead Bodies? Kill'd *Hector* too
with his own Hands, and many other *Gree-
cian* Princes. You can't but rather avow, that
every one wou'd have Laugh'd to fee him
reeling with his ponderous Buckler, or peep-
ing through his Helmet, which the Hump
on his Back fhov'd the Cuirafs above his
Shoulders. In fhort, it had been an indig-
nity to the *Hero* that wore the Arms, as well
as the God that made 'em, won't this hold
good againft your felf now, when you read
over any good Books; for you confound the
fenfe of it as well as the Book? what, tho'
your Hangers on may commend you, yet
when your Back is turn'd they do but laugh
at you. I muft here infert a Paffage that
once fell out at the *Pythian* Games. A very
rich Man of *Terantum*, whofe name was *E-
vangelus*, had a Whim in his Head to get the
Prize at thofe Games, and being not vigorous
enough to Wreftle, nor fwift enough to Run,
he chofe to be condidate for that of Mufick.
Egg'd on by his Sycophants, he came to *Delphos*, and made his Appearance in the Games,
in a Robe of Cloth of Gold, and a Crown in
the Shape of Lawrel, but the Leaves were
Maffy Gold, and inftead of Fruit there were
Knots of large Emeralds: His Harp was
Gold inlaid with Jewels, adorn'd with the

Figures

Figures of *Orpheus*, *Apollo*, and the *Mufes*.
This pompous fhew drew all Eyes upon
him, and every one expected fome wonderful performance anfwerable to fo expenfive
a Preparation ; but when he went to exert
his Faculties, his Voice was out of Tune with
his Harp, there was nothing but Difcord,
and for the Complement of his Shame, going
to ftrike his Harp fomewhat boldly, he broke
three of the Strings. All the Theatre burft
out a Laughing at this, and fo much the more,
becaufe he feem'd to promife fomething very
exquifite ; and the Man that had perform'd
juft before had done tollerably well befides.
When their Laughing was over, the Judges
of the Games had him Lafh'd off the Theatre,
fo away Troop'd the Spark cover'd over with
Blood, and gathering up the Fragments of
his Harp which they kick up and down after
him. Then there came one *Emulus* of *Elis*,
an excellent Mafter, who charm'd the whole
Audience, and was proclaim'd Conqueror,
tho' but mean in Apparel, and an old Rotten
Harp. His Jeft upon the *Terentine* was fmart
enough ; you were Crown'd with Gold and
precious Stones, (fays he) becaufe you were
Rich, and becaufe I was Poor I had only a
Crown of Lawbel ; but notwithftanding my
Poverty I was Crown'd, and your Riches
have made your Infamy more notorious, and
ftifled all Compaffion. There is fomething
very applicable in this ; for I find you are as
little touch'd with the reproaches of Men as
the *Tarentine* was. But to knock thee down
if it be poffible, I will hint upon one Story
more, *Orpheus* being tore to pieces by the

Women.

Women of *Thrace*, and his Head thrown into the River; they fay it floated for fome
time upon his Harp, and as that fent forth
fome melancholly Notes in Honour of the
Hero; fo the Harp being touch'd by the
Breezes, kept time to his Mournful Song.
Thus it came to the Ifle of *Lesbos*, and the
Inhabitants Built it a Sepulchre, where the
Temple of *Bacchus* ftands at prefent; and
the Harp they hung up in that of *Apollo*,
where it continued a great while, till the Son
of *Pittacus* hearing how it wou'd play of it
felf, and Charm Stones and Trees, purchas'd
it at a very confiderable Rate of one of the
Priefts. Apprehending fome Danger if he
play'd on it in the City, at Night he went
out into the Suburbs, where he no fooner
touched the Strings, but inftead of fweet Melody there was fuch a curfed yelling, that
the Dogs all round about him, run upon him
and tore him to pieces, which was the only
thing wherein he was like *Orpheus*. The Art
is not in the Inftrument, but in the hand of
the Skilful. But why go fo far back, fince a
Man in our times paid three hundred *Drachmas*
for *Epictetus*'s Earthen-Lamp, as if his Learning lay in it too. Another gave a Talent for
Peregrinus the Philofopher's Staff, which he
fhews for as great a Curiofity as *Hercules*'s Club,
or the Calydonian's Bore's-Skin of the *Tege-
atæ*, *Gerion*'s Body by the *Thebans*, or the
Head of Hair of *Ifis*, that the *Ægyptians* fet
fo much by. Indeed this Man only exceed
thy Vanity and Simplicity, and his Staff is a
precedent for thy *Collection*. Report goes of
Dionyfius the Tyrant, compos'd a very frivolous

E   and,

and dull Tragedy; and becaufe *Philoxenus* did not applaud it, he punifh'd him very barbaroufly; but afterwards thinking to mend his hand, he bought *Efchylus*'s Note-Book, wherein that incomparable Poet had wrought his Dramatic Compofitions; but alas he perform'd ftill worfe and worfe. Not unlikely your numerous Library turns your Brain, and if you had no Books, you, perhaps, wou'd do much better. Why then fo extravagant in your prices, fo fuperfluous in your Bindings? Are you the better Orator for this, or rather are you not lefs able to fpeak? Thy Debaucheries and Excefles fpeak too lowdly againft thee, and make thee the fcorn and contempt of all Mankind. If fo be thy Books create thofe diforders in thy Brain, you had better be without 'em than with 'em, feeing they help you neither to fay or do any thing well, and are only an expenfive entertainment for Rats, Mice, and Worms, as well as mifery to your Servants, who are continually raked to Death when ever they omit dufting of 'em; you wou'd blufh, but that you have eaten Shame and drank after it, to find that when a Man of Letters happens to extol fome paflages in the Book you carry in your hand, as you never are without one, that you know not what he means nor where to turn to it. *Demetrius* the *Cynic* Philofopher, they fay, finding a Country-fellow reading the *Bacchantes* of *Euripides*, fnatch'd it from him and tore it to pieces, faying, *'Twas better* Pentheus *fhou'd be torn to pieces once by his hands, than a thoufand times by a Fools.* I have thought on it many and many a ferious time, and cannot

yet

yet devise wherefore it is that thou buyest up
such heaps of Books. What has a Man that
is bald to do with a Comb, or an Ennuch
with a Bed-fellow? Looking-Glasses are not
for the Blind, no more than Musical Instruments for the Deaf. Is it out of a vain shew
of thy Wealth that thou lavishest away thy
Substance in un-necessary Expences? Yet I
am positive that if you had not wheedled
your self into an old Man's Will, you had
starved long ago, and sold your Books too.
It must be then that you do it to justifie the
Character that your *Spungers* give you of being
not only a fine Gentleman, but an ingenious
Man, a curious Historian, a profound Philosopher, a quaint Rhetorician, and a knotty
Disputant. You entertain 'em, they say,
with your Harrangues even at Table, and
none will presume to drink till he has bawld
his Throat sore in applauding you. And as
thou art vain and self-conceited, they have
gull'd you into a belief that you are mighty like
the Emperour: and indeed there were such
Alexanders, *Neros*, and *Philips*. But no wonder such an insippid Coxcomb as thou art,
shou'd be led away so, since *Pyrrhus*'s Cour-
tiers made him believe he resembled *Alexander*; till an old Woman of *Larissa* where
he Lodged undeceived him ; for shewing her
one day the Picture of *Philip*, *Cassander*, *Alexander* and *Perdiccas*, he ask'd her which she
thought him the most like to, why in good
truth, said the Woman, you are the likest to
one *Frog* a Cook here in Town, and there
happened to be a Man in *Lariss* of that name
that was not unlike him. I wont tell you

who

who you are like, that wou'd be *too severe* upon you ; but every one looks upon you as a Mad-man for imagining your self like the Emperour, and aping him so much in Dress and Deportment : No wonder then if a Man of so small Judgment in resemblance shou'd mistake himself for a learned Man. But now I have hit it ; You question not but your Fortune wou'd be made if the Prince that loves Men of Letters shou'd take you for a *Doctor.* But think you shameless Wretch, that he don't know thy lewd and vicious Life. Have not Princes Eyes every where, and Ears in every corner, that nothing throughout their Empire can escape their Knowledge ? But all the World is acquainted with thy Debaucheries. Prithee which of thy *Rakes* that have perfected thee in every thing that is Abominable and Obscene, wou'd pass for a *Hercules,* tho' he had his Skin and his Club ? Wou'd not his lewd Behaviour betray the *sham* Hero ? *You may hide an Elephant under his Robe sooner than a lascivious Wretch,* says the Proverb. Then forbear giving thy self such Aires with the Lyon's Skin, the braying shews the Ass. 'Tis not a vast or curious Collection of Books that will draw a Curtain over thy Ignorance, and make you pass for a well read Man ; that Character must be had from Men of Merit and Probity. 'Twere better for you to part with your Books to supply your Debaucheries and Extravagances, either of which folly is enough to eat thee quickly out of doors. If you are capable of Advice, put off great part of your numerous Retinue, and get an ingenious, worthy, difcreet, fober Friend, that will not lead you out of the way, and expofe you when he has done. For I tsok notice 'to-ther Day, that very early in the Morning, one came out of thy Houfe and brag'd of your Debauches, and call'd the People to be Witneffes of it by the marks he had to fhew of it: But I was fo provok'd at him by it, that the Gods and thofe that were by are my Witneffes, I had much ado to forbear beat-ing of him for your fake. If Cuftom has made it difficult to break off your courfe of Lire, then keep your Money for Lewdnefs, not Li-braries. To what end then mighty Volumes pil'd fo loftily one over another? You un-derftand enough for what you Practice. You never fo much as mention Antiquity, yet know all the Poets, Orators and Hiftorians together with the delicacies, and deficiencies of the Tcngue. I might dwell longer upon this Subject, but I muft ask you what Books you generally apply your felf to, *Plato, An-tifthenes, Archilochus,* or *Hipponax?* Or it may be you throw by the Philofophers and Satyrifts, and confult the Orators, did you ever read *Æfchines*'s Harangue againft *Ti-marchus?* But this perhaps you have at your Fingers-end, and fo now apply your felf to Comedy: Have you feen the * *Bapta,* or cou'd you read it without a Blufh? But pray what is your favourite Book? For tho' you have always abundance about you, no body can ever fee you read a Line in any: Is it by Night or Day that you Study, before or after your Debauches? Give over your Studies and indulge your Vices, tho' your

A lovd Comedy like So-dom.

Life

Life is much more infamous than your Learning ; not but that you may juftly apprehend
the fame Reproach that the Women had
from *Phedra* in *Euripides*, and be cautious leaft
the very Walls themfelves proclaim'd thy
Shame : But if you will perfift and die as
you liv'd, be je on ftill, but don't read 'em,
and fince the Ancients never did you good or
harm, let them alone. I know I had as good
fpeak to the Poft, and that you will hold on
your own way, and continue to make your
felf the Laughing-ftock, Jeft and By-word of
all ingenious and learned Men, who will not
fo much mind what is about you, as what is
in you. But you think this will be a Cloak
for your impertinence, as a Scoundrel Sur-
geon *Tops* upon you with a Silver Cafe of In-
ftruments, and knows not the ufe or name of
the beft part of 'em, whereas an Able-Man
with indifferent Tools makes a very good
Dreffing : Nay worfe, thofe Blockheads often lend out their Jnftruments to others that
can make ufe of 'em ; but you are like *Æfop*'s
Dog, that cou'd not eat Hay himfelf, and
wou'd not let the Ox eat any neither. This
is what I thought convenient to fay of your
Studies, and fhall take another opportunity
of giving a full account of the Debaucheries
of your Life and Converfation.

THE
JUDGEMENT
OF THE
VOWELS.

By Samuel Cob, *M. A.*

The Argument.

*This Oration is an Elegant and Jocular Harangue
fram'd after the manner of Judicial Pleading.
Sigma complains of the Violence and Injury of
Tau, that he had Rob'd him of very many
Words, and in a manner turn'd him out of his
proper Possession. First he bespeaks the benevolence of the Audience from a pretence of Modesty, and an excuse of his own necessity · then by
a Transiation he comes to the Subject, which is
this, That none of the Letters ought to be remov'd out of their proper place and order.
Hence he takes occasion to put the Judges in
mind that they do their Duty, and preserve
the Order of the rest, and the Dignity of every
one in particular, to which he subjoyns a little
Narration, which contains the Confirmation of
the Cause. This he amplifies, first with a long*

rehearfal of feveral other Affronts which this Tau *had put upon him the faid* Sigma. *Then he fhows by comparing his own Modefty, and the others Sawcinefs not only towards himfelf, but towards others, Men not excepted, how this* Tau *is hated and detefted by all Mankind.*

In the Reign of Ariftarchus Phalereus, *on the Seventh Day of* October, Sigma *brought his Action againft the Letter* Tau *(the Seven Vowels then fitting upon the Bench to judge in Caufes of Violence and Rapine) complaining of a fcandalous Abufe committed by this malicious Thief, who had rob'd him of all thofe words which are pronounc'd with a double* Tau.

May it pleafe my Lords, the Vowels,

AS long as I was injur'd by this *Tau* in matters of a fmall concern, while he play'd at Petty-Larceny only, and nimm'd here and there what did not belong to him, I contain'd my refentment, and fat down patiently with a little lofs: Befides when I have heard him afpers'd with feveral Calumnies, I have taken no notice, but pretended to be Deaf, according to that ufual Modefty which you are fenfible I have preferv'd not towards your Lordfhips only, but alfo towards the reft of the Syllables. But fince he is arriv'd to that pitch of Covetoufnefs and Folly, that not contented with thofe Injuries which I have hitherto quietly paffed over, he ftill continues his Depredations with greater Violence, neceffity compells me to cite him now before you who are acquainted with both of us. Nor was I in a fmall fear left a Bill of

Exclufion

Exclusion should have pass'd against me. For he will wholly throw me out of my proper place if he thus augments the heinousness of his former Crimes, and should I continue to be silent, there is reason to fear lest I even be number'd among the Letters. Wherefore it behoves not only you, who sit as Judges, but the rest of the Letters, to be very cautious of his attempt. For if it shall be lawful for any one, who has a mind, to thrust another out of his Order by meer force, and that you, without whom nothing can be plainly written, shall allow of it, I see not how any Orders can enjoy their Right and Properties according to the Fundamental Laws of our first Constitution But I think that you will never be guilty of such an oversight as to suffer any piece of Injustice in your Jurisdiction. Nor will you, I presume, if you betrayest the Cause, let this injury pass without satisfaction.) And I wish that the audaciousness of other Letters also had been repress'd, as soon as they began to infringe the Laws. Happy had it been for *Ro* and *Lambda*; they had not to this very day contended about *Kissesis* and *Cephalalgia* Nor had *Gamma* enter'd the Lists with *Kappa,* nor they so often been within an Ace of Daggers-drawing in a Fullers for the Word *Gnaphalon.* Nor had that *Gamma* kept up the Quarrel so long with *Lambda* in borrowing of him *shall I say?* Nay in clandestinely Stealing from him the word *Mogis.* Other Letters also would have been deter'd from attempting any confusion contrary to the Laws. It is fit and decent for every one to keep in the

place which has been allotted him; but to leap the Bounds which he ought not to do is the part of an Infringer and Contemner of Equity. He who firſt gave theſe Laws to us whether it was *Cadmus* the Iſlander, or *Palamedes* the Son of *Nauplius*; tho' others attribute this Proviſion to *Simonides*; whoever he was he did not only determine the Order and Priority, as which ſhould be firſt, which ſecond, but conſulted alſo what Qualities and Powers he ſhould be poſſeſſed of. To you, O Judges, they gave that ſingular honour of being pronounc'd without the aſſiſtance of another. The ſecond place of Dignity they conferr'd on the Semi-Vowels, which cannot be heard, unleſs one of you be added to him. To ſome of the Conſonants they order'd the loweſt Station, and ſuch are the Mutes. But this Raſcal *Tau*, (for he cannot be called by a worſe Name than he has already, and which by the Gods would not be ſo much as heard, were it not for thoſe two worthy and comely Letters *Alpha* and *Upſilon*) this *Tau*, I ſay, has had the impudence to plague me more than ever, inſolently endeavouring to thruſt me out of things and names of Countries, nay, to ingroſs to himſelf the very Conjunctions and Prepoſitions, that I am no longer able to indure ſuch Monſtrous and unheard of Avaricicuſneſs. But it is high time to inform you whence this injury begun. I was travelling not long ſince in *Cybelum* (which is a ſmall Town, and, as I take it, not very unpleaſant; they tell us, it is a Colony of the *Athenians*) I took for my Companion my nigheſt and beſt Neighbour *Ro:* There I
happen'd

happen'd to be acquainted with a certain
Comic Poet call'd *Lyſimachus* (a *Bæotian* by his
Anceſtors, tho' he affects rather to be thought
to come out of the middle of *Attica*) with
this Stranger I firſt took notice of the Rapa-
cious Temper of this *Tau*. For while he made
bold with a few Words calling it *Tettarakonta*,
thereby depriving me of my Kindred, I took
it to be the Cuſtom of Letters which had
been brought up together over and above,
when he took from me *Temſon* and the like,
affirming they were his, I gave him the hearing, and was very indifferent in the matter.
But when from ſuch ſmall beginnings he advanc'd to that high ſtep of Impudence as to pronounce *Cattiteros*, *Kattuma* and *Pitta*, nay, and
laying down all fear and ſhame to call it *Baſi* too
this put me out of all Patience, this rais'd my Indignation, and I fear'd leſt in time ſome Body
or other inſtead of *Suka* would cry *Tuta*. Pardon this juſt Paſſion to one who is caſt down
in Spirit, and deſtitute of all manner of aſſiſtance. But the Danger is not ſmall, nor to
be deſpiſed, when I am depriv'd of my Acquaintance and familiar Letters. My chat-
tering *Pye Kiſſa* he has quite cut ſhort in the
middle, and call'd it *Kitta* : Beſides, he has
rob'd me of my *Poultry*, my *Wood-Pigeon*,
Phaſſa, my *Wild-Ducks*, *Neſſai*, and my *Black-
Birds*, *Koſſuphoi*, can't I cry to the Laws of
Ariſtarchus ? Nor has he ſpar'd my *Bees Me-
liſſai* ; nay, he had the boldneſs to come into
Attica, and againſt all Right take away the
Mountain *Hymettus*, you and the other Syllables being Spectators of it. But why do I re-
count theſe Affronts ? He has expell'd me
out

out of all *Theſſalia,* and will have it call'd
Thettalia. Laſtly, he has driven me out of
all the Seas, and will call it *Thalatta,* and not
Thalaſſa. I can bear Injuries for a long time
together, and of that you your ſelves are
Witneſſes. When did I ever arraign *Zeta*
for taking *Smaragdus* from me, and depriving
me of all *Smyrna?* When did I ever accuſe
Xi, tho' he broke his League and violated all
compact *Xantheke,* being back'd by *Thucydides*
himſelf, who is the Writer of things of that
nature. My neighbour *Rho* may be eaſily
Pardon'd, he being Sick when he Planted my
Myrtles with him *Myrrhina.* You ſee the
eaſineſs and goodneſs of my Temper. But
this *Tau* is a violent Rapparee in his very
nature, nor has he kept his hands from the
other Letters, witneſs *Delta, Zeta* and *Theta,*
and almoſt the whole Alphabet round. Call
in the Evidence, and firſt, if your Lordſhips
pleaſe, let us hear what *Delta* has to ſay. He
has taken from me *Endelecheia,* and which is
repugnant to all Law will have it pronounc'd
Entelecheia. Hear next how *Theta* laments
and tears his Hair, becauſe by his means *He-
tuy* loſt his *Cupping-glaſs, Colocunthe.* Hear
Zeta complaining for the loſs of his Flute
Tunes (*Surizein*) and his Trumpet Tunes
(*Salpizein*) that he dare not now ſo much as
(*Gruzein*) open his Mouth. Is this to be born?
or can any puniſhment be too ſevere for this
notorious Villain *Tau.* Nor is this all, for
not contented to ſpoil his Relations and Kindred the Letters, his Violence has carried
him to make an inſolent attempt upon mankind, which was done in the manner following.

ing. For neither does he fuffer them to ufe their Tongues aright. But now I talk of Tongues he has driven me out of that Quarter, and inftead of *Gloffa* calls it *Glotta*. O *Tau* thou Scandal of the *Tongue*! O thou bafe ufurper of anothers Right! But I will return to him again, and I will ask the Patronage of mankind, whom he has fo much offended. For he endeavours as it were with claim to diftort and tear their Voices. If a Man feeing any beautiful thing and has a mind to call it *Kalon*, he prefently thrufts his Head and compels him to pronounce it *Talon*; fo forward is he to be firft in every thing. Nor does his affronts reach only to private Men, but to that great King whom Earth and Sea obey, and are faid to tranfgrefs the Laws of Nature; that Emperour, I fay, he lyes in wait for, and pronounces him *Syrus* when his name is *Cyrus*. So much in reality. How do Mortals deplore their fad calamity, curfing *Cadmus* a hundred and hundred times for bringing *Tau* into the Alphabet? For Kings, fay they, and Law-givers, when they viewed the Figure of that Letter caus'd Gallowfes to be erected in the fhape of it to hang and punifh Offenders on; and thence that wicked enquirer had its wicked Appellation. For all thofe Crimes how many forts of Death do you think this *Tau* deferves? If you will take my opinion I think it is but juft and reafonable that as he was the firft Caufe of a Gallows being made he fhould take his laft Swing on that very *Engine* which reprefents him; a Death too good for fuch a Hang-Dog as himfelf.

The

The Praise of our

COUNTRY.

By Mr. GILDON.

The Argument.

The Design of this Speech is to shew that our Country is, and ought to be preferr'd to all other Considerations, and this by common Examples of Gods, and Men of several Degrees and Circumstances, a lesson worthy to be learnt in our Modern Times, when foreign Manners and Men are so much in Esteem.

THE celebrated Proverb, that nothing is dearer than our Native Country has long been in the Mouths of every one. But this is not so old and so vulgar as it is true, for there is nothing more pleasing to every Man than his own Country. What is more Venerable and Divine than that? For our Country, that brought us forth, and gave us Nourishment, is the Cause and Source of all that we call Venerable and Divine. Many are pleas'd with and admire the large extent and splendor of Cities, and the Magnificence

of

of their Buildings; but every Man loves his Country. Nor is there any Man so besotted on, or such a slave to the Pleasure of Publick Shews and Spectacles, as to forget his own Country, in the excellence and enchantments of any Sights that can be seen in a foreign Nation.

For this Reason I think him very ignorant of the Honour he ought to pay his Country, who boasts himself the Citizen of a happy and fortunate City; for it is plain, that such a Person wou'd bear with some regret to be born in a Country of but a moderate Fame and Reputation in the World. Whereas I find peculiar Pleasure in paying a Respect and Veneration to the very Name of my Country. For those who make a Comparison betwixt Cities, ought to consider their Largeness, Beauty and Trade or Affluence of all Commodities and Merchandize. But when we come to choose our Cities, no Man makes choice of any more splendid City than his own, but wishes that his Native Country were like those who enjoy the stronger smiles of Fortune and Nature, but yet for all that rejects it not for any other, how Magnificent or Pompous soever.

The same is done by lawful Children and good Fathers, for a Youth of Honour and Honesty will not prefer any Man to his own Father how Great and Fortunate soever; nor does a Father of Sense and Probity ever cherish a Stranger with a paternal Love, whilst he neglects his own Son. So great is the force of Nature in Parents, that Fathers attribute so much to their own Off-spring,

that

that they think them poffefs'd with the greateft Beauty and Bravery, and all other parts
that fhou'd adorn a Man. And he who has
not this Opinion of his Child feems not to me
to look with the Eyes of a Father.

Next the Name of our *Native Country* is
the firft, chief, and moft familiar of all
Names whatfoever. He therefore that wou'd
pay that juft Honour to his Father as both
Nature and Law require, muft by a ftronger
Reafon prefer his Country to his Father.
For this Father, and his Father, and all his
Progenitors and Relations are but the Poffeffion of his Country; and this Nature
reaches up to the very Paternal Gods themfelves. For the Gods themfelves rejoice in,
and are pleas'd with their Country, and tho'
they have regard to all Humane Affairs, as
they ought, looking on the Univerfe both
Sea and Land as their Poffeffion, yet every
God prefers that City and Country where he
was Born to all others what ever. And thofe
Cities are more venerable which are the
places of the Nativity of fome Gods; and
thofe Iflands efteem'd more Divine than o-
thers, where the Nativity of the Gods is Celebrated; and for this Reafon the Sacrifices
are look'd on as moft grateful to the Gods,
which are offer'd to them in places of this Nature.

But if the Gods have fo great a value for
the Name of their Native Country. How
much more ought it to be dear and precious
to Mankind? Every one firft beholds the
Sun as a God in his own Country where he is
Born; which altho' common to all Men
and

and Nations, is not look'd on by every People as of their Country, becaufe it is firft beheld there by them. In his Country it is, that he firft attains to fpeak by learning his Mother Tongue, here he firft comes to the Knowledge of the Gods.

But if any Man be born in a Country, which requires the help of fome other Country for attaining thofe Arts and Sciences, which are not to be learned at home; yet thofe very Arts and Sciences he owes to his own Country. For he wou'd not fo much as have known the Name of a City or Country, had he not, by the Benefit of his own been informed that there was fuch a thing as a City or Country.

The Arts, that all Men apply themfelves to are, I fuppofe, to qualifie themfelves the more for the Service of his Country. And they poffefs Riches, that they may the more liberally contribute to the common Expences of their Country. And that with Reafon, for he who has received the greateft Benefits of his Country ought not to be ungrateful. If in private Affairs every Man is bound to acknowledge the Favour he receives, the Reafon is infinitely ftronger for our Returns to our Country, for the Benefits received from it Every City has Laws againft Children who abufe their Parents; but there is a great deal of Reafon to efteem our Country the common Mother of us all, and we ought therefore to pay our acknowledgements for our Birth and Education, and to refer to her the Regifter of the Laws themfelves.

But no Man is thought fo forgetful of his Native Country, as to neglect it, tho' fome other be his prefent Habitation. For there is nothing fo common i to hear thofe who are in but a mean Condition, extolling the Happinefs of their own, and on the other fide, thofe who have, and by their Wealth live in Magnificence and Pleafure, think nothing wanting to their Happinefs, but that they want to live thus in their own Native Country, for there is a fort of Scandal to live a Stranger out of the place of our Nativity. And we may obferve, that thofe who have arrived at Eminence in a Foreign Country, either in Wealth, or the Glory and Fame of their Deeds, or the Reputation of their Learning, or the Applaufe of their Valour, all make what fpeed they can to return home, as if they cou'd not make a fufficient fhew of their good Fortune among a ftrange People, and in a Foreign Land. And every Man defires with the greater Ardor his Return to his own Country, as he is efteemed the more Worthy by Strangers of the greater Honours and Advantages.

Their Native Country is defireable ev'n to young Men, but thofe who begin to grow Old, as much as their Prudence is greater than that of Youth, fo much the greater is their Defire of returning to their own Country. But when a Man is now in his old Age he wifhes and endeavours to lay down his Life in his own Country, where he firft received Vital Breath, to commit his Body to that Earth whence he received his firft Nutriment, and be bury'd in the Sepulchre of his Anceftors.

cestors. For it seems grievous to every one to be an Exile in a foreign Land, and this Grievance reaches him who lives there even after Death.

Further, we may find what is the Love of a right and legal Citizen to his Country, by those who are only Inmates. For *Foreigners* like Bastards easily overturn the State, as those who neither knew, nor love the name of our Country; but who imagine that they shall every where find a sufficient Quantity of things necessary for their Use, measuring their Happiness by the Pleasure of the Gut. But those who esteem their Country their Mother, love the place of their Nativity and Education, tho' it be but moderate, rough, or Barren, And tho' there be no room for them to praise the Excellence of the Soil, yet will they not be to seek for Topics to extol their Country. And when they hear others boasting of their Fertile Glebe, and Fields beautifully distinguish'd with all manner of Plants; they will not commit the praise of their Country to Silence, or forget to declare its Excellence, but recommend, it as the Breeder of Noble Horses, and Valiant Young Men. And even the Islander himself will make haste into his own Country, and tho' he might live happily abroad, wou'd refuse offer'd Immortality else-where for a Grave in his paternal Soil : He will even prefer the Smoke of his own Country to the Fires of another.

Our Country feems to furpafs all things
fo much in Value, that we find moft of the Legiflators of Cities have inflicted Banifhment
as the laft and moft extream of Punifhments
for the greateft of Crimes.   With the Law-
givers we may place the Generals of Armys,
who exhorting their Men to act Manly, tell
them that the War is undertaken for their
Country ; upon hearing which no Man is
floathful or backward, nay the name of his
Country makes a brave Man of a Coward.

That we ought not eaſily to give Credit to Calumny.

By the ſame Hand.

The Argument.

*The Title ſhews the Summ and Argument of the
following Diſcourſe, that is, that we ought not
eaſily to give Credit to Calumny, becauſe many
Men tranſported by their own Paſſions or Inte-
reſts, will defame innocent and good Men ; and
oppreſs them by Fraud and Injuſtice with ſuch
who eaſily give Ear and Credit to Backbiters.
This Oration is of the Didactic kind, only that
towards the end ſeems to incline to the
Suaſory, &c.*

IGnorance is an Evil it ſelf, and the Source
and Origin of many Evils to Mankind,
not only darkning and caſting a Shadow over
Humane Affairs, but even obſcures *Truth* it
ſelf, and throws the Life of private Men into ſuch a Miſt, that it is not eaſily obſerv'd with
Juſtice. This makes Men wander and grope
about as in the Dark, or rather like the
Blind ſtumbling now upon this and now upon that, which happens to lie in the way.
One thing without occaſion we paſs over un-
regarded; the next which lies directly in
our way, and before our Feet, we cannot
ſee ; but what is remote and from us
at a great Diſtance, we dread as a great
Trouble. In ſhort, in all our Actions we
perpetually Stumble. From this Cauſe and
Spring have the Families of *Labdacus* and
Pelops, and others of that kind furniſhed Arguments for the writing numberleſs Trage-
dys · For you ſhall find that moſt of thoſe
fatal Events, which aſcend the Tragic Scene,
derive themſelves from Ignorance, as ſome
Tragic God. In what I here ſay, I have regard to other Things ; and firſt to thoſe falſe
Calumnys which are directed to the aſſaulting
our Friends and familiar Acquaintance,
which before now have ruin'd Families, and
utterly overthrown and deſtroy'd whole
Cities. This has ſtir'd up Rage and Indignation of Fathers againſt their Children, Brothers againſt Brothers, Children againſt their
Parents, and Lovers againſt the Beloved.
The very Appearance of this has put an end

to multitudes of Friendships, and embroil'd
whole Families.

That we may, therefore, as much as possibly
avoid falling into this Evil, I shall endeavour to
draw the Picture of Calumny to the Life, in
this Oration, with its Origin and Effects.
The Picture that I shall draw of it, I acknowledge to be borrowed of *Apelles* of *Ephe-
sus*, a Painter of great Fame and Reputation,
when he was accus'd of being concern'd in
the Conspiracy of *Theodotas* at *Tyre*, altho'
he had never so much as seen *Tyre*, nor knew
any thing of *Theodotas*, but that he was *Pto-
lomys* Governour of *Phœnicia*; yet *Antiphilus*,
another Painter, who had much the King's
Ear, provok'd by *Envy* or *Emulation* of Art,
accus'd him to *Ptolomy*, as being one of the
Conspirators; and that he was seen feasting
with *Theodotas* in *Phœnicia*, and whispering
him secretly at the Table, and finally con-
cludes that it was by the Advice of *Apelles*,
that *Tyre* had revolted, and *Pelusium* was
taken. Upon which *Ptolomy*, who was a
Man of no great Prudence at the best, but
was fed up in the Custom of a Tyrannical Flattery, fell into such a Passion, and was so disturb'd by this Calumny, that neglecting all
that might lessen the Credit of the Information, or render it more or less probable, (for he
never reflected that they both profess'd the
same Art, or that the Fortune and Power of
a Painter was not of importance and consequence enough to influence such a Revolt, or
that this very Man had been honour'd with
greater Favours by him than any other Painter, nor ever so much as enquired whether

Apelles had touch'd at *Tyre* or not,) gave himſelf immediately up to his Anger, filling
the Palace with Exclamations againſt him as
an ingrateful Man, a Traitor and full of
Treachery and Baſeneſs. And had not every
one of the Conſpirators who were taken una-
nimouſly declared (in deteſtation of the Impudence of *Antiphilus*, as well as in pity, or the
unhappy *Apelles*) that he was in no manner or
way privy to or acquainted with this Deſign,
he had been Beheaded, and tho' guilty of no
Crime, had felt the Puniſhment of the Revolted *Tyrians*.

But the diſcovery of his Innocence is ſaid
to have affected *Ptolomy* ſo much, that he
gave him an hundred Talents, and adjudg'd
Antiphilus to be his Slave. And *Apelles* being
ſtruck with the Reflection on the Danger he
had eſcap'd, expreſs'd his Reſentment a-
gainſt Calumny in the Picture.

On the Right Hand ſate a Figure with
long Aſſes Ears, like thoſe of *Midas*, extend-
ing his Hand to *Calumny* as ſhe approach'd
him at a diſtance. He is attended by two
Women, which, if I miſtake not, are *Ignorance* and *Suſpicion.* On the other part
of the Piece *Calumny* advances in the Figure
of a Woman of extraordinary, nay conſum-
mate Beauty in her Face and Action, expreſ-
ſing Heat, Anger and Rage, bearing in
her *Left-hand* a burning Torch; with her
Right draging along a Youth by the Hair of his
Head, holding up his Hands to Heaven, and
atteſting the Gods to Witneſs his Innocence.
Before her went a pale deform'd Man with a
ſharp look, and a Countenance and Mien like

one that had languish'd long in some Distemper, which you might easily ghess to be *Envy*
Two other Women attended *Calumny*, exhorting and encouraging her, adjusting her Dress, and setting her off with Ornaments, one of these, as he that shew'd me the Picture interpreted it to me, was insidious Treachery, the other *Deceit*. Another Woman followed her in a Mourning and tatter'd Habit, and this they said was *Repentance*, who turning her Face towards her Back, she fixt in her Face with Shame her Eyes flowing with Tears on approaching Truth. In this Piece, thus *Apelles* exprefs'd with his Pencil the Danger he was in.

Let us therefore, like this *Ephesian* Painter, look into the Grounds and Reasons of *Calumny*, having first premis'd a just Definition of it. For this shall be the Method of forming our Image. *Calumny* is therefore an Accusation made against any one in his Absence, and without his Knowledge, and to which Credit is given without hearing both sides, but the Accus'd not admitted to refute the Accuser. This is the Argument of this Discourse. And since here, as in a Comedy, there are three Persons concern'd, the Accuser, the Accused, and he to whom the Accusation is made, let us consider these three several Parts, and what each of them ought to do

Let us therefore first produce on the Stage him that makes the *Calumny,* as being a Person of the first and chief Part. There is no Man so Ignorant but knows how little Pretence he has to the name of an Honest Man, For no
good

good or Honest Man can be the Author of
Evil to his Neighbour. For a good Man
is called and esteemed so for the Benefits he
bestows on his Friends, not for doing Evil
to his Enemys, and creating Hatred and Enmity to them by the appearance and pretence of Benevolence. Whence it will easily appear, that a *Calumniator* is an unjust,
wicked, impious Man, and injurious to his
Friends and Acquaintance. For who is there
that will not allow, that Equality and an e-
qual Regard to Things, so that one shall not
have an Advantage of another, is Justice, but
Inequality, and the Lust of having more Injustice? But who is there guilty of *Calumny*,
but such as are avaritious of more, than they
have, that is, they wou'd engross their Hearer
wholly to themselves, pre-possesses his Ears and
fills them, so as to render them envious to
him, that is to answer in his own behalf a-
gainst the Suggestions of the Accuser. This
is indeed the last Injustice in the Opinions of
the best and most excellent Law givers, *Solon*
and *Draco*; who oblig'd the Senate of *Athens*
by Oath, that in judicial Affairs they should
give an equal hearing to the *Accus'd*, as well
as *Accuser*, 'till such time that the *Culprits*
Cause by plain Evidence becomes either better or worse. For that was look'd on as a
wicked and unjust Judgment, that was past
before the Defence was compar'd with the
Accusation. Nay, we may well say that we
shou'd raise the Indignation of the Gods
themselves, if we shou'd allow the Accuser
free liberty of speaking what he pleases, but
on the other side, stop our Ears to what the

Defendant

Defendant has to fay as to condemn him by the influence of the Plaintiff's Harangue. Calumny is therefore contrary to Juſtice and Equity, and the Oath of the Judges themſelves.

But if the Legiſlators ſeem but of a doubtful Credit to any one, whoſe Decrees direct us to Judge by Juſtice not Partiality, I ſhall quote the beſt of Poets, who has promulgated an excellent Sentence, or rather Law on this Head, when he ſays,

Decide not a Diſpute till both ſides are heard

Here he plainly means, that there is no greater Injury and Injuſtice among thoſe Multitudes that infeſt humane Life more prejudicial and more wicked, than to condemn a Man without hearing him Plead; and this is entirely what a Calumniator does endeavour to effect, by diveſting him, whom he accuſes of all Defence, and leaving him open and ſubjected to the Anger of him, who hears and liſtens to his Calumny, depriving him of all Defence by a Clandeſtine Accuſation. For theſe ſort of Men are Cowards, and dare not ſpeak any thing openly and above Board; but like thoſe who lye hid in Ambuſh throw their Darts from their lurking Places, that thoſe they aim'd at may not be able to reſiſt and oppoſe them Hand to Hand, but muſt Periſh without knowing from whence the Wounds came; which is a very evident Proof, that a Calumniater has nothing to ſay of Truth or Reaſon. For a Man that is Conſcious to himſelf that his

Ac-

Accusation is juft, acts fairly in the Eyes of the Court face to face with Adverfary, he irs and oppofes what he fays; as no Man wou'd have Recourfe to Ambufcade and Surprize, that cou'd worft his Enemy fairly in the Field.

But you fhall obferve this fort of Men moft Converfant in the Courts of Princes, and you will always find them enjoy the Friendfhip of great Men, and the Favour of Sovereigns, that is, they are there where Envy is frequent, Sufpicions innumerable, and many Occafions offer'd of Flattery and Calumny. For where-ever there are larger Hopes always difcovering themfelves, there more Cruel Envy, more Dangerous Hatred, and more Cunning Emulations prevail, there every Man has a watchful and fharp obferving Eye on another, and like Men in fingle Combats, make a narrow and nice Obfervation where his Adverfary is leaft Aim'd or moft naked of Defence. And while every one would have the firft Place, he keeps the next to him as far from it as poffibly he can, and he that is before him he fupplants and roots up. In the Court, if any one be a Man of Policy and Temperance he is the fooner overthrown and deftroy'd, and expell'd with Ignominy. And he whofe Genius is moft adapted to Flattery, is the more prone to this Vice, and in fhort is fure to get the Victory.

The Victor and the Vanquifh'd fall alike
By common fate of War.

Thus

Thus when the Conteſt is for Matters of Moment, they invent various ways of Miſchief againſt one another, of which the moſt Compendious as well as the moſt Dangerous is *Calumny*, whoſe Origin is from Envy fluctuating betwixt Fear and Hope, which produces Events Miſerable, Tragical, and fill'd with many Calamities. Nor is the ſtudy of this Informer eaſy or of a ſimple kind, as it may perhaps ſeem to ſome People, but ſtands in need of a manifold Art, no little Induſtry, and a very exact Diligence. For *Calumny* wou'd not be of ſo dangerous a Nature, did not what ſhe pretended carry the plauſible Face of Truth. Nor cou'd it oppreſs Truth the moſt valuable of all things, but by theſe cunning Arguments it urges to perſuade, and a thouſand Arts to deceive and impoſe on her Hearers.

Beſide the Object of Calumny is always a Man in Favour, and poſſeſſed of Poſts of Honour, which renders him Odious to thoſe below him; for this Reaſon the Darts of all are levell'd at him as the ſole Obſtacle of their deſires; and every one thinks that he ſhall be firſt if he can but remove that great Man out of Favour. There is ſomething like this that happens in the *Gymnic* Games to thoſe who run the Race; when the ſtrenuous Runner having ſtarted from the Barriers minds nothing but his Race, thinking his Feet Tardy by not keeping an equal Pace with his Mind, regarding none of thoſe that contend with him for the Prize, placing the hopes of his Victory in the ſwiftneſs of his Feet. On the contrary his ſloathful and

weak Adverfary defpairing to do any thing
by his Agility turns his mind to fraud and
finifter Arts, and this only ftudy is how to
throw ftops and any hindrance in the way,
by that to prevent the Courfe of the Runner,
which miffing of fuccefs he can never gain
the Victory. The Cafe is much the fame in
our Aplications to the gaining the Favour
and Friendfhips of Great Men, for whoever
is moft Eminent there, is immediately in-
volved in the Ambufhes of their Competi-
tors, by whom for want of Caution, and un-
forewarned he is caught in a Snare and tore
all to pieces. Thefe then come into Favour
and feem to be received into Friendfhip becaufe they have been incommodious and injurious to others.

They are not hafty and carelefs in their
Invention of what may give Credit to their
Calumny, but employing all their thoughts
in the Choife of the Colour, fearing left they
fhould weave any thing into the Body of the
Piece that is diftinct or incoherent. Thus for
the moft part by wrefting and giving a wrong
meaning to the Circumftances of Conduct and
Profeffion of the Perfon, they Accufe, they
render their Suggeftions probable. Thus
they accufe a Phyfician of? Poyfoning;
a Wealthy Man of affecting the Tyranny,
and the Tyrant himfelf of Treachery and
Betraying the People.

Sometimes the Paffions of the Perfon, they
wou'd impofe on fupply matter to the Calumny; to whofe Manners thefe Sycophants
adapting themfelves attain their end. For if
they find him jealous in his Temper they
Whifpe

Whisper to him --- *Such a one tip'd the wink on your Wife at Supper, and looking on her sigh'd most bitterly, your Wife on the contrary gave him a gracious Glance, and other things which lead to Adultery.* But if it be a Person given to the study of Poetry, he cryes out *Philoxenus Laughs at your Verses, Rails at them, and says they are Lobling and unnumerous.* The favourite of a Man that is Religious and Pious is accused of Impiety and Wickedness, as that he is an Atheist and denies Providence. Upon this he that hears it flies out into a Passion, as if Poyson had been instill'd into his Ears, and as is agreeable to the thing, he conceives an Aversion to his Friend without examining into the Matter.

Such things as these for the most part are what are feign'd and invented, and spoken by these Villains, when they are satisfied that they will the most provoke and enrage the Mind of him, that hears them, and knowing very well the prevailing Quality of their Men, and the peculiar excellence of their Adversaries they direct all their Darts that way, that their Hearer being moved only by a sudden Gust of Passion might not have leisure to reflect and examine into the Truth, and then he gives no Ear to him who wou'd clear himself, being already possess'd with an Opinion of the imaginary Crime as if it were real. For that sort of Calumny is the most efficacious which contends with the Hearers desire. Thus one accus'd *Demetrius* the Platonist to *Ptolomy* surnam'd *Bacchus*, that he drank Water in the *Bacchanals*, and that he alone had not put on the Womens Garments. And if

when

when the next Morning he was call'd before
the King, he had not proved by all his Company that he drank Wine, and had on a
Tarentine Habit, that he had beat the *Cymbal*
and Danc'd, he had certainly fall'n a Sacrifice to the Calumny, because he did not approve of the Kings Manners, but was an
Enemy to the Luxury of *Ptolomy.* It was
the highest Guilt imaginable with *Alexander
the Great,* not to adore his beloved *Hephastion.*
For after his Death, *Alexander,* a slave to Love,
wou'd needs add to the Solemnity of his Funeral Rites an *Apotheosis,* declaring him a God.
The Cities immediately built Temples and
Fanes to his Memory, and Consecrated Altars, Victims and Feasts to this new God.
And to Swear by the name of *Hephastion* was
esteemed the most Solemn and Religious of
Oaths, and it was a Capital Offence for any
Man either to Smile at or perform the Ceremonies negligently or without the highest
Zeal and Relegion. His Flatterers finding
this youthful desire of *Alexander* took
care soon to add Fewel and Fire to the Folly,
they soon trump'd up Dreams, Visions, and
Cures for *Hephastion* and declared his Oracles,
in that they offer'd Sacrifice to him as the
associate Judge, and a God *the Driver away
of all Evils.* This at first took with the Vanity
of *Alexander,* which at last past into a Belief
as Truth and Matter of Fact till he began to
boast that he was not only the Son of a God,
but cou'd make Gods himself. How many
of *Alexander*'s Friends do we imagine Curst
this Divinity of *Hephastion* when being accus'd for not Worshipping their common
God,

God, they were Banifhed from Court and thrown out of the King's Favour? At this time there was one *Agathocles* a *Samian*, who was a Centurion under *Alexander* and in his Favour; he with no fmall difficulty Efcaped being thrown to the Lions for being accus'd of weeping as he paft by *Hephæftions* Tomb But *Perdicas* was his Friend and delivered him, Swearing by all the Gods, and particularly by *Hephæftion*, that this new God vifibly appear'd to him when Hunting, and gave him Command to tell *Alexander*, that he muft fpare *Agathocles*, who wept not for him as a Mortal, or as thinking *Hephæftions* Divinity a Jeft, but by having the Memory of their former Friendfhip come into his Mind.

Alexander therefore being thus affected, offer'd the moft appofite Avenue to Flattery and Calumny imaginable. For as when Men befiege a Town they do not Affault the moft lofty and moft Fortify'd Part of the Wall, but that which is Loweft, moft Weak, and worft Defended. And there they make their fierceft Onfet, as the moft ready and practicable place of entring the Town. Thus the *Calumniators* attack the weakeft and moft frail parts of their Hearers Minds, and thofe to which their Approaches are the moft eafy and leaft Guarded, here they place their Engines, and furprize the Fort while they meet with no Refiftance, or any apprehenfions of any Hoftile Force; and being got within the Walls they deftroy all with Fire and Sword. Thus do thefe Fellows, with a Mind they take and reduce to their Slavery.

The Arts they make use of against the Absent are Fallacy, Lyes, Perjury, Prayers, Impudence, and a thousand other Tricks, the greatest of which is Flattery, the near Relation and Sister of Calumny. For there is no one so generous who is not to be subdu'd by the Calumnies of Flattery; and then Calumny undermines and takes away the Foundations. And these are what come from Abroad; but from within there are many to help the Treachery, who assist the Treason, open the Gates, and apply all their Care and Industry, and all manner of ways to take the mind of him they Address to.

Among these the desire of Novelty claims the first Place, and a loathing of the present Condition, which is implanted by Nature in the Mind and Genius of Mankind, which stretches our Credulity to the Belief of ev'n Impossibilites For I know not how it comes to pass, but we find, that we are all pleas'd to hear Informations, and Scandal, that carry pregnant Circumstances of Suspicion. Nay, I have met with some so wonderfully pleas'd with Calumny. as if they were tickled with a Feather. When a Calumniator meets with such Allyes then he pushes on and takes all by Storm; nor does the Victory prove difficult, where there

G

is no Reſiſtance made, but he, who hears, immediately ſurrenders to the Beſiegers; and he who is accus'd is entirely ignorant of the Ambuſcade. For thoſe, who are Calumniouſly inform'd againſt, Periſh like thoſe, who fall in the Sack of a City, they are ſlain in their Sleeps. And that, which is the moſt miſerable Circumſtance of the matter, the poor Man, who is accus'd, knowing nothing of the Tranſactions and Machinations againſt him, approaches his Friend with his uſual Freedom, and a ſerene Countenance, as not conſcious to himſelf of any Guilt; makes his wonted Addreſs, while the unhappy Wretch is ſurrounded with ſecret Dangers, which he does not ſee. Then the *Great* Friend, if he be a Man of an ingenuous and open Temper, Free, and without Apprehenſion, breaks his Anger, and declares his Mind; and having heard his Defence, acknowledges that he has, with too little Ground and Reaſon, been exaſperated againſt his Favourite. But if he be of a more baſe and ſlaviſh Principle, he may indeed receive him, and give him a ſort of fawning Grin or half Smile; but in his Mind hates him, and ſecretly grinds his Teeth, and, as the Poet ſays, *Lets his Anger ſwell within his Mind.*

Then

Then he clandeftinely ruminates on his Refentment. But a Man of this Temper I efteem the moft unjuft and and flavifh of Mankind, who fetting a Seal on his Lips, and the liberty of his Tongue, feeds and nourifhes his Spleen within his Bofom, and encreafes the Hatred conceiv'd in himfelf, while he conceals one thing in his Mind, and expreffes another in his Words, and Acts in himfelf a Tragedy full of various Paffions. And this he does in the higheft Degree, when the Informer feems to do the fame, and appears to have been before a Friend of him, whom he Accufes: For then they are fo far from hearing the Defence of the Accufed, that this will not fo much as hear him fpeak, fo abounding a Credit does that Opinion of their former Friendfhip give to the Calumny. But they do not reflect, that the moft Intimate Familiarity often admits of many Difgufts, and Diffatisfactions; and that fometimes a Man accufes his Companion of Things of which he himfelf is Guilty; while by fuch an Anticipation he endeavours to avoid the Calumny himfelf; and that no Man dares calumniate his Enemy. For

G 2 when

when there is a manifest Cause, the Accusation meets with no Credit. But Men choose to accuse those, to whom they are suppos'd Friends, endeavouring by so plausible a Pretence to engage those, that hear them, when they scruple not to Sacrifice their most Intimate Acquaintance, to their Interest and Service.

Nay, there are some Men, that when they have discover'd that a false Guilt has been laid to their Friends, are asham'd to own their having given Credit to the Imposture, and dare not admit or behold them afterwards, as if they were offended, that they cou'd not find them Guilty of any Crime against them.

The life of Man is repleat with many Evils, but with none greater, than that easie Credulity, which they have for Calumny without hearing the Defence of the Accused. For as *Attia* says,

Mayst thou, O Prætus feel relentless Fate,
Unless Bellerophon perish by his Hate.
Who with audacious Force and Flatte-
                  (strove,
To taint my Honour with adulterous
                     (Love.
     th

tho' she her self had follicitated his Compliance, and found a generous Repulse. And it was a Million to one, but the generous Youth had perished in his Combate with the *Chymæra*, and there found a punishment for his Chastity, and his Modest Regard to the Laws of Hospitality, being assulted by the Insinuations of a lewd lascivious and disappointed Woman. Some such false Suggestions of *Phædra* against her Son in Law *Hippolitus*, made his own Father destroy him, tho' he had been guilty of not the least Impiety or Wickedness

But some may perchance object, that a Calumniator is sometimes worthy of Credit, and that we ought to give Ear to them, who have never been guilty of any such Villainies as we have mention'd. Can History shew us a juster Man, than *Aristides*, and yet he conspir'd against *Themistocles*, and stirr'd up the Minds of the People against him, being tickled with the Emulation of popular Applause, as they say, and Glory. 'Tis true, *Aristides* was otherwise a good Man, but since he was a Man, he was

not

not exempt from Anger, loving some,
and hating others.   And if that Account we have of *Palamedes* be true,
one of the Wiseft of the *Greeks*, and
in all other things a Man of Excellent
Probity, burning with Envy laid Snares
for the Life of a Relation, a Friend
and Companion in the fame Dangerous Expedition.   So Natural, alas!
it is to Man, to fall into this Errour.
Further, What need we inftance *Socrates* accus'd of Impiety, or Treafon
to the *Athenians* ?   What fhou'd we
mention *Themiftocles* and *Miltiades*
after fo many Victories obtained by
them fufpected of Treafon ?   Examples of this kind are without Number,
and thofe known now to every one of
the Vulgar themfelves.

What then ought a prudent Man to
do when any doubts arife about Truth
or Vertue ?   Certainly the fame, that
Homer teaches us in his Fable of the
Sirens ; when he commands us to pafs
by thefe pernicious Pleafures of Difcourfe, that he fhould feal up his Ears,
not open them at all to thofe, who are
prepoffefs'd with any Paffion: but
placing a Porter at their Avenues, that
is Reafon, to examine the Accufations ;
                                                                he

he shou'd admit those which are just and well grounded; but reject and cast aside those, which are Evil and Mischievous. For it wou'd be extreamly ridiculous to set Porters at our Gates, and leave our Ears and Mind open and exposed to every false and unweigh'd Impression.

When therefore any one brings up such Stories winnow well the Matter, and have no regard to the Age, Manners nor Address of the Speaker. For by how much any Man is the more eloquent and plausible speaker, by so much he requires a more accurate Disquisition to examine what he says. We must not therefore give Credit to another Man's Judgment, or rather to the hatred of the Accuser; but must reserve to our selves a Scrutiny into the Tuth, both by attributing Envy to the Calumniator, and by clearing up the Arguments of both sides. And by this means may justly hate one, and embrace the other, which we shall approve of. But before this be done to be mov'd to Anger by Calumny, is an Argument of a very Childish judgment, an abject Mind, and the most Alien from Justice.

But the only Caufe of all this is, *Ignorance,* and that Darknefs and Obfcurity, in which the Manners and Principles of all Men are involv'd. For if any of the Gods wou'd enlighten our Minds, *Calumny* wou'd vanifh into Hell, finding no Place of Refidence, where things were illuftrated by *Truth.*

Charon: Or, the *Contemplator.*

CHARON:

OR, THE

CONTEMPLATOR.

By Mr. Cashen

The Argument.

Lucian in this Dialogue exposes the Folly of Mankind, who making no Account of unavoidable Death, abandon themselves entirely to the Pursuit and Enjoyment of the uncertain Advantages of a short Life, such as Health, Strength of Body, Power, Riches, Glory, and the like. He ridicules also the false Honours given to the Dead, and shews, that all Nature is subject to Age, Disease, and Death it self.

Mercury. Y'Are merry *Charon*, prithee the Jest? and what are the weighty Considerations that mov'd you to quit the Skuller, and come up into the Light you're so great a Stranger to?

Charon Why, faith, *Mercury*, I had e'en a Month's mind to see how Men employ'd themfelves, what Life was, and how great its Pleafures, they fo much bewail the lofs of when they came among us; For not one of them ever made that Voyage with dry Eyes. So like young *Protefilaus* of *Theffaly*, I begg'd a Holy Day from the Prince of Darknefs, laid up my Boat, am come up into the World, and as I take it, have very happily light upon you, for being fo well acquainted here, you'll fhew me all things.

Mercury. I have fomething elfe to do (I thank ye) good Mr *Ferryman*; for *Jupiter* has difpatch'd me on an Errand that relates to Mankind, and you know he's a tefty old God, and fhou'd he take me tardy, he'd condemn me for ever to your Habitation and Complexion; at leaft, ferve me as he did *Vulcan*, give me fuch a kick from the Sky, that whenever I ferv'd him as, Cupbearer, the hitch and limping I fhou'd catch in the Fall, wou'd make me the Sport of the Company.

Charon. What! then you'll take no notice of your Comrade and Mate, but let him wander about the Earth? 'Twou'd indeed become Mrs *Maia*'s Son to remember, I never put him to the Swab, or Oar, though a lufty broad-back'd Fellow; but you lay at your length and fnoar'd on a Voyage upon the Hatches; unlefs perhaps you met fome pratling Deceas'd, who entertain'd you at his own ridiculous Charge, till we had made our courfe, whilft I, *Jove* help me, old as I am, tugg'd eternally at both Oars. But, my dear little *Mercury*, for God's fake take me along with you to fee fome Sights before I go, for elfe I fhall ftumble in the Light, as Men do in the Dark, and your Favour will be always moft gratefully remembred by your Friend and Servant.

Mercury. Now am I in bodily Fear, that this damn'd Peregrination of ours will coft me fome broken Bones at leaft; but (hang it,) there's no refifting ones Deftiny, and what wou'd not one do to ferve ones Friend. But 'twill be impoffible for you to fee every thing, for that wou'd be the Bufinefs of many Years, and *Jupiter* wou'd have me cry'd by all the Beadles of Heaven, fhou'd I ftay: Nor cou'd you difcharge your Offices to the Dead; and fhou'd you let 'em ftick a hand any time, *Pluto's* Kingdom muft fuffer by it, befides that plaguy Publican *Æacus* wou'd keep an old pother, fhou'd he be behind in his reckoning of the *Poll-money.* But however, let's confider what's to be done, that you may know the principal Matters.

Char. Nay, take you care of that, for I'm a perfect Stranger, *Mercury.*

Mer. In fhort then, we muft get to fome high Place, and from thence furvey all. Cou'd you come up into Heaven with me, we might without more ado, through a Tube of Clouds, take a view of the whole World; but that may'nt be neither, for you being always with *Ghofts* and *Hobgoblins,* muft not come into the Court of *Jupiter.* 'Tis high time to look out fome convenient Mountain or other.

Char. When we made a Voyage together,
you know, *Mercury,* what I us'd to say to
you, if the Wind happened to blow fresh
in our Teeth, and the Waves to rise, and
you ignorantly would pretend to advise,
either to take down the Sails, shorten the
Course, or run the Vessel adrift, I often bid
you hold your prating, and let me, that
knew what was to be done, look to the
Boat; so now that you're at the Helm
do what you think fit, and I will sail by
your Steering, like a Beaco.

Mer. You'ie i'th' right on't, old Boy, I
do know what is proper, and will find a
Prospective, but the Question is now, whether *Caucasus;* or *Parnassus,* that's higher,
or *Olympus* that's highest of all, be the
more convenient Place; but now I think
on't, while I'm staring at that same *Olympus,* we shall need your Help.

Char. You may use me, to my Power,
I'll obey you

Mer. The Poet *Homer* tells us, that the
two Sons of *Alœus* had resolv'd to pluck
up *Ossa* by the Roots, clap it upon *Olympus,*
Pelion upon that, and so make a Ladder of
Mountains to scale Heaven; but the Youth
paid for their impious Frolick, now we,
who intend no Affront to the Gods, may
safely pile Mountain upon Mountain,
that we may have the fairer Prospect

Char. And think ye that we can pile
Pelion and *Ossa* one a-top o'th' other?

Mer. Why not? Are not we God
strong, as those Boys?

Char. Ay, but 'tis a woundy Task, let me tell you that.

Mer. 'Tis so indeed; but you *Charon* know nothing of the Poets, that old famous *Homer* cou'd heap ye up Hills on Hills, give you a lift to the Sky, and I wonder you should think much of that, since you know how *Atlas* supports Heaven; and may be you have heard too of my Brother *Hercules*, who succeeded him while he rested himself

Char. I have heard such Stories, but you and the Poets look to the truth of 'em

Mer They're true, as Oracles Why should those wise Men lie so? Let us then pluck up *Offa*, as that Mason *Homer* directs in his Verses, next *Pelion*, shaded o'er with Trees, see how easily and poetically we have done it already. Now let's see if we are high enough, or must we raise it higher. Oh! we're yet at the very bottom of the Sky, for we can scarce see *Ionia* and *Lydia* on the East, no more, than *Italy* and *Sicily* on the West, the *Danube* on the North, and only *Crete* on the South, and scarce that too; wherefore we must clap *Oeta* upon these, and *Parnassus* upon 'em all.

Char. Agreed, but let's look to't, that in raising our Work so very high, we don't make it dangerous, and so tumbling along with it, find by the bitter Experience of broken Pates, that we have reason to curse this new *Homerical* way of Building.

Mer.

Mer. Have a good Heart, *Charon*, all's
safe, lift *Oeta* there; here *Parnaſſus*, ſo I'll
try again . O ! 'tis very well, I can ſee every thing, and come you up now.

Char. Lends your Hand, *Mercury*, for
(believe me) 'tis no Mole-hill you'd have
me climb.

Mer If you wou'd ſee all, *Charon*, I
muſt tell you, to be very ſafe and very
curious, are hardly conſiſtent. But, here
take hold of my Hand, and ſet your Foot
faſt. 'Tis very well, now you're up, and
ſince *Parnaſſus* has two Peaks, let each ſit on
one, and look you round and conſider every
thing.

Char. I ſee a large Country, and a Lake
that waſhes it, with Mountains and Rivers bigger than *Cocytus* and *Phlegeton*, and
Men, but they are very little, with their
Hives

Mer. Thoſe are Cities you call Hives.

Char. Why, look ye *Mercury*! to how
little Purpoſe have we made ſuch work
with theſe Mountains ?

Mer. What's the matter ?

Char. The matter! I can ſee nothing
here ; I wou'd not look down upon Towns
and Mountains, as upon thoſe in a Map,
but I wou'd ſee Men themſelves, and what
they're doing, and hear what they're ſaying, as when I firſt met you, and you
ask'd me what I laugh'd at, I had heard
ſomething, and was much pleaſed with
it.

Mer. What was that ?

Char. A Fellow being invited by his Friend to Supper, told him, he'd be with him the next Night, and while the Words were yet in his Mouth, a Tile fell from the House (Heaven knows who threw it down) and knock'd him on the Head, so I laugh'd at him for not keeping his Promise, and now, that we may hear and see better, let us get down again.

Mer. Not so fast, I'll take care of that, for by a Spell of old *Homer*'s, I'll give a long Sight, and as soon as I have pronounced the Charm, take notice you doubt no more, but see every thing clearly.

Char. Come then, let's hear it, say on.

*Mer. From his dark Eyes I did remove the
    Clouds,
And he saw clearly who were Men, who
Gods.*

Char. Bless me!
Mer. What! don't you see yet?
Char. See! I marry that I do, *Lynceus* was blind to me; so that now I'd have you teach me all things, and answer my Questions; but let me ask you in *Homer*'s Verses, to shew you, that (as simple as I sit here) I can admire and understand a good Saying when I hear it.

Mer. But how do you pretend to know any thing of him, having never been out of your Sculler?

Char. Why look ye now! must you always have a Fling at my Profession? When I ferry'd him over, I heard him sing a great many Catches, of which I remember some still, and we were then in no small Danger, for when he begun that unlucky Song, (I'm sure it was to the Passengers) *Neptune* gathered the Clouds, strikes the Seas with his Trident, and raises all the Waves, which (together with the Storm brought on by those damn'd Verses) had like to have overset us   Then *Homer* (being Sea-sick) spews out a whole Load of Poetry upon *Scylla*, *Charybdis*, and the *Cyclops*.

Mer 'Twas no hard matter then to have remembred something of that large Vomit

Char But tell me,

> *What Fellow's that, who stalks so like a God*
> *Tall, brawny, straight, and in his Should'e*
>   *broad ?*

Mer. That's *Milo* the great Wrestler of *Crotona*, so famous among the *Greeks* for carrying a Bull half a Mile.

Char But, *Mercury*, how much more justly are all their Praises due to me, who, when Death, that unconquerable Enemy, has laid him upon his Back, will take that same *Milo* and ferry him over to eternal Darkness, nor shall he know by whom he was foiled, and it shall give him infinite Trouble, as often as he remembers his Crowns and his Glory, though now he prides himself in the Applauses of his Strength   Wou'd one believe he ever considers he must die?

Me

Mer How, Fool, wou'd you have him think of Death in so prosperous a Health?

Char. Well; let him pass, when he takes our Voyage, how shall we laugh at his Cost? we shall break many a Jest upon that Strength, when he shall be so little able to carry a Bull, that he shan't lift a Flea. But what reverend Man is that there? he's no *Greek* by his dress.

Mer. That's *Cyrus*, *Cambyses*'s Son, who brought over the Empire of the *Medes* to the *Persians*, has lately subdued the *Assyrians*, took *Babylon*, and is now preparing a War with *Lydia*, that he might establish himself an unlimited Empire upon the Conquest of *Crasus*.

Char. Where is that *Crasus* you speak of?

Mer. Turn and look upon that Cittadel encompass'd with a triple Wall; 'tis *Sardis*, and you may see *Crasus* himself seated upon a Throne of Gold, talking with *Solon* the *Athenian*. Shall we listen?

Char. By all means.

Crasus. And now, my Guest of *Athens*, that you have seen my Riches, my Treasures of uncoin'd Gold, and precious Furniture, give me your Thoughts of my Condition, and whom do you take to be the happiest Man?

Char How will *Solon* answer the Fool?

Mer. No Impertinence, good *Charon.*

Solon There have been but very few happy, *Crasus*, but of those who fell in my Knowledge, *Cleobis* and *Bito* seem the Favourites of Heaven.

Char.

Char. He means (I'll warrant ye) the Sons of that Argive-Priests, who were found dead together, next day after they had drawn their Mother's Chariot to the Temple.

Crœſus. Be't ſo ; let them have the firſt Place: Who fills the next ?

Solon. Tellus, the *Athenian,* who having liv'd well, dy'd for his Country.

Crœſus. Poor Wretch ; then am not I happy ?

Solon. I can yet make no Judgment , you have not reach'd the end of your days, and Death alone can ſhew us nicely, who has ran the Race of Life moſt happily.

Char. Well ſaid, *Solon,* (i'faith) thou doſt not forget us, but think'ſt (and truly too) that our Boat is the beſt Judge in this Caſe But who are thoſe Fellows *Crœſus* ſends away loaden, and what is it they carry ?

Mer. He's conſecrating golden Ingots to *Apollo,* as a Thanks-offering for that Oracle, by which he ſhall ſhortly be undone, for 'tis a ſuperſtitious Bigot.

Char. Then that's Gold that looks with a paliſh Brightneſs, 'tis the firſt time I ever ſaw it, tho' I heard on't ſo often

Mer. That's the dear glorious Name for which the World's in Arms.

Char. For my part, all the good I ſee in it is, that it tires thoſe that carry it.

Mer. You are ſafely ignorant what Wars, *Treaſons, Robberies, Perjuries, Murthers, Chains,* how many *tedious Voyages,* hazardous *Ways* of Traffick, and how ſevere Slaveries that Metal engages Mankind in.

Char.

Char. And is it for thofe Reafons preferable to Brafs ? I know Brafs ; my Paffengers pay their Fare in Brafs.

Mer. No, the plenty of Brafs makes it lefs valued ; there is but little Gold, and that the Miners dig very deep for too ; for it comes out of the Earth, as Lead and other Mettals do.

Char. Ridiculous Folly of Men, who fo eagerly thirft after that, which they muft purchafe with Pain, and keep with Care, and whofe very Enjoyment muft coft 'em their Peace.

Mer. But you fee *Solon* feems to have no regard of it, but defpifes the *Barbarian* and his Vanity ; and I think is going to ask him fomewhat. Let's hearken.

Solon. Tell me, *Cræfus,* do you think *Apollo* ftands in any great need of what you fend him ?

Cræfus. Yes, by *Jupiter* do I, for all his *Delphos* can't fhew fuch another Offering

Solon. And you believe you bring the God in your Debt, and make him happy, by giving him to poffefs your Golden Ingots.

Cræf. And well I may.

Solon. You'd have one think, *Cræfus,* that Heaven's a Commonwealth of Beggars, if the Gods muft come to *Lydia* for Gold when they have occafion for it.

Cræf. What Place can afford 'em that plenty our *Lydia* can ?

Solon. But let me know, *Cræfus,* whether there be any Iron in *Lydia* ?

Cræf. None at all.

Solon.

Solon. Why then you want the better Metal of the two.

Cræf. Wherein is Iron to be preferred to Gold.

Solon. If you will anfwer, and keep your Temper, you may foon know.

Cræf. Then go on and queftion me *Solon*

Solon. Whether is to be valued moft, he that keeps, or the thing that is kept?

Cræf. He that keeps, certainly.

Solon. If, therefore, *Cyrus*, (as 'tis reported) fhou'd make War upon *Lydia*, wou'd you make your Army's Swords of Gold, or Iron?

Cræf. No doubt of Iron.

Solon. Yet, fhou'd you not procure it, your Gold wou'd be plunder'd by the *Perfians*.

Cræf Have a care what you fay, Friend

Solon. Nay, the Gods forbid it fhou'd come to that, but you feem now to confe the preference is due to Iron

Cræf. What then, wou'd you have me fend Iron Ingots, and call back my Gold?

Solon Nor has *Apollo* occafion for Iron, but whether you confecrate Brafs or Gold, or whatever Metal it is, you but provide a Booty for the *Phocians*, *Beotians*, or it may be the *Delphians* themfelves, or fome Tyrant or Robber; for the God cares but little to deal with Goldfmiths.

Cræf You always quarrel with me about my Riches, and envy me.

Mer. That *Lydian* there, *Charon*, can bear an honeft freedom of Speech and
Truth

Truth, but thinks it a strange thing for a poor Man to contradict him without trembling; but he shall one Day remember *Solon*, when, being taken Prisoner by *Cyrus*, he shall be forc'd up the Funeral Pile alive; for to the Day I heard *Clotho* reading the Destinies of Men, among the rest, that *Cræsus* shou'd be taken Prisoner by *Cyrus*, *Cyrus* himself be slain by that Queen of the *Massagetes*. Do you see that *Scythian* Woman yonder, managing a white Horse?

Char. I do, who is she?

Mer. That's *Tomyris*, who with her own Hand shall cut off the Head of *Cyrus*, and throw it into a Vessel of Blood; but do you see that *Cambysses* his Son there? He shall succeed his Father, and when by a Thousand wild Follies he has run over *Lydia* and *Ethiopia*, he shall then fall stark mad, and as soon as he has kill'd *Apis*, shall die.

Char. Oh Comical! Can any one see these Fellows despise others, and be so dully patient, as not to break his Spleen at them? For who wou'd think, that yonder Man shall shortly be a Captive, or this have his Fool's-head pickled in a Vessel of Blood? But who's that, *Mercury*, who buttons on his Purple Robe, whose Head a glorious Diadem does crown.

And to whose Hand obedient Cook does bring.
from Men of Fish a Tributary Ring,
And who of yonder Isle do's boast himself the King,

A a 2.

Mer. *Charon,* you handfomely enough tack Rhime and Profe together, that's *Polycrates* the Tyrant of *Samos,* who thinks himfelf compleatly happy, yet fhall be betray'd to *Oratas* by his Domeflick *Meandius,* in a Moment be ftript of all his Happinefs, and crucify'd, for I remember *Clotho* faid fo too.

Char. Gramercy *Clotho,* bravely cut off their Heads and crucifie them, that they may know that they are but Men; let 'em be lifted higher, that they may be crufh'd with the greater Fall: And I'll laugh a 'em when they come into my Boat, naked of all their Glory, Crowns, Gold and Purple.

Mer. And it will all come to that, don't you fee a confus'd Multitude, *Charon,* where fome Travel, fome make War, fome wrangle at the Lawyers Bar, fome exercife Husbandry, others let out their Money to Ufury, and others beg.

Char. I fee indeed an undiftinguifhable Crowd, a Life full of Trouble, and the Cities like the Hives of Bees, where every one has his Sting to wound his Neighbour fome, though very few, drive and are driven downwards; but what is that Troop that buzzes round 'em?

Mer. Thofe, *Charon,* are their Paffions Hopes, Fears, Madnefs, Pleafure, Avarice, Anger, Hatred, and the like: From thefe proceed the Ignorance of the Mob, and the fame Breaft are lodged, by them both Anger, Hatred, Jealoufie, Blindnefs, Ignorance, and Covetoufnefs. Fear and Hope flutter above 'em, and Fear fometimes ftrikes 'em with a chilling Horror, and other times but fhakes 'em with a fhort Ague fit; Hope lifts 'em above themfelves, and when they think they're moft fecure of their Wifhes, they grafp the Air, and the deluding Joy is flown away, as you fee in *Tantalus* below. Now if you'll turn your Eyes this way, there are the *Parcæ* diftributing to each his Fate, whence on the flender Threads of Life they all depend.

Char. I fee, and 'tis a moft fine Web, to which they are all faften'd, they are link'd too one to another·

Mer. They are fo, for 'tis decreed, that this Man fhall kill that; that again do the fame civil Office for a Third; this fhall inherit yonder's Eftate, though his Thread be fhorter; and this their being linkt together fignifies: Each Man hangs by a Thread, and this, who is fo lifted up, fhall tumble with a mighty Noife, foon as his Load fhall become too heavy for the Thread; while yonder Man, who is rais'd but little from the Earth, drops down in Silence, and his very Neighbours are fcarce aware of his Fall.

Char. How extravagantly ridiculous are thefe things you tell me, *Mercury.*

Mer. So very ridiculous, that Words are too fhort to reach the heighth of their Folly. For, firft, their Defires are *exorbitant*, from which *juft Death* fnatches 'em away in the ftrength of their Hopes, and though the Envoys and Minifters of Fate are fo numerous, as *Fevers, Confumptions,*

Rotten

Rotten Lungs, *Daggers*, *Poisons*, *Affassines*, *Judges* and *Tyrants*, yet never does the melancholy Remembrance of 'em damp or divert 'em from the *mad* Chace of Pleasure, but soon as they find the sad mistake, nothing is to be heard but *Woe* and *Lamentation*, *idle Sighs*, and *unrelieving Alasses*! But had they earlier consider'd they were mortal, and that it was but a short time they were allow'd to travel o'er the Stage of Life, that leaving all that's dear behind 'em, they must pass from the World as in a Dream, they wou'd then live wiser, and die with less Concern; while, as it is, they expect an Immortality of Pleasure; when ever the Executioner rushes in upon 'em, and drags 'em off with a swift *Fever*, or a slow *Consumption*, how are they grieved to be divided from what their foolish Wishes perswaded them to be *Eternal*? Look on that Builder there, and think what wou'd he not rather do, though he now industriously presses on the Workmen to the finishing his House, did he believe it shou'd no sooner be built, but that he must die, and leave the Possession of it to his Heir, e'er he poor Wretch shall have had once the Pleasure of supping in it. He who hugs himself in his becoming a Father, entertains his Friends at a Feast of Joy, and calls the Boy by his own Name. If he knew the Child shou'd never out live his Seventh Year, wou'd he, think you, be so wanton at his Birth? The reason is, he looks upon himself, as happy in a Son who shall hereafter be crown'd in the O-

lympic

lympick Games, and obferves not his Neighbour carrying out his Son to the laft Fire, nor looks foward to what end awaits him. You fee fome fighting about the Bounds of their Poffeffions, fome heaping up Wealth they are none of 'em ever likely to enjoy.

Char. I have feen, and wonder what they find fo agreeable in Life, that they fhou'd fo lament the lofs of it.

Mer Now, fhou'd we examine the Condition of Princes, who feem to be placed out of the reach of *ill Fortune*, we fhou'd find their *Troubles* out number their *Joys*, and fee e'en them too rack'd with *Fears*, *Treafons*, *Factions*, *Hates*, *Anger* and *Flatteries*, and though we take no Account of the Griefs and Difeafes common to them with other Men, 'twou'd require no lefs time to reckon up the Sufferings peculiar to their Condition, than thofe of the *lower Poverty*

Ch. Then, *Mercury*, let me tell you what I think Mankind and their Life here refemble moft You may have feen, among the Bubbles of a rapid Stream, that make up the Froth, fome bigger, and rifing over others, fwell higher, and laft longer; fome lefs, that are fooner broke, and loft in the Stream; fome others, that as if they were made only, that they might perifh, fall in the very Moment they are rais'd Nor can it indeed be otherwife. Such is Man's Life, they all rife with a Breath, fome higher, fome lower, fome to a longer, fome to a fhorter Continuance, but they are *all* broke at laft.

Mer. You come nothing fhort of *Homer*, in his Comparifon of Man's Life, who likens them to the Leaves of Trees

Char. Yet fuch, as you fee 'em, how do they contend for Empire, Honour and Riches, which they muft all quit, and come down to us with a *fingle Half-penny* Let us then, being in this high Place, with a loud Voice, preach to 'em, that they leave off to weary themfelves for no Price, and keep their laft Hour before their Eyes Come, I'll fpeak to 'em thus : Hold, *Madmen*, you fhan't live for ever, and what is this you purfue fo eagerly ? Nothing of all you prize fo much here, fhall you carry with you at your Death; you fhall all go naked hence ; your Houfes, your Poffeffions, your Gold fhall be referved for others, and fhall for ever change their Mafters. Now cou'd I warn 'em thus, do ye think they wou'd manage themfelves more prudently.

Mer. You're very wife I'll warrant you, you don't know I fee how Ignorance has blinded 'em, you can't bore their Ears with an Augre, they have ftuff'd 'em fo full of Wax, like the Comrades of *Ulyffes*, when he apprehended their hearing the Songs of the *Syrens*. How then cou'd they hear though you fhou'd bawl till you fplit again ? For what *Lethe* does with you, Ignorance does here ; yet are there fome who have kept themfelves free to difcover things, as they are, and diftinguifh Truth from Falfhood.

Char. Then let me preach to them

Mer. How needlefs is it to tell 'em, what they know as well as you? Don't you fee how they feperate themfelves from the Crowd, and laugh at 'em preparing themfelves for their Journey to you? And they are hated too by thofe, whofe Follies they blame.

Char. Brave Fellows, but there are few of 'em !

Mer. And they're enough too, but let's defcend now.

Char. There's one thing more, *Mercury,* which, when you have taught me, your Inftructions will be compleat. I wou'd fee where they lay the dead Bodies

Mer. They call 'em *Monuments,* *Tombs,* and *Sepulchres.* Don't you fee thofe *Heaps,* thofe *Pillars* and *Piramids* at the Gate of the Cities? Thofe are the *Repoſitories of the Dead*

Char What then, do thofe yonder a-noint and put Crowns upon Tomb-Stones? I fee others there building up a Pile, and having dug a Trench round it, burn on it fumptuous Banquets, and pour Wine and Mead, as near as I can guefs, into the Trenches.

Mer I don't know how the Dead are concern'd in it, *Charon,* but thefe Fools believe that the Ghofts returning from Hell, flutter about, and drink in the Smell and Smoak, and Mud they make here.

Char What thofe eat and drink whofe Souls are cover'd with Mofs? how ridiculous it is for you to talk fo, who coming

down every day with the Dead, know
that they can never return again; And in
deed, my Passees were no less so, if I
shou'd be oblig'd, not only to carry 'em
down, but to bring 'em back again to eat
and drink   O sots! what Madness is this,
you little know how wide the distance is
between the *Living* and the *Dead*, and how
Matters are carry'd among us.

Where they an equal Honour share,
Who buried or unburied are,
Where Agamemnon *knows no more*
Than Irus *he contemn'd before*
Where fair Achilles *and* Thersites *lie,*
Equally naked, poor, and dry,
Wander alike through Vales and Hills,
Be set with Flowers of Daffodils.

Mer. Bless me! how much have you
learnt from *Homer?* But since you desire
it, I'll shew you *Achilles's* Tomb. Look
there, that which lies near the Sea, upon
the Promontory *Tigeum, Ajax* is buried over-
against him in *Rhæteum.*

Char. Those are not great Monuments,
but shew me those Cities of which we
heard such great Things below; *Ninive*
the City of *Sardanapalus, Babylon, Mycene,*
Cleone, and *Troy* it self; for I remember,
that for these Ten Years past I have carried over many from thence; and though I
scarce brought away my Boat from it, I
never wanted a Fare.

Mer

Mer. Ninive is utterly demolish'd, so
that it is a hard matter to know where it
was; yonder is *Babylon*, beautified with so
many Towers, fortified with such a great
Wall, which shortly shall be no more, and
in no better Condition than *Ninive*, but
for *Mycene* and *Cleone*. I'm asham'd to shew
you them, for you'll hang *Homer* when
you go down, for so magnifying two such
paltry Villages, and keeping such stir with
'em in his Verses. But they were formerly
pretty Places, though they are now lost,
for Cities die as well as Men, and what
is more wonderful, Rivers too, so that
there remains nothing of *Inachus*, that
fam'd River of *Argos*

Cur. What is it you praise *Homer?* and
where are those Names of great *Ilium* and
fair *Cleone?* but in the mean time, who are
those fighting there, and what do they
knock one another o'th' Head for?

Mer. They are the *Lacedemonians* and
Argives, and that is *Othryas*, who being half
dead, is yet raising a Trophy to his own
Name.

Char. What was this War undertaken
for?

Mer. For the very Field they fight in.

Char. O foolish Men! who are ignorant,
that though they possess'd the whole *Pello-
ponesus*, they should scarce receive a Pearch
length from *Æacus* But others will turn
this Field to better Uses, and plough where
that Trophy's built

Mer. So it ſhall happen indeed, but let's deſcend, and leave the Mountains where we found 'em, and let's be gone, you to your Sculler, I on my Errand ; I'll bring ſome Dead to you e'er long.

Char. You have oblig'd me, *Mercury,* and I'll put you in the Liſt of my beſt Friends, for the aſſiſting me in this Peregrination　But how are unhappy Men employ'd! Kings guided Bricks , magnificent Sacrifices and Battles ' but no thought at all of *Charon.*

T H E

THE
IMAGES.

Lycinus and *Polystratus*

Translated by Mr. Vernon.

The Argument.

This Dialogue gives the Draught of a compleat Woman, both in Mind and Person.

Lycinus I Proteft, my dear *Polyftratus*, I have fuffer'd the fame, from the fight I had juft now of a beautiful Woman, which they did who look'd upon the *Gorgon*'s Head; and as that Fable goes, from a Man, I am, almoft, become Stone, ftiff and cold with the very wonder

Polyftratus Indeed, the fight you fpeak of muft be extraordinary, and almoft miraculous, if a Woman can put *Lycinus* befides himfelf. For that pretty Boys had the effect upon you, is no News; fo that the whole Mountain *Sypilus* might fooner be remov'd, than you from gaping after, and fometimes like *Tantatuls*'s Daughter,

B b 4   from

from shedding Tears over them. But pre-
thee let us hear at length who this _Petri-
fying Medusa_ is, whence came she? that I
may see her, for I humbly conceive, you
would not envy a Man the sight of her,
nor will rack your self with Jealousy, since
I too must be petrified just by you for my
Curiosity.

Lyc. But first be well assur'd, that should
you only see her from a Balcony, she immediately strikes you dumb, and leaves
you as fix'd and immoveable, as a Statue.
But if you think this slight, and not so
dangerous, (for perhaps the Wound which
is made by your seeing her is not mortal)
what if she should chance to turn about
and spy you, what Art then could draw
you from her? You are chain'd and fet-
ter'd, and she draws you where she pleases,
as a Loadstone does Iron.

Pol. I prithee, good _Lycinus_, leave framing
to your self an Idea of some wondrous Beauty, but tell me in plain Terms, who she
is.

Lyc. You think, then, I perceive, I have
spoken too much; whereas I my self fear,
upon your seeing her, I may then be
thought unable to commend her enough,
so far does she surpass all that I can say.
But for telling you who she is, is more
than I can do. She has great Observance
paid her, a very noble Retinue, a great
number of Eunuchs and waiting Women:
in short, every thing about her, bespeaks
her somewhat greater than any private
Person.

Pol. Did you not enquire her Name?

Lac. No indeed, not I; only in general I learnt, she is of *Ionia*: For one of the Company turning to his next Man, cried out, as she passed by, such usually are your *Smyrna* Beauties, and 'tis no wonder if the fairest of the *Ionian* Cities produce a Woman the fairest of her Sex. I have some reason likewise to believe, that he was of *Smyrna* who cried out so, such a Pride he seem'd to take in her.

Pol. In good troth now, *Lycinus*, any one would take you for a Stone, by your management of this Affair, who had not the sense either to follow her, or to learn from that *Smyrnean*, who she was. But however, describe her Person, as exactly as you can, by that means I shall soon know her.

Lyc. Do you know what your Request is? Such an admirable Piece cannot be expressed by any Words, much less by mine. No not *Apelles*, nor *Zeuxis*, nor *Parrhasius*, those most famous Artists are sufficiently qualified for this Work, no nor even *Phidias* or *Alcamenes*, were they now living I shall grosly debase the Original through my unskilfulness

Pol. But pray thee, *Lycinus*, what kind of Face had she? for it is not so bold an Attempt, if you describe to your Friend this Image, and what Lineaments it has.

Lyc. However, I think I shall be less bold, if I call to my Assistance some of the ancient Artists, that they may make a Draught of this Lady.

Pol.

Pol. What makes you mention them? how can they come at your Call, who have been dead so long since?

Lyc. Easily enough, I warrant you, if you'll not think much to answer me a Question or two.

Pol. Pray try me.

Lyc. Have you ever travell'd to *Gnidos, Polystratus?*

Pol. Yes, I have.

Lyc. I hope you have seen their *Venus* there?

Pol. Ay, the very best of *Praxiteles's* Pieces.

Lyc. Have you heard the Story which the Townsmen tell of her, how one was enamour'd with the very Statue, who hiding himself privately in the Temple, did, as much as was in his power, commit a Rape upon it. But you shall know more of this some other time. But come answer me, for her Statue at *Gnidos* you say you have seen, did you ever see that of *Alcameres* at *Athens* in the Garden?

Pol. I had otherwise been justly esteem'd the most careless Person in Nature, had I overlook'd that Image, *Alcamenes's* Masterpiece.

Lyc. I will make no question then, *Polystratus,* but you have often gone up the Cittadel, and seen *Sosandra* by *Calamis* Hand.

Pol. O! very often.

Lyc. Well, these are sufficient for my Business. But which of all *Phidias's* Pieces do you most admire?

Pol. Which, but that at *Lemnos*, upon which *Phidias* himself vouchsafed to infcribe his Name; and next, his *Amazon*, refting upon a Spear.

Lyc. Moft curious Pieces indeed, my Friend, fo that we fhall need no other Artifts Come, I will now prefent you with a Picture, as well as I can do it, compos'd of all thefe you juft mention'd, containing whatever is illuftrious in each of them.

Pol How can this be done?

Lyc Without any difficulty; if trufting the Images to the management of a Difcourfe, we leave her to put them together, in the beft method fhe can, obferving carefully Mixture and Variety.

Pol. A good Contrivance; let her take them therefore, and begin, for I long to fee what ufe fhe can make of thefe, or how from this Medly, fhe can compofe one entire Piece, whofe Parts fhall agree amongft themfelves

Lyc Behold, then fhe prefents to your View the growing Picture after the Compofure. From the Statue of *Guidos* fhe fhall take the Head, for fhe will need no other Parts, they being Naked. As to the Hair, the Forehead, and well-turn'd Eyebrows, let her have them as *Praxiteles* has fafhion'd them. But as for the Eyes which roll and languifh with a graceful Sparklingnefs, let them be obferved too accordingly as *Praxiteles* has form'd them. But her Cheeks, and the fore-parts of her Face, fhe fhall take from *Alcamenes*, and that Image of his in the Garden. From hence too, fhall be

ex-

expreffed the Extremity of the Hands, and
well proportion'd Wrifts, the limber Fin
gers, ending in a fine, flender Make. As
for the whole Draught of the Face, the
Tendernefs of the Checks, with a Nofe or
juft Size, *Phidias* and his *Lemnian* Statue
fhall furnifh her with; and his other, the
Amazonian, fhall fupply the neat clofure of
the Mouth, and the whitenefs of the
Neck, and the Whole, *Calamis* with his
Sofandra fhall varnifh o're with a becoming
Modefty, her fmile too fhall be foft and
fecret like hers. Here likewife fhe may
fit her felf with a convenient modeft Drefs,
only her Head fhall be bare, and open
Her Stature, be what it will, fhall rather
refemble that at *Guidos*, than any other
Take this too from *Praxiteles*. What think
you, *Polyftratus*, is the Image like to be
Beautiful, efpecially when it has received
its finifhing Stroak

Pol. What, my Gentleman, have you
omitted any Excellence in that Image. af
ter the heaping upon it all thefe Perfecti
ons?

Lyc. Not tre leaft, my Friend, unlef
you think that the Colours and Ordinance
of the whole, does contribute little to
the making up a Beauty. 'Tis that, th
where Black is neceffary, it fhould be ex
quifitely Black, where White, a moft per
fect White, with a natural Red flowing
o'er the whole, and hence I fear the moft
difficult part is ftill wanting But where
fhall we be furnifhed with the Materials
fhall we fend for the Painters, particu

ly those renown'd for mixing Colours, and laying them on with great Skill and Artifice? Let them be sent for; *Polygnotus*, and the celebrated *Euphanor*, *Apelles* and *Aetion* too, alloting every one his proper Task. *Euphrates* shall paint the Hair, in Imitation of his *Juno*; the Beauty of the Eye-brows, with the Rosie-Cheek, shall be committed to *Polygnotus's* Skill, to be copied after *Cassandra* in the common Hall at *Delphos*. He shall likewise prepare the Drapery finely work'd, that as much as ought, may sit close and strait, but the greatest part, hang loose, as flutter'd by the Winds. *Apelles* shall form the other Parts, like those of *Pacata*, not altogether Pale, but moderately enliven'd with Red. The Lips shall be such as *Aetion's Roxana*. But above all, we must consult *Homer*, the Prince of Painters, although *Euphanor* and *Apelles* were by. The Colour then which he bestow'd on *Menelaus's* Thigh, describing it to be like a piece of Ivory, lightly stain'd with Purple, with that Colour let him draw the whole Neck and Nature. Let the same paint the Eyes also, making them Ox-like, large and black. But *Pindar* the *Theban* Poet must share with him in his Work, the Eye-lids shall be his care. *Homer* shall make her of a pleasant Countenance, with white Arms, and Rosie Fingers. To conclude, he shall with more Justice compare her to the Golden *Venus*, than he did formerly old *Briseus* his Daughter. Thus much shall be Statuaries, Painters, and Poets Work. But for the exact Beauty of the whole, it shall

be

be committed to one of the Graces, nay to
all together, though never so many of
them, and to all the little Loves dancing
to and fro; And now, who is there able
to imitate this Part to the Life?

Pol. O *Lycinus*! your Image is Divine,
no doubt dropt from the Heavens, being
one of those which are there fashion'd,
But what was she doing when ye saw her?

Lyc. She held a Book in her Hand, open-
ed in the middle, and seem'd to have pe-
rufed the first Part, and was then reading
the second. In her passing by, she discoun-
led with one of her Retinue, of what I
know not, for she spoke not loud enough
to be heard. However, happening to smile,
she discover'd her Teeth, *Polystratus*: Good
Gods! How white! How admirably siz'd!
What an equal Distance! In order they
grew like a Bracelet of Pearl, all neatly
polish'd, and of equal Bigness; and yet
they receiv'd new Lustre from the Red-
ness of her Lips, they stand according to
Homer's polish'd Ivory, fashion'd in Form
of a Saw, being not as you see in many
People, some broader than the rest, other
jetting forth, these wider, but all of one
quality, the same Colour, the same Bigness, and the same Distance. In short
she was a very Miracle; a Wonder exceeding any mortal Beauty.

Pol. Hold a little, *Polystratus*, I know
perfectly the Woman you describe, but
by these Characters, and the Country
You said, as I remember, she had a great
many Eunuchs following her, and some
                                    Soldie

Soldiers too. O my honeſt Friend, you have been telling me all this while of the moſt Illuſtrious Queen of the Great King.

Lyc. What is her Name?

Pol. A moſt ſweet and lovely one *Lycinus* the ſame with that of the moſt beautiful Wife of *Abradatus*: You muſt needs remember I know perfectly, who have ſo often heard *Zenophon* ſpeaking in Praiſe of a certain diſcreet and beautiful Lady.

Lyc. I do very well indeed, *Polyſtratus,* and methinks I am as much effected, as if I ſaw her, when I ever read him. I ſeem almoſt to hear her ſpeak, when ſhe there recounts what ſhe did, and how ſhe puts on her Lord's Armour, and how ſhe ſends him forth to Battle.

Pol. But, alas, my Friend, you have ſeen her but once only, like a tranſient Flaſh of Lightning, deſcribing thoſe things in her which are obvious to every Eye, ſuch as her Body and her Shape As for her Endowments of Mind, you have been no Spectator of them, nor know the Beauties of that Part, ten Thouſand times more Divine, than thoſe of her Body. But I am no Stranger even to thoſe, being acquainted, and often converſing with her, as her Country-man; and you very well know, I always prefer an eaſie Temper, and a civil obliging Carriage, mixt with a good Education, befoe any thing of a Beauty, as deſerving really in themſelves to be preſeir'd before thoſe outward Excellencies, For what an abſurd thing would

t

it be to fee a Man enamour'd more with
fine Cloaths, than with the Body that
wears them? Not but I think that the
perfect Fair, where Beauty of Soul and Body jointly confpire. For I can eafily point
you out not a few, who having the Character of compleat outward Make, yet
fpoil all by their Deformity within, fo
that their Beauty, immediarely upon their
fpeaking, decay'd and withered, being
found fault with, and a Blemifh caft upon
it, becaufe it was unworthily in League
with a wicked Miftrefs, the Soul. Such
as thefe, methinks, are not unlike *Egypt-
an* Temples, their fabrick is Beautiful
large, built with Stones of great Value
guilt with Gold, and adorn'd with Statues
of the beft Hands. But when you come
within, and expecting to fee their God,
you find either an Ape or ftork, a Goat
or Calf. You may meet with many Women of the fame Nature with thefe Temples. Therefore outward Beauty is not
enough, unlefs adorn'd with that, which
more truly fo; I don't mean Purple Robe
or Pearl-Necklaces, but fuch as Difcreti-
on, Courtefie, and good Nature, and the
like, the Graces and true Ornaments of
this Lady.

Lyc. Wherefore, good *Polyftratus,* repeat
my Difcourfe with one of the fine nature, as the Proverb goes, or heaping your
Bufhel, if you pleafe, for you may allow
it. Shew me a Picture of her Soul, that
that I may no longer admire her only by
Halves.

Pol My Friend, you set me about no small Task, for 'tis not equally difficult to commend things obvious to every Eye, as to illustrate by Words, what is more abstruse and hid; and likewise I seem to be at a loss for some Fellow-workmen, not Statuaries or Painters, but Philosophers, that my *Image* may be fram'd by their Rule, and may appear fashion'd after the old way of Working. But, however, let us settle to it. In the first place then, she speaks clear and eloquently, so that *Homer* could have better affirm'd of her, than he did of that old King of *Pylos*, That Words flow'd sweeter than Honey from her Tongue. The Accent most agreeable, neither too harsh, which is the Property of Man, nor over shrill, that being effeminately weak, but such as we find in Youth, when Down buds upon their Chins; sweet and pleasant, gently sliding to our Senses, which being ended, there remains a sort of humming, and as it were Relicks buzzing in the Ear, which like an *Eccho* prolongs our Hearing, and leaves upon the Soul some sweet Foot-steps of a found full of Rhetorick and Persuasion. But should she once sing with this Musical Voice, especially to her Lute, it would be high time for the *Halcyons*, the Grashopper, and the Swan to be mute and silent. Should you alledge *Philomela Pandion's* Daughter, her various Notes would not secure her, from being esteem'd unskilful, and without Art. Nay, *Orpheus* and *Amphion*, two such Leaders of their Auditors;

tors, that Stones and Woods, things without Life, danc'd to their Mufick, even
they, I fay, would throw away their Harps,
and ftand liftening to her Melody; for to
obferve fo exactly every Rule of Harmony, as never to tranfgrefs a Note, and
fcarce to meafure the whole Song by feafona-
ble Rifings and Fallings of the Hand, befide, to make the Lute anfwer exactly to
the Voice, and the Quill, and Tongue to
go the fame Pace; add to this a neat touch
of the Fingers, with an eafy Motion of
the other Limbs, Whence I pray, fhould
that *Thracian* have thefe Excellencies, or
the Herdfman, who followed his Harp and
his Sheep at the fame time upon Mount
Cithæron? So that, *Lycinus*, did you but
hear her Sing, you would not only endure
that effect of the *Gorgon*'s-Head, of being
chang'd all into Stone, but would know how
powerful the *Syrens* Mufick was. You
would, I am fure, be enchanted, quite
forgetting your dear Countrry and Acquaintance; nay, fhould you wax up
your Ears, this Melody would make it
way through; and then when 'tis heard
fo charming is it, that you would turn
it a Leffon of fome *Terpfichore*, or *Melpo-
mine*, or even of *Calliope* her felf, made up
of a Thoufand different Charms. To fpeak all
in a word, think me to have heard fuch an
Harmony as was fitting to come from thofe
Teeth and Lips: Since then you have feen
her, whom I fpeak of, imagine too you have
heard her. But the Exactnefs and perfect
Eloquence of her Tongue, and the Purity of
the

the *Ionic* Dialect, and her ready Faculty and sweetness of speaking extempory in common Conversation, being full of the *Attick* Graces, tho wonderful, are scarce to be admir'd, because, as these are Hereditary to her, deriv'd down from her Ancestors, so that it can't be expected otherwise, she her self being half an *Athenian*, by reason of a Colony transplanted from thence. Nor would I have it admired, that she delights in Poetry, and applies her self to it, since she is a Country-woman of *Home*. You have now, *Lycinus*, one part, her sweet Voice and Singing. Consider then now the rest, for I purpose, not like you, to set to view one Image compos'd of many, this is poorly done, and like a Sign-Drawer, to jumble together so many Beauties, and at last, to send out a Piece with many Heads, altogether disagreeable to it self. But all the Vertues of the Soul shall each singly be describ'd on a Picture resembling exactly the Original

Lyc. You promise me, *Polystratus*, a Holy Day, and a noble Feast. You are like, I see, to repay me with over-measure, heap on, I pray, for nothing you can do, can more oblige me.

Pol. Since Learning therefore ought to have the Preference of every thing, that is praise-worthy, particularly that of Contemplation, let us frame this Image various, and of different Forms, that even in this way of yours we may not seem inferiour to you. Let her be painted then, as one who has drank of all the different Streams of *Hilicon*, not as *Clio*, *Polymnia*, and *Calliope*, and the other Mufes, learned in one Art alone, but let her have all in general, not excepting thofe of *Mercury* and *Apollo.* Whatever Poets have adorn'd in Verfe, whatever Hiftorians have recorded, or Philofophers extoll'd, with all thefe let this Image be beautify'd, not fo, as to be only lightly coloured, but as if it plung'd to the bottom, even to Satiety, in Paint of a perpetual Dye. You muft pardon me, if I cannot produce an Original after this Model, for amongft all the Ancients, no one is recorded to have had fo comprehenfive a Knowledge. Therefore, if you think fit, let this be laid up as finifhed, for if I may judge of my own Work, 'tis not to be blam'd.

Lyc. Moft beautiful in truth, *Polyftratus*, and abfolutely perfect in every Stroke

Pol. In the next Place, muft be defcrib'd, an Image of her Wifdom and Underftanding, for this we fhall want a great many Patterns to go by, efpecially of Ancients, and one of later Date, and that *Ionic.* The Painters and Workmen to be employ'd here, muft be *Æfchines*, *Socrates's* Friend, and *Socrates* himfelf, the beft of Artifts in Curiofity, imitating an Original, as painting with an excellent Grace and Beauty That famous *Afpatia* too, of *Miletum*, with whom *Pericles*, that wonderful Man, confulted, fhe fhall be propos'd, as no contemptible Pattern of Underftanding How great foever her Skill be in Affairs her Sagacity in relation to Government her Readiness and Acuteness, all shall be transferred to our Image, precisely to a Hairs breadth, excepting only, that she is painted within the Compass of a small Tablet, but this other is a very *Colossus* in her Size

Lyc But what talk you thus for?

Pol Because *Lycinus* affirms, that two Images, not of equal Bigness, may be yet like one another Thus the ancient Policy of *Athens*, and the present Power of *Rome*, are not equal, no nor any thing near it; so though this resemble in Likeness, yet in Magnitude the other surpasses, as being painted on the broadest Table But for a second and third Example, *Theano* and the *Lesbian* Poetress, shall be produced, to whom we add *Diotima*. *Theano* shall bestow upon us her greatness of Mind, *Sappho* her agreeable way of Conversation. As for *Diotima*, she shall not only resemble her, in that which *Socrates* admires so justly in her, but in all her other Wisdom and Prudence. Thus you have this part, *Lycinus*, let this be laid aside

Lyc. Wonderful indeed, *Polystratus*! But prithee, my Friend, paint also her other Graces, her Kindness, Affability, and Mildness of Temper, with her Charity towards the Poor and Indigent.

Pol Let her then be likened to that other *Theano*, *Antenor's* Wife, to *Areta*, and her Daughter *Nausicaa*, and if there be any other, who amidst the great Plenty of Things have born their Fortune modestly. After this, let Chastity be drawn, and

that not without Friendliness toward her
Acquaintance ; that she may be as pure
as that Chast Daughter of *Icarius*, descri-
bed so by *Homer*, for such is his Character
of *Penelope*, or else in truth of *Abradatus's*
Wife, this Lady's Names-sake, whom a
little before we mention'd

Lyc This part too, *Polystratus*, you have
drawn most beautiful, and now your I-
mages are almost finished, for you have tra-
vers'd o'er the Soul, and have commended
every part of it.

Pol. Hold, not all over, for her greatest
Praise is yet behind. 'Tis this, I mean,
that abounding in such Plenty, yet in her
greatest Prosperity, she is never cloth'd
with Pride, nor in Confidence of her Fortune is lifted above any thing, that is human, but instead of this, we find her containing her self in a Level, favouring of
nothing insolent, or disdainful, but carrying
her self familiarly to those, who visit her
kindly receiving them, by taking of their
Hands, and shewing great respect to them
Which sort of Carriage becomes the more
delightful to those, they converse with, by
how much proceeding from Superiour
there appears nothing of Haughtiness, being such, who use their Power, not for their
own Pride, but for the good of other
These seem to me most worthy of the
good things, which Fortune disposes of,
and these alone can be secure from the in
vidious Eye. For no one envies his Superiour, if he sees him moderate in his Prosperity, and not like *Homer's Ate*, stalking
proud

proudly upon the Necks of Mortals, and trampling under Foot his Inferiours, which is the Custom only of base Souls, through Ignorance of what Fortune is. For when she lifts them on a sudden to a wing'd and lofty Charoit, not dreaming of any such thing, they rest not satisfied with their present State, nor cast an Eye downward, but still contend higher. Whence it comes to pass, that like *Icarus*, their Wax soon dissolving, and their Wings falling to pieces, they tumble head-long into the Surges of the Sea, laught at, and derided by all Men. But they who use their Wings like *Dædalus*, and soar not over high, considering they are made of Wax, who order their Course, as most becomes Men, and are content to be carried just above the Waters, so as their Wings may be always moisten'd by them, and not aspire towards the Sun, these fly both safely and prudently. For this Quality should every one praise this Lady, and therefore she deservingly receives, as a reward the Prayers of all, that these Wings may remain with her always, and a Stream of good Fortunes may continually attend her.

Lyc. May it be so, say I, *Polystratus*, for she is not to be esteem'd, as fair *Hellen* was, for her comely Body only, but she is much more beautiful and lovely, in that she fortifies her Soul with these Excellencies 'Twas becoming the Dignity of so great a King, so good and so gentle a one, to be blessed with this Good, among the many other he enjoys, namely, that such a Wo-

man

man should be born in his time; and being his Queen, should affectionately love him, for that Wife is no small Blessing, to whom one might reasonably apply that of *Homer*, that she contends with the Golden *Venus* for Beauty, and equals even *Minerva* in Working · For, says the same Poet, not one amongst all the Women put together, may be compar'd to her, either for Body, Nature, Mind, or Workmanship.

Pol. You say right, *Lycinus*, if you think fit, let us now join the Images, that which you have made of the Body, with the other which I have made of her Soul, and these united from many into one, and regist'd in some Book, let us publish them, to be admir'd by all those, that are, or ever shall be, for this must needs be of longer Durance, than had it come from *Apelles*, *Parrhasius*, or *Polygnotus*, and shall be more graciously receiv'd, than those of their making; it being not made with Wood or Wax, or Colours, but fashion'd according to the Invention of the Muses. An Image the most absolutely perfect, presenting at once the Beauties of the Body, and the Virtues of the Soul.

A
DEFENCE
OF THE
IMAGES.

By Mr. Vernon.

Polyſtratus. I Am very ſenſible, *Lycinus,* ſays the Lady, of your great Reſpects to me, and the Honour you have beſtow'd on me in your Book; for no one certainly did ever ſo extravagantly extol a Woman, but he who writ with an Eſteem for her; but that you may know my Temper, in ſhort, 'tis this, My Diſpoſition is particularly averſe to Flatterers, who ſeem to me no better than Impoſtors, and Men of ſlaviſh Nature. But, for their Praiſes, if any one in Commending me, makes an intollerable, fulſome Hyperbole, I bluſh preſently, and am almoſt ready to ſtop my Ears, eſteeming it rather Mockery, than any juſt Praiſe: For Praiſes are only ſo far tolerable, as the Perſon prais'd, knows every thing which is ſaid of him to be his due;

due; and when it exceeds that, 'tis foreign and meer Flattery. Not but that I have seen some pleas'd, said she, when any one in praising them, has adorn'd them in their Compliments, with that, which is not in them, as if indeed one should bless an old Man by bestowing on him Youth again, or a deform'd Person, with the Beauty of *Nireus* and *Phaon*; for they think their Shape will be chang'd, by vertue of their Praises, and themselves become young again, as before them *Pelias* imagin'd. But the Case is otherwise; for Praise would deservedly be much esteem'd of, was it possible to enjoy any thing by the benefit of such Hyperboles. But since 'tis not so, methinks, said she, their Condition is much the same, as if a Man should put a beautiful Mask upon an ugly Face, and thereupon he should think himself a Beauty, tho' it is liable to be pluck'd off and defaced, by every one he meets, and therefore the more expos'd to Laughter, when his Genuine Countenance appears, which before he had conceal'd under a Vizard. Or, as if a Dwarf putting on Buskins, should contend for Stature, with one taller by half a Yard, if measur'd upon even Ground. She mention'd one possess'd with such a Folly as this was. There was an Illustrious Lady, said she, otherwise fair and beautiful, but short, and wanting much of a just Height; whom a Poet prais'd in his Verses, particularly amongst other things, for her Beauty, and large Stature, even so far as to liken her

Talnes

Talness and strait Make, to a Poplar Tree. While the poor Lady was tickled with this Praise, and as if she had grown higher by the very Verses, clap'd her Hand for Joy. The Poet seeing her thus pleas'd with his Praises, often repeated them, till a certain Man of the Company, leaning down, whisper'd him in the Ear, Heark you, Sir, pray leave off now, for fear you make the Lady rise up. She told a Story too of *Stratonice*, Wife to *Seleucus*, who did something like this, but more ridiculous, who offering a Prize of a Talent, to any Poet, who should write the best in praise of her Hair, though she was Bald, and had not the least Lock upon her Head. But in this Condition as she was, and every one knowing this to have befel her, by reason of a long Sickness, yet she patiently heard the damn'd Poets call her Hairs Violets, knitting up some tender Locks, and comparing them to Parsly, though there was no such thing about her. She laugh'd at such as these therefore, who deliver'd themselves up to Flatteries, withal, adding, that not in Praises only, but Pictures too, many People desir'd to be thus flatter'd, and deceiv'd. For, said she, they are most taken with those Painters, who will draw them most beautiful; nay, some there are who instruct their Artists, either to leave out a part of their Nose, or to paint their Eyes somewhat blacker, or to add any other thing they desire should be in them, forgetting all the while they adorn a strange Picture, that does not at all resemble

them

them. This, and such like, she said, commending you for most part of your Book, but not enduring that Passage, where you compare her to Goddesses, such as *Juno* and *Venus*. For such Comparisons, said she, far exceed mine, nay, every mortal Beauty Neither was I so vain, as to desire of you to compare me to those Heroines, *Penelope*, *Areta*, and *Theano*, much less to the two divinest of all the Goddesses, repeating this very often, That she had a superstitious Fear and Dread in every thing relating to the Gods. I tremble therefore, says she, lest I be thought like *Cassiope*, seeking after this sort of Praise, who she was only equal to the Nymphs, remaining still a Votary to *Juno* and *Venus* Wherefore. *Lycinus*. she commands you to alter this, or she will call the Goddesses to witness, you writ it against her Content Moreover, she would have you know, your Book mightily troubles her, in going about, in the Dress it wears now, as not being compos'd religiously and piously enough, in respect to the Gods. She imagines too, this will reflect on her, as Irreligious and Prophane, if she permits her self to be compar'd to that Statue at *Gnidus*, or in the Garden She remembers you, and what you said of her in the latter end of your Book, where you stile her Modest, without Pride, not lifting her self beyond Humane Measure, but taking her flight, almost level with the Ground But that you, in saying this of her, advance her above the Heavens, even making a Com-

pa..

parifon between her, and the Goddeffes.
She defires you, not to efteem her more
unadvis'd, than *Alexander*, who, when an
Artift promis'd to transform even *Athos*,
and fafhion it fo like him, that the whole
Mountain fhould bear the Image of a King
grafping two Cities in his Hands, encou-
rag'd not fuch a Prodigy of a Promife, but
thinking the Adventure greater than his
Ability, hinder'd the Man from contriving fuch an improbable *Coloffus*, and
commanded him to let *Athos* fland in its
place, and not to diminifh fo vaft a Mountain into the refemblance of fo fmall a
Body. She prais'd *Alexander*, for his great-
nefs of Mind, and faid, he had rais'd himfelf a Statue, greater than that *Athos*, in
the Opinion of Pofterity, who would never forget this ftory · For it is the fign of
no little Mind, to difpife fo ftrange and
fingular an Honour. She therefore praifes
your Workmanfhip and Skill, in framing
the Images, but does not own them for her
Picture, being unworthy of fuch Comparifons ; nay, not having the leaft Affinity
with them, nor any Woman in Being.
Wherefore fhe returns you all the Honour
of this fort, and admires your Originals
and Patterns, but withal, would have you
beftow on her Humane Praifes only, and
not make her Shoe fo big for her Foot,
left, fays fhe, in my walking with him,
he fo confounds me, I can't fpeak She
charg'd me to tell you this alfo, I have
heard, faid fhe, many affirm (how truly
you Men know beft) that 'twas not permitted

mitted to the Olympick Conquerors, to erect themſelves Statues, greater than their Bodies; but that the *Grecian* Judges, did take care, that not one exceeded the Standard, and that by the Conſent of the Champions, each Statue ſhould be diligently examin'd. Therefore take care, ſid ſhe, leſt we be accus'd, for falſifying the Meaſure and Proportion, and ſo the *Grec* Judges ſhould demoliſh our Image too To this effect, ſhe ſaid. But now, *Lycinus* think how you may alter your Book, and expunge ſuch Paſſages, and not offend thus againſt the Gods, ſince you ſee how ſhe was diſpleas'd at it, and trembl'd when 'twas read, deſiring the Gods to have mercy on her. And indeed, ſhe is to be excus'd, if ſhe ſuffers any thing incident to her Sex, nay, to ſay Truth, I thought myſelf ſaying ſomething, to this purpoſe For upon the firſt hearing, I ſpied nothing amiſs, looking meerly upon what was writ but when ſhe pointed it out to me, I began my ſelf to think as ſhe did, and was affected juſt ſo, as is uſual in viſible Objects. For if we behold any thing very near, juſt under our Eyes, we can't exactly diſtinguiſh, but if we look afar off, at a due diſtance, every thing appears in its true Proportion, what is well, and what is otherwiſe. Now to compare her, a mortal Woman, to *Venus* and *Juno*, what is but plainly to diſparage the Goddeſſes For in ſuch Compariſons as theſe, the Meaner does not become ſo much Greater by the Compariſon, as the Greater is leſſened sen'd, by being drawn down to something, so much inferiour. As for instance, if two should walk together, the one very tall, the other very low of Stature, and both these were to be made equal ; so that one should not exceed the other, this could not be effected, by the shorter stretching himself, though he rais'd himself a-tip-toe, but if both would appear of the same Height, the Taller must stoop down, and make himself lower. Just so is it, in such Images, a Man does not so much become greater, if any one compares him to God, as Divinity must necessarily be impaired, by being bent to that which is beneath it ; but if for want of earthly Instances, one was necessitated to stretch his Words to Heavenly, such a Man would be less suspected he did it through Impiety ; but you, tho' you had Women of such admirable Beauty, ventur'd to resemble her to *Venus* and *Juno*, when there was no need . Therefore, *Lycinus*, remove away this excessive and odious Character. For this is not according to the Custom, who at other times are not so forward, and liberal in your Praises ; but now, I know not how, you are on a sudden chang'd, and become very prodigal, and you who before were so sparing, are most extravagant in your Commendations But think it no Disgrace to you to correct your Dialogue after the Publication, for they say, *Phidias* himself did so, after he had finish'd his *Jupiter* for the *Eleans*. For standing behind the Doors, when he first expos'd his Work

to

to publick View, he heard what they found fault with, and what they commended. One blam'd the Nose as too thick, another the Visage, as too long, another found fault with a third thing. By-and-by, after the Beholders were gone, *Phidias* locks himself up again, and corrects and alters his Statue, according to the Opinion of the greatest part, for he did not lightly esteem the Judgments of such a Number of People, for that many of Necessity, must see farther, than one Man, though he be *Phidias* himself. This she gave me in charge to you, which I press home upon you, as your Friend and Well-wisher.

Lyc. Well, *Polystratus*, I never took you for so great an Orator before. You have produc'd so long an Oration, and so grievous an Accusation against my Book, that you have left me no Hopes for an Apology. But in this you have not done according to the Rule of Judicature, especially you, *Polystratus* in contemning my Book unheard, no Advocate being present to defend it for as the Proverb goes, *I think it very easie for him to win the Race, who runs by himself.* Therefore 'tis no such wonder if we are overcome, when there was no Hour-Glass set up, nor we permitted to make our Defence. But that, which is most unreasonable, is, that you are both Accusers and Judges. Which therefore do you advise me to, you'll rest satisfy'd with your Decree, I should be still, or as the *Hymerean* Poet did, write a Recantation?

on? Or else will you suffer me to make my Appeal to some other Judges?

Pol. With all my Heart, if you have any thing that is worth alledging · For you make not your Defence before Adversaries, as you call us, but before Friends, for I am ready to stand by you in the Tryal.

Lyc But that troubles me, *Polystratus,* that I shall not plead my Cause, when she is present, it would be much better so. But now I am commanded, I must defend my self: If you will therefore be as trusty a Messenger, from me to her, as you were from her to me, I will hazard a throw upon the Die.

Pol As for that, *Lycinus,* fear not but you shall find me no ill Representer of your Defence, only endeavour to be brief in what you say, that I may the more easily remember

Lyc. But I need have a very long Oration, to answer so grievous a Charge, however, for your sake, I will abridge it. Carry then to her this from me

Pol. By no Means, *Lycinus,* but speak you as if she her self was present, and afterwards I will personate you before her.

Lyc Therefore, *Polystratus,* seeing you will have it so, (say) she her self is present, and did before speak all which you reported to me from her. But I am forc'd now to make a second Beginning; for I will not scruple to tell you what has befallen me. You have made the Business, I can't tell how, seem more dreadful to me; and as

D d

you may perceive, I fweat and tremble all over, and think in a manner I fee he., which very thing mightily diftracts me But, for all this, I will begin, for 'tis impoffible to draw back, when fhe is prefent

Pol. And in truth, fhe carries in her Countenance a great deal of Clemency, fhe is all Pleafantnefs and Mildnefs, as you may fee, therefore begin your Speech with Courage.

Lyc I (O' moft excellent Woman) in my great and immoderate Practices as you ftile it, cannot fee any thing, which I have faid of you, to match that Encomium you produce of your own felf, namely, your having in fo great efteem, the Honour due to the Gods. This almoft furpaffes the whole which I have faid of you, but I hope you will pardon me for omitting that Character in your Picture, which efcap'd me through Ignorance, or elfe I would have painted none before it. Wherefore, upon this Account, I am fo far from thinking my Praifes extravagant, that I fear, I have fpoken, much below the Dignity of the Subject. Confider therefore what an Excellence I have omitted, how weighty and ferviceable to demonftrate good Manners, and an upright Mind, for they who pay not a flight Devotion to the Gods, are commonly moft juft in their Dealings with Men. Therefore, if I were to alter my Oration, and correct my Image, I fhould not dare take the leaft away, but would add this at the top and crown of the whole Work

All

And indeed, I muſt confeſs I am indebted
to you much of Thanks upon this Score,
for that, when I was commending your
Modeſty of Temper, and telling how your
preſent Plenty of Things made you no way
loſty, or ſupercilious, than in blaming this
put of my Diſcourſe, have confirmed the
Truth and Sincerity of my Praiſe. For not
greedily to catch at ſuch Praiſes, but to
bluſh at them, ſaying, they are too great
for your Merit, is the Index of a Moderate and humble Diſpoſition. But farther,
the more you are thus diſpos'd towards Pa-
negyricks, the more do you manifeſt your
ſelf worthy of the moſt exalted one, and
your Caſe is almoſt arriv'd to that Saying of
Dogenes, who, when a certain Perſon ask'd
him, how he might become Famous? an-
ſwered, by contemning Fame. For I my
ſelf ſhould ſay, was I ask'd, who moſt deſerv'd Praiſe, he that leaſt of all deſir'd it.
But this perhaps is beſide the Purpoſe, and
far from the Buſineſs. That which I am to
Apologize for, ſeems to be this, that in
framing your Beauty, I liken'd you to
that Statue at *Gnidos,* and to that in the
Garden, to *Juno* and *Minerva.* Theſe, it
ſeems, you think beyond Meaſure too big
for your Foot. Concerning theſe, I anſwer,
though there goes an old Proverb, which
ſays, *Poets and Painters are accountable to none;*
and I think Panegyriſts too, eſpecially if
they go upon the Ground, as we do, Step
by Step, and are not carried beyond Bounds
for Praiſe is a thing that is free, no Law
confining it, but this is the only Rule ſhe
D d 2   obſerves,

obferves, fo to reprefent the Perfon prais'd, as he may be worthy our Wonder and Imitation. For my part, I will not go this way to work, leaft you fhould think I do it for want of any other Method. But this I fay, that the matter of Commendatory Orations, is fuch as the Panegyrift muft needs make ufe of Images and Comparifons, for in this almoft the Skill and Art of Painting well confifts, and what is well, may chiefly be judg'd this way. No by putting like to like, nor by making the Comparifon with what is more vile, but by fcrewing up what you praife, to fomething as far as poffible its Superiour As for Example, was any one to praife a Dog, and fhould fay, he was greater than a Fox or Cat, would you think fuch a one knew the Art of Praifing? Without Queftion you'd fay no. Nay, fhould he affirm him to be equal to a Wolf; neither fo would he beftow any great Praife. How then fhall he give him his due Praife By comparing him to a Lyon for Bignefs and Strength, as when the Poet praifes *Orion's* Dog, he calls him the Lyon-Tamer for this is the perfect Praife of the Dog Again, had any one a mind to praife Milo of *Croton*, or *Glaucus* of *Caryftos*, or *Polydamas*, and fhould fay either of them were ftronger than a Woman, would you not deem him worthy to be laugh'd at for his frantick Commendation? Or if he fhould fay he was fuperiour to any fingle Man, neither would this have been fufficient Praife. But after what manner does *mer*, that famous Poet, honour *Blaucius*, when he says, that not *Pollux*'s Courage dar'd to engage him, no nor *Alcmena*'s hardy Son ? Do you see to what Gods he compares him, or rather sets him before them ? And yet *Glaucus* was not angry in being extoll'd equal to those Gods, who are the *Ephori* and Overseers of the Combitants. Nor did they revenge either him or the Poet, as one blasphemous in his Praises ; but both were in Honour and Esteem with all the *Greeks*, *Glaucus* for his Valour ; but the Poet, amongst his other Excellencies, for this particular part Wonder not therefore, that I, about to take your Picture, us'd an Example more sublime than ordinary, it being absolutely necessary for a Panegyrist, and the very Nature of the Discourse requiring it. But since you mention'd Flattery, and shew'd an Aversion to those who practis'd it, I must praise that in you, nor can I do otherwise. But I will distinguish to you, and define what is the Business of a Praiser, and the Extravagancy of a Flatterer. A Flatterer therefore, (as one who praises for his own Ends) having little regard to Truth, thinks he ought to praise every thing by Hyperbole, so that lying impudently, and adding a part of his own, he fears not to make *Thersites* handsomer than *Achilles*, or to affirm *Nestor* to be the youngest of all the Warriors, who came against *Troy*. He boggles not to swear, that *Cræsus*'s Son is more quick of Hearing than *Melampus*, and *Iphenus* sharper sighted than *Lynceus*,

if he has only hopes of gaining, tho'
never so little, by his Lies. Was the
other to praise such as these, he would not
thus play the Counterfeit, nor give them
any thing, that is not in them, but the
Gifts of Nature they enjoy, tho' not
very great, these would he take and im
prove, making them seem greater. If he
was to praise a Horse naturally swift and
nimble, as we know those Creatures are,
he would venture to say,

He flew o'er bearded Corn, nor broke an Ea.

And again he would not stick, saying,

The Course of Horses swift as the Wind.

Or was he to extol a fine House rich
furnished, he wou'd say,

Such is the Palace of Olympick Jove

Now a Flatterer would have applied a
Verse to a Swine-herd's Cottage, if he had
hopes of getting the least Penny from him
Like *Cynæthus,* Flatterer to *Demetrius Po-
orcetes,* who having exhausted all his store
of Flattery, commended *Demetrius's* be
troubled with a grievous Cold, that he
coughed very musically. But this was
the only difference between them, that
Flatterers, to curry-favour with the
they praise, boggle at no sort of Lyes
that Panegyrists only endeavour to raise
Truths by magnifying them. But the

they do not a little differ, that Flatterers
as much as possible they can, use Hyperboles, the others even in them are moderate, and keep within Bounds These
few Marks, I have given you out of an
infinite Number of Flattery and true
Praise, that you may not suspect immediately, all who profess the Art, but may
distinguish, and measure each of them by
their proper Rule. If you please therefore, come on, and apply both Rules to
what I have said of you, that you may
see which it resembles most, this or that.
Now, if I had affirmed of some ugly deformed Creature, that she was like the
Statue of *Venus* at *Gnidos*, I had been deservedly censured for a Cheat, and a
greater Fawner, than even *Cynæthus*; but
affirming it of such an one, as we all
know, my Boldness was not at a great distance from Truth. But now perhaps you
will say, or rather have said, that it was
granted you to praise my Duty, but then
you ought to have bestow'd Praise, which
would not have been envied, and not to
have compar'd a frail Mortal with Goddesses, But I (most excellent Lady) for it is
come to that, that I must declare the Truth,
have not compar'd them to the Goddesses,
but to the publick Works of the best Artists, fashion'd in Stone, Brass, or Ivory.
And to liken Man to the Workmanship of
Man, is neither Impious, nor Irreligious,
unless you take this to be the true *Minerva*,
which *Phidias* has carv'd out, or this to the
Heavenly *Venus*, which not many Years

since *Praxiteles* made at *Gnidos*. But take heed, least this be prophane, to entertain such Notions of the Gods, whose true Images, I conceive, can't be exprefed by Man's Imitation. But if I had compar'd you to them, 'twas not my own, nor did I first cut out the way, but many of the Poets, and those eminent too, did it before me, especially your Fellow-Countryman *Homer*, whom I will now raise from his Grave, to plead for me, or else there is no way for him, but that he be taken in the same Net with me. I will ask him therefore, or you instead of him, (for you remember and relish the most excellent Passages of his Poems) how think you of that, where he affirms of the Captive *Briseis*, that *like the Golden* Venus *she bewail'd* Patroclus? And by and by he adds, as if it were not enough to compare her to *Venus*,

Thus said the Crying Woman Goddess-like

Therefore, when he says such Things as these, do you abominate his Book, and throw it away, or give you him leave, to take his Liberty in his Encomiums? But if you do not allow him, the whole Series of Time does, nor has one appear'd, who has found this Fault in him, or who durst to lash this Image of him? Or who has branded these Verses as spurious, by setting an Obelisk upon you. If then he is permitted to compare a Barbarian, and to this all over in Tears too, to the Golden *Venus*, may not I, not to mention your Beauty, be-

çause

cause you can't hear it with Patience, may not I, I say, compare to the Images of the Goddesses, a good-humour'd Lady, almost always smiling, which is a Quality we have in common with the Gods. But in his describing *Agamemnon*, see how sparing he is of the Gods, and how he produces them as Patterns to the exact forming him, how he says,

> *His Eyes and Head were like* Jupiter's, *his Belt like that of* Mars, *his Breast like* Neptunes.

And as it were dividing the Man Limb by Limb, comparing them all to the Images of so mighty Gods   And again, he says, he is like to *Mars* that Man-flayer, and so others he compares to others of the Gods.   That *Phrygian* he Son of *Priam*, he calls Divinity-shaped, and *Peleus's* Son oftentimes the God-like *Achilles*.   But I will return to Examples of Women-kind, you have heard him say somewhere,

> *Such-like descends* Diana *from the Hills.*

But he does not only compare Men to Gods, but even *Euphorbus's* Hair to the Graces, and that too when it was stained with Blood   In short, there are so many Examples of this fort, that scarce a part of the whole Poem but is adorn'd with these Divine Images of the Gods Therefore, let either these be blotted out, or let me have the Liberty to dare the same thing.

Similitudes

Similitudes and Comparisons are so absolute
at Will, that even *Homer* sticks not to illustrate even Goddesses from Inferiours.
Therefore *Juno*'s Eye he calls Ox-like, another compares *Venus*'s Eye-lids to Violet.
But who has not heard of the Rosie finger of
Aurora, tho' never so little vers'd in his
Poems; and indeed the Commendation of
any Shape is moderate, tho' it be said to
be like even a God. But how many are
there, who, have imitated their Names,
and have been call'd *Bacchus's*, *Vulcans*,
Jupiters, *Neptunes*, and *Mercuries*. The
Queen of *Evagoras*, King of *Cyprus* was na-
med *Latones*, and yet the Goddess was not
displeas'd, tho' she could have transformed her, as she did *Niobe*, into a Stone. I
pass by the *Egyptians*, who tho' most Superstitious Observers of the Gods, make
use of their Names, even that it would
tire me to rehearse, for the greatest part
of them are from Heaven. Therefore
you have no Grounds of being possess'd
with Fear, at my Praises. For if my
Book contains any thing against the Gods,
you are not liable to be question'd for it,
unless you think you may be accus'd for
Hearing. But the Gods will punish me, because they have punish'd before me *Homer*
and other Poets, tho' as yet they have
not punish'd the very chief of the Philosophers, who said, That Man was the Image
of God. I have much more to say to you,
but for this *Polystratus*'s sake will end, that
he may remember what has been said.

Pol. I don't know whether I shall be able, *Lycinus,* for in saying as you have, you have discours'd very long, beyond the running of your Glass, but however, I will try to remember you, and as you see, will immediately post to her, which my Ears stopt up, that nothing else may enter in, and confound their Order, and so I perhaps be hiss'd at by the Spectators.

Lyc. It ought to be your care, *Polystratus,* to represent me the best you can. I for my part, having delivered you my Play, will now withdraw. When the Judges Sentence is declar'd, I will then again appear, and see what Issue attends this Controversie.

THE

THE
Stygian Passage :
OR, THE
TYRANT.

By Captain Sprag.

The Argument.

As this Author in his Dialogue of Menippus, *describ'd the Ends and Punishments of wicked Men, reciting the very Decree, whereby their Souls are ordain'd to wander into* Asses. *So here-under the Person of* Megapenthes *he exposes the Life of Tyrants, their Customs, and the end of their way of living; what Pains and Racks of Mind after this Life remain for them; and these he amplifies by a certain Antithesis, when he compares the Cobler* Micyllus *and* Cyniscus *the Philosopher, with the Tyrant, insinuating that they who greedily hunt after Power and Riches, and for the most part lead filthy, lewd, and wicked Lives, in their very Souls suffer the most grievous Death, that can be imagin'd* gin'd. But on the contrary, they, who have a *Mind* free and remote from worldly things, and such, as are really the *Beginnings* and *Causes* of all *Mischiefs* ; and prefer *Vertue* before any thing, the *Mob* desires, aud admires those are wont to contemn *Death*, and are not easily frighten'd with any *Lashes* of *Conscience* ; but of those he treats after his own peculiar *Way* and *Design*, feigning by a certain fabulous *Dramma*, a *Transportation* of *Ghosts* over *Acheron*, which, whilst this *Usurper* was to be ferry'd over, a great *Delay* is caus'd by his *Reluctarce*, and endeavours to avoid *Death*, which being heinously taken by *Charon*, and others, *Mercury* at length taking him by the *Collar*, compels him into the *Boat* by the *Assistance* of poor *Cyniscus*, and *Micyllus*, and then after the *Voyage* is over, he again feigns him desiring to evade the *Judgment* of *Rhadamanthus*, but there being brought before him, and accus'd by *Cyniscus*, he is at last condemn'd to the highest *Punishment*.

Char. COme on ho! *Clotho*, the Skiff hath been long since ready, and well fitted for the Passage, the Balge-water is pump'd out, the Mast set, the Sail abroad, all the Oars are lash'd, and nothing on my part hinders, but that we may get up our Anchor, and break Ground. But *Mercury* stays, who shou'd have been here long ago Besides, fee the Boat is empty of Passengers, which might have made three Trips to day, and now it draws towards Evening, and we have not gain'd one Farthing of a Fare. In the mean time,

Pluto,

Pluto will fufpect that I fail in my Bufinefs: and that when 'tis the fault of another; for that good and fweet Captain of the Dead, as if he were one of the Ghofts, hath taken a Draught above of the Water of Oblivion, and doth not remember to return to us. He is either Wreftling with Striplings, or playing on his Harp, or pronouncing his Harangues; fhewing his Folly. Or elfe the pretty Gentleman is thieving fomewhere in his Return to us, for that alfo is one of his Faculties. He takes a great deal of Liberty with us, especially, fince he is ours, at leaft the half part of him.

Cloth. But how do you know, O, *Charon* whether fome Bufinefs hath not fallen out for him; and if *Jupiter* hath not occafion for his help in the Affairs above; for he alfo is his Lord and Mafter.

Char. But yet not fo, *Clotho*, that he fhou'd above meafure Lord it over our common Servant; I have never detain'd him beyond the time he fhou'd return, but I know the reafon well enough, for here with us is nothing but Daffodil, Wafers and Jumbles, and Funeral Oblations, as for the reft, 'tis Fogs, Clouds and Darknefs, but in Heaven all things are clear, there's *Ambrofia* and *Nectar* in Plenty therefore it feems to me to be much fweeter to ftay with them, but he ufes to fly away from us, as if he had made his efcape out of Prifon, and all the time he fhou'd come down to us, he is flow, and at laft comes, but unwilling.

C

Cloth. No more of that, *Charon*, for here he is, look ye, he's bringing with him a huge Number, or rather driving before him with his Rod a mighty Shoal, like a Flock of Sheep But what is the matter, for I percieve one amongſt them to be bound, another ready to burſt with Laughter, and another with a Budget and Cudgel, and don't you ſee *Mercury* himſelf flowing with Sweat, his Feet all Duſty, and puffing and blowing, as if his Mouth was full of Air, What's the Buſineſs, *Mercury*? Why ſuch haſte? You ſeem to us diſturb'd?

Mer. What ſhou'd it be elſe, *Clotho*, but that by purſuing this Raſcal, who ran away from us to Day, as I had like not to have viſited your Boat to day?

Cloth. Who is he, or what was his meaning to ſhirk away ſo?

Mer. This is certain, he had rather live, he is either ſome King, or Tyrant, as one may gueſs by his howling, he complains he is depriv'd of ſome vaſt Happineſs.

Cloth. And did the Fool run away, as if it were poſſible to ſurvive when the Thread of his Life failed?

Mer. Did he run away, ſay you? If that moſt generous Perſon, with a Cudgel had not aſſiſted me, and bound him faſt when we took him, he had got clear from us, for ſrom the very Inſtant, that *Atropos* delivered him to us, hang'd an Arſe and reſiſted, clapping his Feet ſo cloſe to the Ground, that he hath not been very manageable

nageable for us to drive him ; sometimes
he would beg, and entreat, requesting to
be dismiss'd a little, and promising he
wou'd give huge Rewards for it : But I, as
it was fit, wou'd not part with him, knowing what he ask'd to be impossible. However, when we were got even to the very
Gates, and I had made up my account of
the Dead to *Æacus,* and he had computed
them all over by the Tally sent him by
thy Sister, I know not how, but the wicked Varlet sneakingly stole away from us,
so that there was found one dead Man
wanting in my Tole. Then *Æacus,* knitting his Brows, said to me, *Mercury,* don't
use thy pilfering in all things ; let thy
Foolleries in Heaven suffice thee, the things
of the dead are accurately manag'd, and
in no wise possibe to be conceal'd from us,
you see my Tally had a Thousand and Four
mark'd on it ; But thou want'st one of the
Number, except thou wilt say *Atropos* has
put a Trick upon thee. Then I, blushing
at his Words, suddenly called to mind
what had happen'd on the way, and when
in looking all about, I cou'd in no wise discern the Fellow, I perceiv'd his Escape,
and follow'd, as fast as I cou'd, to the way
that leadeth to Light, and this best of Men
going along with me, and hoisting away,
as it were, out of a Goal, we caught him
in *Tanarus,* so near was he to have gotten
from us.

    Cloth. And, we, *Charon,* all this while,
had been condemning *Mercury* of Lazi-
ness.

Char. Well, but why do we ſtay any longer, as if we had not loitered enough already?

Cloth. Thou ſay'ſt well, let 'em get aboard, and I taking the Regiſter in my Hand, and ſitting upon the loweſt Step of the Ladder, as my Cuſtom is, will inform my ſelf concerning every one of them as they enter, who they are, from whence they came, and after what manner they died? But, *Mercury,* do thou rank and put them in Order; but firſt caſt in theſe little Children, for what can they anſwer to me?

Mer. Look here, Ferry-man, there's 300, counting thoſe, who were dropped at other Folks Doors.

Charon. Good lack! how delicate a Fare, but thou bring'ſt ſuch, as are too green for us

Mer. Wou'd you have us, *Clotho,* put in with ſuch as them, ſuch whoſe Deaths were never lamented?

Cloth. Do you mean the old Folks? Yes, for what does it import me to make my ſelf Buſineſs, by ſearching out after the things, that were before *Euclide.* Come hither all of ye that are turn'd of Sixty. Ho la! what's the Matter? They do not hear me, their Ears are ſtuff'd up with Age, 'twill be beſt ſuddenly to tranſport 'em.

Mer. See here's 400, bating two, all withered, over-ripe, and gather'd in their proper Seaſon.

E e

Cloth.

Cloth. Yes, certainly, since all of 'em are like dry'd Grapes. Bring the wounded too, *Mersury*, but first of all, tell me after what manner they departed this Life, I my self will inspect the Inscriptions upon 'em, it was decreed, that yesterday Eighty four of them that were at the Battle in *Media*, shou'd be slain, and amongst 'em *Gobares*, the Son of *Oxiartes*.

Mer. They are all here.

Cloth. And the seven who kill'd themselves for Love, and the Philosopher *Theagenes*, because he cou'd not possess the Whore of *Megara*, that he was in Love with.

Mer. They are all present.

Cloth. But where are those who for the desire of Empire were butcher'd by one another?

Mer. They stand here.

Cloth. And he that was kill'd by the Adulterer, and his own Wife.

Mer. Behold he is before you.

Cloth. Now bring those, that were condemn'd by the Judges, I mean those, that were hang'd and crucify'd, but where are the seventeen whom the High-way Men kill'd.

Mer. They are present, those that you see wounded are they, wou'd you have me bring out the Women with 'em too.

Cloth. Yes, and the Shipwrack'd, for they died together, and in the self-same manner, and those likewise, who died by the Feaver, and the Physician *Agathocles* along with 'em, but where's *Cyniscus* the Philosopher, who was to die, as he was eat ing the Supper of *Hecate,* and sacrific'd *Egges,* and the crude Cuttle-Fish

Cynisc. I stand, before you, best *Clotho,* but what Injury have I done, that you have left me so long amongst the Living? for you have almost crowded my whole Spindle, and although I have endeavour'd to break the Thread to come hither, yet I know not how, but it was not to be broken

Cloth. I left thee to be an Inspector and Physician of human Sins, but come aboard now and good luck to thee

Cynsf Not I, till we have driven the bound Man on board, for I fear least he move even you from the Sentence, by his Solicitations

Cloth Bring him in, let me see who he is.

Mer. 'Tis *Megapenthes* the Son of *Lry-des* the Tyrant.

Cloth Come up here.

Mege No good Lady, *Clotho,* do but permit me to go back a little while, I will voluntarily return, without any Bodies calling me.

Cloth. What is the reason, that thou woud'st live again

Megap Suffer me first to compleat the Building of my House, which I left but half finished

Cloth Thou doatest, come in.

Megap. I do not ask much time, O Destiny, give me leave only to stay this one day with 'em above, until I shall give Orders to my Wife concerning my Estate,

and shew her where the great Treasure is
I had buried in the Ground.

Cloth. Well, thou shalt not obtain it.

Megap. Must therefore all this Money be
lost?

Cloth. For that matter, take heart, for
Megacles thy Sister's Son shall have't

Megap. O Affront! that very same Enemy, whom out of Scorn I have not dispatch'd.

Cloth. The very same, and he shall survive thee forty years, and a little more
too, and get thy Wardrobe and thy whole
Treasure

Megap. You do me Injustice, *Clotho*, in
giving what is mine to my most mortal
Enemies.

Cloth. Did'st not thou seize all the E-
state of *Callimachus*, murthering him, and
cutting the Throats of his Children while
he was living?

Megap. But now all he had was mine.

Cloth. But now the time of thy possel-
sing of 'em is compleated.

Megap. Hear, *Clotho*, what I say to you
in private, no body hearing of us. Withdraw then a little, if you will suffer me to
run away, I'll give you 1000 Talents of
Coined Gold

Cloth. D'you keep your Gold and Talents in mind still Blockhead?

Megap. And if you please, I will throw
thee two Baskets which I got when I slew
Cleocritus, either of 'em is a hundred
Weight of Talents of pure Gold.

Cloth. Pull him in there, for by his good-will he will not come at us.

Megap. I call ye to witness that the Walls remain unfinish'd, and the Dock for Ships, which had I lived five days longer, I had perfected.

Cloth Take thou no care for that, another will finish 'em.

Megap But I expect this Boon from you, which is altogether reasonable.

Cloth. What's that?

Megap That I may only live so long as to subdue the *Pisides*, and put the *Lybians* under Contribution; and then having e-rected a most stately, magnificent Monument for my self, I will engrave upon it all the great and warlike Actions I have atchieved in my Life-time.

Cloth. Hold, thou dost not ask to tarry one day, but twenty years almost.

Megap. I'm ready to give you Pledges for my speedy Return, and if you please, I will deliver to you my beloved Succes-sor.

Cloth. Oh Rascal! whom thou hast so often pray'd on Earth to survive thee.

Megap Formerly I did pray so, but now I percieve what is more for my Interest.

Cloth. In a little time he will come unto you, the new King will dispatch him.

Magap. Yet this you shall not deny me.

Cloth. What's that?

Megap. I wou'd fain know how my Af-fairs go now I am dead.

Cloth.

Cloth. Hear it then, thou wilt be more tormented, by knowing *Midas* thy Slave shall love thy Wife; he hath long since made her his Strumpet.

Megap. What! that cursed Villain, whom I made free at her Perswasions

Cloth. And then for thy Daughter, she shall be reckon'd amongst the present King's Harlots; the Statues and the Monuments which thy City formerly erected for thee, are all broken down, and make Sport to all the Spectators

Megap. But tell me, shall none of my Friends resent such Proceedings?

Cloth. Who was ever thy Friend? Or who had ever any just Cause to be so? Art thou ignorant, that all thy Adorers and Extollers of every thing thou cou'd'st do or say, did it either through Hope or Fear, being Friends of the Goverment, and siding with the Times

Megap. But when they sacrific'd at their Banquets, with a loud Voice, they wished many and good things for me, every one of 'em was ready to die before me, if possible, and to conclude, I was the only Oath they swore by.

Cloth. Yesterday therefore, thou gotten thy Death by supping with one of 'em, for the last Pot that was given sent thee hither.

Megap. That was it that I tasted so bitter, but what did he mean by so doing?

Cloth. Thou delay'st too much, thou ought'st to come in.

Megap. One thing most mightily afflicts me, *Clotho*, for which I could wish to live again for a very little Season.

Cloth. What can that be? It seems to be something of very great Importance.

Megap. *Carion*, one of my Houshold Servants, so soon as ever he perceived that I was departed this Life, about the Evening Twi-light, entring into my Bed-Chamber, which was then empty, for no body look'd after me, lay with my Concubine *Glycerium*, with whom he had been formerly common, then shutting the Door fast, as if no Body had been within, after he had taken his fill of Lust, looking upon me, said he, Thou wicked Fellow, thou hast often buffetted me when I did not deserve it, and so saying, he struck and cuff'd me In fine, when he had spit upon me, and bid me packing in the Region of the Damn'd, out went he, but I swelled with Anger, tho' I had not wherewithal to revenge my self upon him, because I was cold, and had no Blood in me, besides, my wicked Maid hearing the Noise of some coming, rubb'd her Eyes with her Spittle, and as if she had lamented for me, went away howling, whom if I catch?

Cloth. Leave off your Threats, and come aboard here, 'tis high time for thee to appear before the Judgment.

Megap. And will any one dare to pronounce Sentence against a King?

Cloth. Against a King no Body will, but *Rhadamanthus* will against a dead Man,

whom

whom thou shalt find to be most equitable, giving every one his due according to his Merits; wherefore now delay not.

Megap. O Destiny! make me some poor private Person, and a Slave, instead of a King, only permit me to live again a little.

Cloth. Where is he with the Cudgel? Haul him by the Foot, *Mercury*, for he will never enter by his Good-will.

Mer. Follow now Runagate; take him Ferry-man, and this Fellow, see that he be lash'd to the utmost.

Megap. But 'tis fit I shou'd have the great Cabbin.

Cloth. Why so?

Megap. Because I was certainly a King, and had my Guards without Number.

Cloth. And did not *Carion* justly give thee a twitch, when thou hast been so cruel? Thou shalt have a little Tyranny shew'd thee by taking the Cudgel.

Megap. And does *Cynifcus* give me the Cudgel? Have I not lately almost faiten'd thee to the Cross, because thou wert too free, sharp and reprimanding.

Cloth. And therefore thou shalt be close lashed to the Mast.

Micyllus Tell me, *Clotho*, do you make no Account of me, because I am poor, must I therefore be the last of all that come aboard.

Cloth. Who art?

Micyllus. I am *Micyllus* the Cobler

Cloth. And is Delay troublesome to thee? Do'st not see how much this Ty rant promises to give to be loose but a little?

tle? I admire that flaying is not defirable to thee.

Micillus Beft of the Deftinies, hear me, that Gift of the *Cyclops* doth not very much delight me, to be devour'd the laft; for whether firft or laft, the Teeth are ftill the the fame. The Rich and the Poor are not alike, our Lives (as we may fay) are diametrically oppofite, for this Tyrant, who in his Life-time feem'd fo happy, terrible to all, and admir'd by 'em, leaving behind fo much Gold and Silver, and Raiments, Horfes, and Dainties, lovely Boys, and beautiful Women, is juftly afflicted and griev'd to be taken away from them, for I know not how, but the Soul, as if 'twere faften'd with Bird-Lime, ftick clofe to thofe People; nor will it eafily fly from them, as being long fince addicted to them; but rather, as if the Bond by which they happen to be bound, was not to be broken, when any are taken off by force, they howl and roar very loudly, and tho' in other things they are couragious, yet in this way that leads to the Shades, they are found to be Cowards, like difpairing Lovers, fhe looks ftill backwards, and defires to fee, at a great Diftance, the Things that are done amongft Mortals, as this Fool did running out of the way, and here by importuning of you; but I who in my Life-time left no Pledges behind me, no Grounds, no Number of Houfes, no Gold, no Houfhold Stuff, no Pomp, no Images, was altogether ready for Death; and as foon as ever *Atropos* but wink'd upon me,

throwing

throwing willingly away my paring Knife,
and Shoe Sole, and having the Laft in my
Hand, (I, unfhod as I was) without rub-
bing out the Wax, follow'd, nay rather
went before; looking ftill downwards, for
nothing that was behind cou'd ftay or re-
cal me, and truly I perceive all things
are very fine amongft you; for to me it
feems the fweeteft thing in the World
that the Degrees of Honour fhou'd be e-
qual to all Men, and none more eminent
than his Neighbour, and I conjecture, no-
body here demands Ufe-Money of his
Debtors, and no paying of Contributions,
and what goes furtheft with me, no one
frozen in Winter, nor indifpofed, nor buffetted by the more powerful, but that human Affairs are turn'd quite topfie-turvy;
for here we who are Poor, do laugh and
are merry, but the Rich are doleful and
mourning

Cloth I have feen thee laughing this
good while, *Mycillus*, but what was it that
chiefly mov'd thy Laughter?

Mycil. O Goddefs, for whom I have the
greateft Veneration, living near this Tyrant, I very exactly obferv'd his Proceedings, and then he feem'd to me not
inferior to a God, for when I minded the
Flower of his Purple Robe, and the Croud
of his Attendants, his Gold, and Cups fet
with Jewels, and his Silver-footed Bed,
I blefied him, befides the Favour of fuch
things as were prepar'd for his Supper,
did very much affect me; and therefore I
look'd upon him to be a Man more than
human,

human, and thrice happy, yea, much more comely and tall, by the Success of his Fortune, raising himself more loftily by a whole Royal Habit, walking stately, regarding of himself, and astonishing others, but after he deceas'd, and was stript of all his Pleasures, he appear'd to me very ridiculous, and I the more derided my self, for admiring the Villain, esteeming of his Happiness only by his Splendor, and declaring him bless'd for his Scarlet Neither was he only a Sport to me, but I cou'd not forbear laughing, when I saw the Usurper *Gnipho* sobbing, and repenting the Methods he had taken not to enjoy his own Cash, but to die without so much as tasting of it, leaving his Estate to his Nephew *Rhodocanes*, for he was the nearest in Kin to him, and next Heir at Law, especially, when I called to mind how pale and wan he was, making his Countenace sorrowful with Cares, and rich only in the Fingers wherewith he counted his Talents and Ten Thousands, gathering together by Degrees, what was in a very short time wasted, by the fortunate *Rhodocares*, but do not we get away, for we will laugh out the rest as we sail, when we see them lamenting

Cloth. Come aboard then, that the Ferryman may get up his Anchor

Charon. You Sir, whither go you, the Boat is full, stay there, I will give you a Cast over to Morrow morning.

L. cyl.

Micyl. You do me Injury, *Charon*, to leave a poor dead Man behind you, certainly I will accuse you of Injustice before *Rada-manthus*; miserable me, now they sail, and I shall be left all alone here, but why do not I strive to swim to them, for I do not fear drowning when I'm tir'd, being dead already, especially, since I am so poor that I have not one Farthing to give to the Ferry-man for my Vassage.

Cloth. What's the matter? Stay *Micyllus*, for tis not lawful for thee to pass over.

Micyl. But it may be I may swim ove. before you

Cloth. By no means, but bring the Bark nearer, and let's take him in, *Mercury*, pull him in there.

Cloth Where shall he sit now, for thou seest all is full.

Mer. Upon the Shoulders of the Tyrant, if you think fit.

Cloth. *Mercury* hath contriv'd it very prettily, come aboard there, and tread upon the Neck of this Villain; we shall have a good Passage.

Cynis. 'Tis fit, *Charon*, I tell you the truth, I truly have not one Farthing to give you for my Passage, for I have nothing in the World but the Satchel and Staff you see here, but if you would have me Pump and Row, I am ready, nor shall you have any reason to complain, provided you give me a good pliable strong Oar.

Charon. Row then, let that be enough to take from him.

Cyn. Is it requisite that I give you a Song?

Char. Yes, for thou well knowest how to give the Mariners a Lesson.

Cyn. I know many, *Charon,* as you are sensible, but these Mariners are too abstreperous, so that our Song will be spoil'd.

Rich Man Alas! alas! my Possessions

Another. Well-a-day my Fields! miserable Man that I am, what a stately House have I left behind me?

Another. Oh! how many Talents will my Heir squander away, which he has got from me?

Another. Woe! woe to my Infants

Another. Who will dress my Vines that I planted last Year?

Mer. *Micyllus,* bemoanest thou nothing, it is not fitting for any to sail without Tears.

Micyl. Fie upon't, I have no cause to lament when I have a good Passage

Mer. However, for Complaisance sake whine a little

Micyl. My Shoe-Soles! Oh my old Lasts! Lack-a-day my stinking Shoes! I shall no more, unhappy Man, be starved from Morning till Night, nor shall I any more go half naked, and gnashing my Teeth for very Cold Who shall have my Cobling Knife? Who shall enjoy my Awls? Sure here's Lamentation enough, for we are almost at the end of our Voyage.

Char. Come on, first pay that Fare, and give me thine also, so I have gotten from every one. *Micyl.* give me the Farthing

Micyl. You Joak, *Charon*, or as one may say, you write in the Water, if you expect one Farthing of *Micyllus*, for from the beginning, whether a Farthing be round or square, I know not.

Char. A very pritty gainful Voyage to day; but get ye out together, I will go to the Horses and Oxen, and Dogs, and the other Animals, for 'tis fit that they have their Passages.

Cloth. Take and carry them away, Mercury, but I'll sail back to the Shore o'th' other side, and bring along with me *Indoputes* and *Heromithres*, the Sons of *Cyrus*, for they have kill'd one another by this time, by fighting for the Bounds of the Dominions.

Mer. Yes, Sir, let's be going, but see that you all follow me in order

Micyl. O ftrange! What a Mift's here? Where is now the fair *Micyllus*, or which fhall any one know, if *Joan* ben't as fair as my Lady? For all things are alike, and of the fame Colour. Here is no Degree of Comparifon of Fairnefs, my courfe Mantle, that feem'd before very mifhapen, is now become equal to Royal Purple, for they are both of them without any Luftre and wrap'd up in the fame Darknefs; But whither art thou gotten *Cyniscus*?

Cyniscus Here am I, *Micyllus*, and if you think good, let us go together

Micyl. You fay well, give me your Right Hand, tell me, for you have been initiated in the *Eleufinian* Mufteries, do the things there feem like unto thefe.

Cyf

Cynif. You fay right, behold a certain Perfon comes, carrying a Lord, looking terribly and threatning, Is it not *Erinnys*?

Micyl. It feems to be her by her Drefs

Mer Look you, *Tifiphone*, take thefe four Thoufand and four here.

Tifaphon. *Rhodamanthus* has expected you long fince.

Rada Bring *Erinnys* there, and *Mercury*, be thou Cryer, and call 'em all over

Cynif. O *Rhadamanthus*, for *Jupiter*'s fake, I befeech you firft of all to examine me

Rhoda. For what reafon?

Cynif. I defire I may accufe a certain Perfon, that I am confcious he has done fuch things in his Life-time, for I fhall not be worthy of Belief, except it be firft apparent, what manner of Perfon I have been, and after what fort I have lived.

Rhada. Who art?

Cynif Oh, moft worthy Judge, I am *Cynifcus*, by Profeffion a Philofopher.

Rhada Come then, come firft to thy Tryal, *Mercury*, call the Witneffes againft him.

Mer. If any manner of Perfon hath any thing to fay againft *Cynfcus*, let him come forth here; no body comes, but this is not enough, *Cynfcus*, undrefs, that we may confider what Marks you have gotten

Cynf Where have I been ftigmatiz'd?

Rhada. So many ill things as a Man commits in his Life-time, fo many invifible Brands he carries in his Soul.

Cynf Look, I am naked therefore, fearch for the Brands you fpeak of

Rhada

Rhada. He is altogether pure, except some three or four Scars, which are very obscure, and almost wore out; What's these here? These are the Traces and Marks of a Burn; but I know not how they are effac'd, or rather cut out, how comes that to pass, *Cyniscus*, after what manner are you become pure.

Cynis. Formerly, when I was wicked for want of Instruction, and thereby had contracted many Marks, as soon as ever I began to Philosophize by little and little, I washed all the Spots out of my Soul.

Rhada. Certainly thou hast us'd a most excellent and present Method to go into the Islands, live with the best, but first accuse the Tyrant, as you term him, call others

Micyl. My Affair, *Radamanthus*, is little, and needs but small Enquiry, I am ready before you, and stark naked, therefore inspect me.

Rhad. Who art thou?

Micyl. *Micyllus* the Cobler.

Rhada Well, *Micyllus*, thou art delicately pure and unbranded, go thou to *Cyniscus* now call out the Tyrant.

Mer Megapenthes, Son of *Lacydas*, come forth, whither dost thou turn? Come hither, I call the Tyrant, take him by the Collar *Tisiphone*, and drag him before us and now *Cyniscus*, accuse and convict him for the Fellow is near us

Cynis. Altho' in general there's no need for you may know what he is by his great scars, yet, however, I will display the Mar

and make him more notorious, by what I
have to fay to you. As for this moft ac-
curfed Villain, I think fit to pafs over all
the Rogueries he did as a private Perfon,
but after he had aflociated with the moft
defperate People, raifed Guards, and advanc'd himfelf to be chief of the City, he
murther'd Six hundred, without hearing
their Caufe, taking away all Mens Eftates,
and arriving at the very heighth of Riches,
he never omitted any fort of Luft, but
ufed all manner of Cruelty and Injuries
againft the Citizens, corrupting the Virgins, debauching the young Men, and in-
fulting all manner of ways over fuch, as
were fubjected to him, then for his Pride
and Infolence, and roaring againft all he
met with, you cannot execute Juftice e-
nough upon him, for 'twas eafier for any
one to look upon the Sun, than earneftly
upon him   And who is able to reckon up
his new Punifhments to fatiate his Luft,
who did not abftain from his very intimate
Friends ? And that you may know this is
no vain Calumny againft him, call thofe who
have been murther'd by him, all thefe,
O *Rhodamanthus*, were butcher'd by this
Villain, fome treacheroufly taken out of
the World, becaufe they had beautiful
Wives, others, becaufe they ftomach'd to
fee their Children abus'd; fome becaufe
they were rich, others becaufe they were
good, and prudent, and in no wife pleas'd
with his Proceedings.

F f   *Rhada.*

Rhada. What fay'ft thou to this, thou Caitiff?

Megap I have committed the Murthers he fpeaks of, but as for all the other Points, the Adulteries, lying with young Men, and Whoring with Virgins, in all thefe Things *Cynifcus* accufes me of falfly.

Cynif. Oh *Rhadamanthus,* I will produce Evidences of it.

Rhada Whom do you mean?

Cynif. Mercury, call me hither his Lamp and his Bed, when they are come, they'll teftifie what Things he has done to their Knowledge.

Mer. You Bed, and Lamp of *Megapenthes,* come into the Court here

Rhada Tell us what you know of *Megapenthes* in this matter, fpeak firft, *Bed*

Bed All's true that *Cynifcus* hath objected, but I am afham'd, Lord *Rhadamanthus,* to tell you all he hath done upon me, they are fo Beaftly.

Rhada. Thou doft manifeftly convict him, tho' thou canft not endure to declare them, but now, *Lamp,* give in thy Evidence.

Lamp Truly, what he did in the Day-time, I know not, but what he did fuffer in the Night, I am afham'd to tell you, but I have obferved many things, which are not to be expefs'd, exceeding all Villainy, altho' very willingly I did not fuck in the Oil, defiring to be extinguifh'd, but he ufed me in all his Wickednefs, and contaminated my Light.

Rhada. Here's Evidence enough, pull off his Purple, that we may see the Number of his Scars; good-lack, he is quite black and blew, and quite mark'd all over, or rather of a Sky Colour by his Brandings; after what manner therefore shall he be punish'd, is he to be cast into the fiery *Phlegeton*, and given to *Cerberus*.

Cynif. By no Means, but if you please, I will propose to you a new sort of Punishment, and very agreeable for him.

Rhada. Tell it, and on that Condition, I will give you the greatest Thanks I can for it.

Cyn.f. 'Tis the Custom, I think, for all who die to drink of the Water of Oblivion.

Rhada. Yes.

Cynif. Then let him only of all others, be without drinking of it.

Mer. Why so?

Cynif. Because he will be severely tormented, when he remembers what a base sort of a Person he was, and how powerful upon Earth, and recollect his past Pleasures?

Rhada. Right, let him be condemn'd, let him be bound fast to *Tantalus*, and let him for ever remember what he did in his Life-time.

THE
TYRANT-KILLER,

By Mr. Hill

The Argument.

*As for the Argument of this Declamation, it is
subjoyn'd by the Author himself, the Oration
is of the judicial kind, the state of the Que
stion consists in the quality of the matter, for it
is chiefly enquired whether he may be thought
worthy the Reward due to the Slayer of a Tyrant, that hath only killed the Son of a Tyrant
or not. Nevertheless there is likewise a point
of Law, for it is also disputed who may be
properly called a Tyrant-killer, and concerning
the Tenor and purpose of the Law in this case
The Proem or Preamble is almost spent in
gaining the attention of the Auditory, and ex-
plaining the nature of the Action, whilst the
Plaintiff, in like manner, shews the Scope of
his Petition, together with the Greatness and
Novelty of his Enterprise, excepting that in the
mean while he endeavours to procure favour
for himself, from the consideration of the Merit of the Fact, and at the same time to excite
ill-will against his Adversary through suspicion.
In the Narration he proceeds to discant on
the Grievousness and Cruelty of the Tyranny,
and transfers the whole Cause thereof on the
Tyrant's Son, to the end, that it might seem as*

ij

if he had attack'd the Son before the Father of
set purpose; then he gives an account of the
manner how the Slaughter was committed, and
of his own design.   Here ensues the Proposi-
tion or Petition it self, and at length the Confirmation, wherein he first shews the Equity of
his Demand, by an amplification of the Events
and Benefits occasioned by this Attempt, compared with the Adversary's Objection.   Afterwards in the Words of the Law, he propounds
the Definition of a Tyrant-slayer, prov'd from
the nature thereof, viz. that this name ought
to be appropriated not only to one, who hath kil-
ed a Tyrant with his own Hand and Sword,
but also to one that destroys him by another Person, or by any means whatsoever.   Moreover, he
argues from the end of the Law against the
Letter.   In fine, after the manner of the Rhe-
toricians, he makes a Re-capitulation; in
the Design, or Intention, the Endeavour, the
Action, and those too by way of comparison, or
disposition are amplified, and lastly the Event
is considered   The Perotration or Conclusion
consists of pathetical Expressions, for the Orator endeavours to move the Affections of the
People in his own behalf, from the manner and
Instrument of the Action, as also a certain Hy-
potyposis or Example taken from the Person
of that Tyrant, in a representation of his Sayings
and Actions   In the end he reports the Proposi-
tion, and leaves, as it were, a remembrance of
the signal Services lately perform'd by him in
the Ears of his Auditors.

A certain Person went up into a Citadel, on purpose to kill a Tyrant, but not finding him there,
slew his Son and left the Sword in the Body:

But when the Tyrant came and saw his Son
dead, he dispatch'd himself with the same Sword.
Whereupon the Assassin who had storm'd the
Fort and perform'd this Exploit, demanded
the Reward, decreed by the Law, for the Slay-
er of a Tyrant.

HAVING slain two Tyrants on the
same day (most awful judges) one
of whom was well advanc'd in years, and
the other in the prime Vigour of his Youth,
ready to succeed the former in the committing of enormous Crimes, I come only
to sue for one Recompence for both, being
indeed the only Person among all those,
who ever undertook to assassinate a Tyrant, that remov'd and destroy'd two Malefactors with one Stroak, *viz.* by killing
the Son with a Sword, and the Father,
through the means of the natural Affe-
&ion, which he bore to his Off-spring
Therefore the Tyrant hath suffer'd con-
dign Punishment for the Crimes lately per-
petrated by him, since he first liv'd to see
his Son taken away by untimely Death,
and afterwards (which is a very unlawful
thing) was constrain'd to be his own Executioner. Indeed, the Son perish'd by my
Hand, and being slain, afforded me his
Assistance for the accomplishing of another
Slaughter; and that he, who had been a
Coadjutor to his Father, while living, in
so many unjust Actions, after his own
Death, became (as far it was possible) the
Murderer of his said Parent. Therefore I
am the Person that has put an end to the

Tyranny, and my Sword hath performed all these notable Exploits. But I
have chang'd the Order of the Executions,
and have made an Innovation with respect
to the manner of dispatching those wicked Wretches, by killing with my own proper Arm the lustier of them, that was able
to defend himself, and leaving the elder
only to the Management of my Sword
alone On which Account I thought to obtain
somewhat more of you, and to receive Rewards equal, in number, to the Persons
slain, in regard that I have not only deliver'd you from present Calamities, but also from the fear of any for the future,
and have render'd your Liberty firm and
permanent, since there is no longer left an
Heir of such detestable Outrages

In the mean while, nevertheless, I stand
in Jeopardy, after having atchiev'd so remarkable Enterprizes, of being oblig'd to
depart from your Presence without a Reward, and of being alone depriv'd of that
Recompence, which the Laws, that have
been preserved by me, apparently allow.
Wherefore my Adversary, who contradicts
it, seems to me to do so, not thro' any
Zeal for the Benefit of the *Commonwealth,*
as he insinuates, but by reason of his grief
for the Loss of the deceased Tyrants, and
desire to be avenged of the Author of
their Deaths. However, I must entreat
you, right honourable Judges, patiently
to give Ear to me a little, whilst I more
particularly rehearse the Mischiefs that
arise from Tyranny, altho' I confess they

F f 2   can-

cannot but be already well known to you,
since by this means ye may the better understand the Greatness of the Service done
by me to the State, and may be so much
the more delighted, in considering from
what Misfortunes ye have been lately delivered. For we have not sustain'd (as it
hath often happen'd to some other People)
a simple Tyranny, and one Servitude, neither have we been subject to the Dominion
of one Lord, but alone of all those, that
were ever affected with the like Calamities,
have had two Tyrants instead of one, oppress'd with a double Injury However,
the o'd Man was much more moderate,
as being less prone to Anger, more gentle
in punishing, and slower in the prosecuting
of Pleasures, by reason that Age had now
abated the Vehemency of his Appetite,
and restrain'd the Eagerness of his Pass-
ons Besides that, (as they say) he was
usually first excited by his Son, even a-
gainst his Will, to the committing of any
Outrages, not being himself, very much
incl a'd to Tyranny, but willing to comply with his Humour : For he bore too exceeding an Affection toward his Son, as in
effect he plainly shewed, his Son was all in
all, and he altogether obey'd him, offering
whatsoever Injuries he thought fit, punishing whomsoever he appointed, and in every
thing diligently observing his Orders In
fine, the Son apparently tyranniz'd over
the Father, who was only, as it were, the
Minister of his exorbitant Passions. In
deed, the young Man resign'd the He

nour to the other, by reason of his Age,
and abstain'd only from the Title, nevertheless, he actually exercis'd the Tyranny,
and was himself the Head thereof. And
altho' he receiv'd the Defence and Safety
of the Principality from his Father, yet
he alone enjoy'd the Advantages of the
Oppressions. For he was the Person that
enroll'd the Guard, that kept the Watch and
Ward, that put to Death those Wretches
who were tyrannically oppress'd, that defended those, who endeavour'd to lay any
Snares, that took away the Striplings, and
that violated the Sacred Rites of Wed-
lock To him the Virgins were brought:
Lastly, if any Murders, any Banishments,
Robberies, Confiscations of Goods, Tortures and other Outrages were committed,
all these were the Effects of the young
Tyrant's Audaciousness. Moreover, the
old one follow'd the Advice of his Son,
became an Abettor of his unjust Actions, and
only approv'd his Villainies, insomuch, that
an intolerable Yoak was laid on our Shoulders, for when the Passions of Mens minds
assume an absolute Licentiousness, thro Sovereign Authority, they soon break forth vio
lently into all manner of enormous Disoders.

But that which more-especially afflicted
me, was the Consideration, that this Servitude could be of long Continuance, nay,
rather everlasting, whilst the Commonwealth was successively transmitted from
the Possession of one Tyrannical Lord, into
that of another, and the People, as it were,
by right of Inheritance, were render'd
Vas-

Vaſſals to a profligate Wretch. For from hence ariſeth no ſmall Comfort to others, in arguing and diſcourſing thus one with another, certainly his Power will e'er long be reſtrain'd, or he will die ſuddenly, and within a little while we ſhall be ſet at Liberty But none of theſe things were then hop'd for, in regard, that we plainly ſaw an Heir of the Tyranny already prepared Therefore none of the Gentlemen, nor even thoſe that were of my Opinion, durſt make any Attempt, ſo that the Recovery of our Freedom was altogether deſpair'd of, and it ſeem'd abſolutely impoſſible to ſuppreſs the Tyranny, more eſpecially, ſince ſo many Enemies were to be oppos'd However, all theſe formidable Obſtacles did not terrifie me, neither did I ſhrink back, after having reflected on the difficulty of the Enterprize, neither did I dread the Danger. Thus I alone, alone I ſay, march'd up againſt ſo great and potent a Tyrannical Power, or rather not alone, as being accompany'd with my Sword, which fought together with me, and in part ſlew the Tyrant, whilſt Death on all ſides preſented it ſelf before my Eyes, and nevertheleſs, I doubted not but the common Liberty would be redeem'd by my Slaughter.

Therefore, when I had broke thro' the firſt Watch, and not without much Oppoſition, oblig'd the Guards to retreat, killing every one that ſtood in the way, and removing every Obſtacle, I made up to the principal Head of the Work, to the only

Streng

Strength of the Tyranny, and to the main Source of our Calamities. Then having storm'd the Rampart of the Fortress, where the young Tyrant appear'd, valiantly defending himself, and endeavouring to resist my Force at length slew him with many Wounds. Now the Tyranny was already abolish'd, my Design was then already accompl'sh'd, from that very time we were all absolutely free; except this, that the old Tyrant remain'd alone, unarmed, destitute of Attendants, depriv'd of those his numerous Guards, altogether abandon'd, and no longer worthy to fall by the Hand of a generous Assailant. That Instant, right worshipful Judges, I mused thus in my Mind, all things have been well manag'd, all things have been brought to Perfection, all things have succeeded according to Expectation, but after what manner shall he that survives be duly punish'd? Indeed, he is unworthy to be put to Death by me, or my Hand, more especially, if after the performing of so memorable, juvenile, and noble an Exploit, the Glory of the former Slaughter should be thereby eclipsed. Therefore, a convenient Executioner is to be sought for, but after so signal a Calamity, let him not gain such an Advantage from hence, let him take a view of the Corps, let him be tortur'd for a while, and let the Sword be laid near him, whereto I will commit the rest. Having thus determin'd the matter, I departed far from the Place; but he soon did what I had before conjectur'd, namely, flew the Tyrant, and put an end to my Tragedy.

Where-

Whereupon I am come to you, bringing along with me a popular Form of Government, bidding every one to be of good Cheer, and proclaiming the joyful Tydings of Liberty. Go to now, enjoy the Fruit of my Labour; the Citadel (as ye plainly see) is clear'd from lewd Miscreants, none commands Tyrannically, ye have Power to confer Honours on whomsoever you shall think fit, as also to administer Justice, and plead according to Law. But consider, that all those Benefits have accrued to you thro' my means, as the effect of my Valour, and thro' the Slaughter of one Person, after whose Death his Father was no longer able to live. Therefore I judge it convenient, that you should allot to me a Reward suitable to these Merits, not that I am greedy of Gain, or sordid, or determined to serve my Country, meerly for Profit, but as only desirous, that my Service might be encouraged with some Gratuity, and not altogeter disparaged, as also that my Atchievements may not be render'd inglorious, by being adjudg'd to be unprofitable, and unworthy of any Recompence. However, this Adversary contradicted and affirms, that I do not Justice in desiring to be gratify'd, and receiving a Pension, insinuating at the same time, that I am not the real Destroyer of a Tyrant, and that there was nothing done by me, according to the Tenour of the Law, but that somewhat is yet wanting to my Exploit, as a necessary Qualification for the demand ing of a Reward. Therefore I would willingly ask him these Questions; What more do you require of me? Did not I form the Design? Did not I go up and storm the Fort? Did not I kill one of the Tyrants? Did not I set the People at Liberty? Does any one domineer? Does any one command Arbitrarily? Does any absolute Lord threaten? Hath any one of the Malefactors escap'd my Fury? Certainly it cannot by any Means be avouch'd. On the contrary, all things are full of Peace, all the Laws are restor'd, the Liberty of the Commonwealth, is manifest; the Democracy is firmly establish'd, Marriages are no longer violated, our young Men are secure, our Virgins are safe, and the City as yet celebrates the publick Happiness with solemn Festivals. Who then hath caus'd all these Events? Who hath put an end to those Misfortunes? Or who hath procur'd these Advantages? Indeed, if any one of my Predecessors hath a right to this Honour, I willingly renounce the Recompence, and desist from suing for any Favour: But in case I alone have transacted all things, by couragiously attempting, exposing my self to Danger perplexing, destroying, and harrasing the Enemies of the State, and punishing some of them by others, why dost thou go about to detract from the Reputation of my signal Services? Why do'st thou endeavour to render the People ungrateful to me? For thou did'st not kill the Tyrant.

Moreover,

Moreover, the Law hath appointed a Reward for the Slayer of Tyrants, but I pray tell me what difference is there, whether any one should kill him in Person, or procure his Death? None at all in my Opinion. The Lawgiver had apparently regard only to the Freedom of the People, to the Democracy, and to the removing of Calamities: He hath decreed Honour for this Enterprize, and hath determined it to be worthy of a Retribution, which you cannot deny to have happen'd thro' my means. For if I have slain him without whom the other was not able to live, I my self have accomplish'd the Slaughter, I have actually kill'd the latter, but by the Hand of the former. Therefore do no longer nicely dispute concerning the manner of his Death, nor make Inquisition how he perish'd, but whether he be now destroy'd, and whether I were the cause of his Destruction. Indeed, you seem also to demand thus much of me, and so calumniate those Persons that have deserv'd well of the Commonwealth on this Account, whether any one of them hath assassinated a Tyrant, not with a Sword, but with a Stone, or a piece of Wood, or after any other manner whatsoever. But what if I had besieged the Tyrant with Famine in his strong Hold, and drove him to the utmost Extremity, would you even then require the Slaughter to be perform'd with my own Hand? Or would you tell me that somewhat was wanting for the Satisfaction of the Law? And that too, when the
prosigue

profligate Wretch was more cruelly put to Death. Examine this one Matter of Fact, make this Demand, enquire diligently into this Affair, whether any of the Malefactors as yet survive, or whether there remains any expectation of Fear; or whether there be left any Remembrance of the Calamities? But if all things are purged and pacified, it is the part of a slandering Sycophant, by finding Fault with the manner of the Action, to endeavour to deprive any one of that Reward which is due to his Industry or Merits.

Indeed, I remember it to have been pleaded in Law, unless perhaps, by reason of long Servitude, the particular Ordinances have slipt out of my Mind, that there is a double Cause of Death, *viz.* 1 If any one hath kill'd another himself. 2 If one hath not done it in Person, nor committed the Fact with his own Hand, but only reduc'd him to Extremity, and given occasion, or hath been in any wise accessory to his Slaughter, the Law determines, that the like Punishment ought to be inflicted on both, and that too with very great Equity, for it defines the Audaciousness of the Attempt to be equal to the Fact, and then it would be superfluous to enquire into the manner of the Murder. On which account you are apt to judge, that such a Person, who thus destroys another, ought to be punish'd as a Man-slayer, and by no means to be acquitted, nevertheless, you will not vouchsafe to allow to one, who hath in like manner perform'd

some

some notable Service to the Commonwealth,
a Recompence commensurate to his Merits. Certainly, you cannot argue, that
I did unwittingly, and that some prosperous Event happen'd beyond my Expectation; for what else could I fear, when the
more sturdy Tyrant was Slain? Why did
I leave the Sword in the Wound, unless
I had plainly foreseen the very same Occur-
rence, which afterward fell out accordingly? Unless perhaps you will say, that he
who perish'd was not a Tyrant, nor had
this denomination, and that on that account you cannot allot much Reward, as
if he had been actually destroy'd; but it
cannot be averr'd Now that the Tyrant
is slain, will you deny a just Recompence
to him that was the cause of his Death?
Oh strange Nicety! Art thou so sollicitous
to know after what manner he died, whilst
thou enjoyest Liberty? Or rather dost thou
require somewhat superfluous of him, who
hath restor'd the Democracy? The Laws
you have already acknowledg'd, searche
into the principal Matter of Fact, but take
no Cognizance of any of the Means, nor
makes any other scrupulous Enquiry. The
why, if any one had only expell'd a Tyrant, would he not receive the same Pension, as is due to the Slayer of a Tyrant?
He would certainly, and that too on very
good Grounds, since he had introduc'd
Freedom instead of Slavery.

But the deliverance which I have procu-
cur'd, doth not imply Banishment, nor
the fear of a second Usurpation; but an

abfolute Removal thereof, an utter De-
ftruction of the whole Tyrannical Off-
fpring, and an entire rooting out of all the
Mifchiefs. In truth, Gentlemen, proceed
(if you fhall think fit) to a ftrict Examination of every Article, from the beginning to the end, particularly, whether
any thing appertaining to the Law, be
omitted, or whether any of thofe Qualifications be wanting, that are requifite in a
Slayer of Tyrants. Firft then it is neceffary, that he fhould be of a generous Difpofition, and a Lover of his Country; being ready to expofe his Perfon to any Danger for the Benefit of the Republick, and
to redeem the common Safety, even with
the Lofs of his own Life. Have my Endeavours been herein deficient? Have I
fhew'd my felf effeminate? Have I floth-
fully turn'd back, after having forefeen
the Dangers thro' which I was oblig'd to
pafs? This cannot be avouch'd. Conceive therefore, that I remain only in this
Station, that I was willing, and had determin'd to make thefe Attempts, even, altho' no Advantage fhould arife from thence,
and that I now Demand a Retribution, as
a publick Benefactor, only for fixing fuch
a Refolution.

Furthermore, fuppofing, that I were not
able to accomplifh my Defign, and that
another Perfon fhould have flain the Tyrant after me, tell me, I pray, would it be
abfurd, or unjuft for the State to afford a
Recompence? More-efpecially, if I faid,
O fellow Citizens, I have determined, refolved,

attempted,

attempted, and have also endeavour'd to put my *Design in Execution, I* alone am worthy to be *rewarded,* What Answer would you then return? However, now I do not plead thus, but that I have ascended into the Fort, run a great Risk, and perform'd almost innumerable Exploits, before the Slaughter of the Youth. For you cannot imagine it to be easie and feasible to repel the Watch, to subdue the Guards, and for one single Man to defeat so many Indeed, this is almost the greatest Enterprize of all in the killing of the Tyrant, and as it were, the main Scope of the whole Work. For it is not a matter of much difficulty to oppress the Tyrant himself, but to remove those Ostacles that secure and maintain the Tyranny, which difficulty, whosoever hath surmounted, he hath rectified all things with prosperous Success, and that which remains is of little Moment. But I could never have come near to attack the Tyrants, unless I had before assaulted and subdued all the Centinels and Guards with whom they were encompassed.

I shall add nothing more, but still continue to insist on the same Argument, I have broke thro' the Watch, overcome the Guards, and render'd the Tyrant destitute of Attendants, unarmed and naked. Do I then seem to you to be worthy of Honour after these Transactions or not? Or do you still require of me a farther slaying? Indeed, if you are desirous thereof, it is in no wise wanting: I have not en-

encountered the Enemy without Bloodshed, but have committed a great and noble Slaughter, *viz.* of a vigorous Youth,
and one that was formidable to all, thro'
whofe means the other his Father was fafe
from Snares, on whom alone he relied, and
who in a manner fupplied the place of many Life-Guards. Therefore, I pray, do I
not well deferve a Reward? Or is it fit that
I fhould be defrauded of the Honour due
to fuch remarkable Atchievements ? What
if I had flain one of the Partifans of the
Tyrant, or one of his Minifters of State,
or one of his honourable domeftick Servants? Would not this feem to have been
a confiderable Attempt, to have enter'd
into the middle of the Citadel, and fo have
ftabb'd one of the Tyrant's Friends in the
midft of fo great a Multitude of armed Men?
Now reflect a little on the Quality of the
Perfon flain. He was the Son of a Tyrant, nay rather, he was the crueller Tyrant, an inexorable Lord, more fevere in
inflicting Punifhments, more violent in offering Injuries, but the greateft Misfortune confifted herein, that he was the Heir
and Succeffor of all, and able to render
our Miferies perpetual Are you rather
defirous, that this only were perform'd by
me, and that the Tyrant were yet living
in Exile ? Neverthelefs, I would demand
a Recompence even on this Account What
fay you? Will ye not allow it? Did ye not
fufpect, and were ye not afraid of him alfo? Was not he an abfolute Lord? Were
not his Oppreffions intolerable ?

Now

Now therefore, obferve the main Scope of the matter, I have very well accomplifh'd (according to my Ability) that which the Adverfary requires of me, and have kill'd the Tyrant, thro' the Slaughter of another, not fimply, and with one Stroak, as it were moft to be wifh'd for, with refpect to one that was guilty of fo great Crime; but after I had firft caus'd him to be tortur'd with exceffive Grief, and prefented to his View that which was moft of all believ'd by him, miferably lying proftrate on the Ground, namely, his only Son, in the prime of his Youth, (who altho' a lewd Wretch, nevertheleſs flou rifh'd, and was like his Father) now befmear'd all over with Blood and Gou. Thefe are the Wounds moft afflicting to Parents ; thefe are the Weapons of the juſt Slayers of Tyrants, this is a Death proper for cruel Ufurpers of the Peoples Liberties, this is a Vengeance adequate to the Merits of fuch notorious Crimes. But to die fpeedily, to expire immediately, and not to behold fuch an Object, amounts to nothing worthy of the Punifhment of a Tyrant. For I was not ignorant, good Sir, I was not ignorant, nor indeed any one elfe, how great an Affection he bore toward his Son, and how unwilling he was to furvive him, tho' never fo little a while. Perhaps this paffionate Love may be common to all Fathers, but in him it was fomewhat more abundant, than in others, and that too deſervedly, fince he was very fenfible, that this young Heir was the only Perfon that ſup-

porte

ported and maintain'd the Tyranny; as also, that he alone was ready to expose himself to Danger for his Father, and establish'd the Safety of the Empire. Insomuch, that I well know that he would soon die, if not thro' extream Affection, yet at least thro' Despair, as concluding, that no Advantage could any longer proceed from his Life, when the Security which accrued to him from his Son, was entirely taken away.

Therefore I took care that all these Passions should at once confusedly seize on his Mind, *viz. Natural Affection, Grief, Despair, Fear,* and a Dread of what might happen for the future. I made use of these Auxiliary Forces against him, and at length compell'd him to take that fatal Resolution. Thus he perish'd for your Sakes, Childless, Sorrowful, Lamenting and Weeping, having bewail'd his Misfortunes with extream Grief, indeed not of long Continuance, yet such as was sufficient for a Father. Lastly, which is the most lamentable Catastrophe of all, he laid violent Hands on himself, which manner of Death is the most miserable, and far more grievous, than if it were caus'd by another. Where was I furnish'd with the Sword? Doth any one else own or lay Claim to it? Did this Weapon ever belong to any other Person? Who brought it into the Fort? Who made use thereof before the Tyrant? Who sent it to him? O Sword! the Partaker and Successor of my glorious Atchievement, after so great Dangers, after so many Slaughters, we are contemned, and esteem'd as unworthy of a Reward, For if I should demand a Gratuity of you only on the Account thereof, if I should say, O ye worshipful Judges, when such a Tyrant was desirous to die, and perceived himself to be unarmed at that time, this my Sword was serviceable to him, and in fine, co-operated with us all in the Recovery of our Liberty, certainly ye would judge that it well deserv'd some Honour and Recompence. Would ye not also make some Retribution to the Author of so great an Advantage to the Republick? Would ye not enroll his Name among those of the Benefactors of the State? Would ye not carefully lay up your Sword amidst other Sacred Monuments? Nay, would ye not reverence it as it were a kind of Deity?

Now consider a while with me, what the Tyrant might probably have done and said before his Death When the young Man who was slain by me, and stabb'd with many Wounds in the more visible Parts of his Body, to the end that his Father might be most exquisitely tortur'd and perplex'd even at the first Sight, cried out miserably, calling for his said Parent, not as an Assistant or Defender (for he knew him to be old and infirm) but only as a Spectator of their Domestick Calamities, I who was the Author of the whole Tragedy, retir'd in the mean time, leaving the dead Corps to the Actor, together with the Scene, the Sword, and other Appur-
tenances

tenances of the Play. But as foon as the
other came near, and faw his only Son
fcarcely breathing, weltring in his own
Blood, and full of Slaughter, having alfo
perciev'd that his Wounds were very clofe
one to another, many in Number, and
Mortal, he cried out thus *O Son! we are
deftroy'd, we are flain as Tyrants, where is the
Murderer? Why doth he keep me? To what
end doth he preferve me, who have been before
kill'd in thy Perfon, O my Child? Doth he
defpife my old Age? Surely he forbears to difpatch me, and prolongs my Slaughter of fet purpofe, as if I ought to be punifh'd with a linge-
ring Death.*
 The Tyrant having uttered thefe Words,
fought for a Sword, for he was unarmed,
relying altogether on his Son's Defence.
But neither was this Inftrument wanting,
as having been already prepar'd by me, and
left on purpofe to accomplifh the future
Exploit. Whereupon, drawing it out of
his Son's Wound, he brake forth into thefe
pathetick Expreffions: *O Sword! thou haft
indeed killed me a little before, now therefore
put an end to my Miferies; afford fome Comfort
to a forrowful Father; help his aged and unhappy Hand; flay, deftroy the Tyrant, and deliver
him from his Grief: Would to God I had met
with thee in the Beginning, would to God I had
taken up the firft place in the Slaughter; I fhould
have perifh'd indeed, but only as a Tyrant, and
believing that I had an Avenger as yet furvi-
ving; but now, alafs! I fhall as it were Child-
lefs, and even deftitute of a Slayer.* Thus the
unfortunate Wretch, whilft he pronunc'd

thefe

thefe Words, ftruck the Sword thro' his
Body, trembling, and fcarcely able to give
the fatal Blow ; in eed, he was defirous
to do it fpeedily, but had not Strength fufficient to commit the Fact

Obferve then, I pray, how many Punifhments are here? How many Wounds
How many Deaths? How many Slaughter s
of Tyrants? How many Rewards meri-
ted? In fine, ye have all feen that vigorous
young Man firft lying proftrate on the
Ground, which was no fmall nor eafie Work
to be perform'd ; afterward the Corps of
the elder Tyrant laid near the other, and
the Blood of both mingled together. Behold thefe glorious Victims of Liberty and
Victory, which my Arm hath facrific'd to
your Safety ; behold the noble Atchiev-
ments of my Sword. But the Sword it
felf remains in the midft, between both
the dead Bodies, fhewing how worthy it
hath been of its Mafter, and teftifying at
the fame time, what faithful Service it
hath done for him. Gentlemen, this Enterprize, which hath been accomplifh'd by
me, would be of lefs Moment, were it not
more illuftrious on the account of its Novelty. Wherefore, I am the only Perfon
that have entirely abolifh'd the Tyranny
But the whole Work may be divided into
many Parts, after the manner of Stage-
Plays ; for, the firft Act of this Tragedy
was acted by my felf, the fecond by the
Tyrant's Son, and the third by the Father,
whilft the Sword was ferviceable to us in all.

DIPSAS.

By Mr. Hill.

The Argument.

This is a kind of Preface, of the same Nature as some of the former, wherein the Author declares his Affection towards the Auditors, or whosoever they were, with whom he then convers'd, by making this Comparison of the Viper, called Dipsas. *For as an insatiable Thirst seizeth on those Persons who are stung by these sorts of Serpents, insomuch, that the greater quantity of Liquor they drink, their Drowth is so much the more inflam'd; so he likewise profess'd himself to be transported with a certain unsatiate desire of their Conversation. And that the oftener he enjoyed it, the more it was coveted by him. Moreover, as for the Sting of the* Dipsas, *and that deadly Thirst thereupon ensuing, You may find almost the Discription, and Example, of one* Aulus, *an Ensign in* Cato's *Army, who perished after the same manner as the Man on whom the Epigram of the present Narration was made, in the Ninth Book of* Lucian, *where all the other kinds of Snakes here mentioned, are reckon'd up together, with a Fa-*
ble

ble, shewing why Africa *abounds, and is so extreamly infested with Serpents.*

THE Southern Side of *Africa*, is only a vast Plain of profound Sand and Soil, being every where a parched Desart, and extreamly barren, not bringing forth any Grass, Herb or Plant, and destitute of Water; but if any be found in some Caverns or Holes of the Earth, after a few Showers of Rain, it is altogether muddy and stinking, so that it cannot be drunk, even by those that are never so thirsty, for which causes the Land is become uninhabitable. For who can dwell in such unpleasant, scorched-up, and noisome Regions, where the Air it self is, as it were, on Fire, and the Sand so hot, that it renders the Ground altogether unpassable The *Garamanthes* alone, a neighbouring Savage Nation, lightly armed, and that live generally in Tents, and are much addicted to Hunting, do sometimes make Incursions into these Countries, during the Winter Solstice, more especially when they observe the Weather to be rainy, at what times the vehement Heats are much abated The Sand being moistned, becomes in a manner pervious. Their Sport is in hunting of wild Asses, and large Ostrages that fly on the Ground, but chiefly of Apes, and sometimes Elephants; for these Animals alone, are capable of enduring Thirst, and the excessive Heat of the Sun. And the *Garamantes*, as soon as they have spent the Provisions they brought along with

them

them, speedily return, fearing least the Sand, when inflamed again, should obstruct their Paffage, if not absolutely hinder their Retreat; so that, being as it were caught in a Net, they must inevitably perish, together with their Prey; for it is impossible to shun it, if the Sun, darting its Beams with greater vehemency on the humid part, (which adds Fewel to the Fire) should thereby cause a more consuming Heat, and soon dry up the parched Ground.

But all the above mentioned Inconveniencies proceeding from the Heat, Drought and Solitude of the Earth, will seem to be more tolerable than those which I shall now rehearse, and on this account that Region is altogether to be abandon'd, wherein are nourish'd divers sorts of creeping Things, and Monsters terrible for their Form, Magnitude, and Number, but more especially by reason of the Strength of their Poison.

Some of these lie hid in the bottom of the Sand, and others crawl about the Surface of the Earth, *viz* swelling Toads, Asps, Vipers, horned Serpents, venemous Flies, Javelins, Snakes that have Heads at both ends, Dragons, and two kinds of Scorpions, one whereof is terrestrial, gliding on the Earth, of a prodigious Size, and full of turning Joints. The other is Aerial and Volatile, having thin skinny Wings, such as those of Bats, Locust, and Grass-hoppers, many noisome winged Fowls of the like Nature, render that part of *Africa* inaccessible. But of all the Serpents usually bred

E

in the Sands, the moſt obnoxious is that which the *Grecians* call *Dipſas*, being of no very large Dimenſions, and reſembling a Viper Nevertheleſs, its Sting is violent, and its Poiſon groſs, immediately exciting inceſſant Pains; for it cauſeth a burning Heat, together with Putrifaction and Inflamation, inſomuch, that they that are ſtung cry out, as if they lay in the midſt of a Fire.

But their greateſt Affliction and Anguiſh proceeds from hence, that they labour under a Diſtemper of the ſame Name with the Serpent, that is to ſay, an inſatiable Thirſt It is alſo chiefly to be admired, that by how much the more they drink, ſo much the more eager they are ſtill to quaff, and their ardent deſire of Drinking is continually more and more encreaſed.

Neither can this exceſſive Thirſt be extinguiſh'd, altho' you ſhould even give them the whole River of the *Nile* and *Danow* to drink, but their Diſeaſe would be more enflam'd, by moiſtening it, as if one ſhould endeavour to quench a Fire with Oil. The Phyſicians affirm this to be the cauſe, that the groſs Poiſon afterward dilated with the Drink, becomes more quick in its Motion, being thereby rendred (as it is probable) more moiſt, and farther diffuſed thro' the Body.

Indeed, I never ſaw any one afflicted with this Diſtemper, and God grant, that ſo dolorous an Object may not be preſented to my view; neither can I forbear applauding my own Conduct, in not adventuring

turing at any time to enter into the Continent of *Africa*.

However, I have heard of an Inscription, which one of my Friends (as he told me) had read on the Pedeſtal of a Statue, erected for a certain Perſon who periſhed after this manner, as he was travelling out of *Africa* into *Egypt*, thro' the Plain called the *Grand Syrtis*, or *Quickſand* ; for there is no other Road that leads to this Country. My Friend declares, that he met with the Tomb of the ſame Perſon built on the Seaſhoar, and even waſhed with its Waves, whereto was affix'd a Monument, ſhewing the manner of his Death, on which was carved the Figure of a Man, as *Tantalus* is uſually repreſented, ſtanding in a Pool, and drawing Water to drink, whilſt the little Beaſt, or Serpent *Dipſas*, cloſely embraces him, and environs his Legs.

Divers Women are alſo repreſented, carrying Water, and pouring it on his Body ; and near it lie ſeveral Eggs of ſuch Oſtridges as I have already intimated to have been hunted by the *Garamantes*. Moreover, an Epigram was ſubjoin'd, which it may not be improper to incert.

> *Thus* Tantalus *is wrack'd with tort'ring Pain,*
> *Whilſt poiſonous Vapours run thro' every Vein*
> *The ſubtil Venom ſtill augments its Rage,*
> *Th' exceſſive Drowth no Waters can aſſwage.*
> *Ye Daughters of the* Argive *Prince, your Skil*
> *This leaky Veſſel ſurely ne'er can fill.*

There

There were in like manner four other Verfes, concerning the Eggs, and how the Traveller was ftung in taking them up; but I have let thofe flip out of my Mind. The Neighbouring People gather the Eggs, and preferve them with no fmall Diligence, not only for eating, but to make Veffels and Cups of the Shells, when empty, for they cannot there form any Earthen-Ware, by reafon that the Soil is univerfally Sandy, but when large Eggs are found, two Cups may be made of every Shell, for each half is a fufficient Covering for a Man's Head.

Thus thefe Serpents lie in Ambufh near the Eggs, until any one approach, then they fleal off the Sand, and bite the unfortunate Wretch, who endures the Tortures even now mention'd, perpetually drinking, yet ftill thirfting, and never fatisfied.

I have gone thro' this Difcourfe, not defigning to difpute with the Poet *Nicander*, nor to give you to underftand, that I am not ignorant of the nature of the *African* Vermine and Infects; for this Skill is more laudable in Phyficians, to whom this Knowledge becomes extraordinarily neceffary, to the end, that they may be able to prefcribe proper Antidotes for fuch Maladies.

But in truth (Gentlemen) I my felf feem to be affected with the like Paffion toward you, as much as thofe Perfons covet Drink, that are ftung by the Serpent *Dipfas*, pray be not difpleas'd then at this Comparifon,

parifon ; for the oftner I have had the
Honour of your Company, fo much the
more ambitious am I ftill to enjoy it;
and by an intolerable Thuft, I am enfla-
med, infomuch, that it feems an Im-
poffibility ever to be fatiated with the
Fruition of fuch excellent Nectar, and
that too with very good Reafon ; for where
fhould I find fo clear and pure a Fountain :
Wherefore I hope (Gentlemen) you will
excufe my Boldnefs, if I alfo being ftruck
to the Heart with this moft delectable and
wholfome Sting, fhould immerge my felf
all over in the Torrent of your Favour,
laying my Head under the Source   Heavens grant only thefe Emanations from
you may never fail, and that when your
ardent defire of Hearing fhall begin to
abate, you may not leave me gaping and
ready to perifh by Thirft, which with refpect to you, will be everlafting, and nothing can hinder me from continuing ftill
to participate of thofe refrefhing Streams,
fince, according to the Judgment of wife
Plato, in the Enjoyment of good Things
there can be no Satiety.

THE

THE
SHIP:
OR, THE
WISH.

By Andrew Baden, *M. D.*

The Argument.

In this Dialogue, Lucian *laughs at the fond Desires and Appetite of Men, that they should
place their* Summum Bonum, *in the desired
Possession of those Things, which, if after all
their Labour and Industry they can acquire,
will render them more liable to a greater Share
of Trouble and Danger ; and to that end here
is represented* Adimantus, *coveting immense
Riches ;* Samippus *Power and Empire,
and last of all* Timolaus, *desiring nothing
more, than the Fruition of all the pleasurable
Things of the World. All whose Wishes,*
Lucian *confutes in such a manner, that he
proves any thing rather than Happiness is to
be expected from those Enjoyments,*

Lycinus, Timolaus, Samippus, Adimantus

Lycin. **D**ID not I say, a fresh Corps
might escape a Vulture's Eye,
or a young Gull the Tricks of an inveigl-
ing

ling Jilt, sooner than *Timolaus* would miss any strange Sight, tho' at a Miutes Warning he was to ride Post to *Corinth* to see it, he is so very curious after any thing that is odd

Timol. What should I do, *Lycinus*, having no Business upon my Hands? But to employ those Intervals of Leisure, in satisfying my Curiosity, and when I heard that vast Ship was arriv'd at the *Piræum*, being one of the Corn-Vessels from *Egypt*, but to go and see it. And I believe, that neither you, nor *Samippus*, had any other Business out of Town, as well as my self.

Lycin. Why, 'Faith that's true; and *Adimantus* came with us too, but we have lost him since in the Croud, and can't imagine what's become of him, for as we were all going aboard together, and *Adimantus* was leading me up the Ladder, he being Slipshod, drop'd his Shoe, and from that time to this, I neither saw him aboard, nor since we came ashoar

Sam.p. You know, *Lycinus*, where he left us, think, then, at what time that handsome young Fellow came out of his Cabbin, that was dress'd so delicately, with his Hair tied up behind, and brought curling before to each side of his Face. Besides, if I know *Adimantus*, I am apt to believe his tender Nature would feel some Concern, he being very apt to simpathize in any Affair of Love, and this was the Reason he bad adieu to the *Egyptian* Sailors.

Lycin. But yet *Samippus,* the Lad did not feem fo charmingly handfome, as to be able to furprife *Adimantus,* whom fo many Beauties follow at *Athens,* genteel, all eloquent and diverting in their Difcourfe, and behaving themfelves with a becoming Grace, whom it would be an incumbent Duty on all to admire. But this Fellow, befides his Buff-colour'd Skin, has very thick Lips, and too weak and flender Legs, he will talk indeed a rude Argument pretty roundly in *Greek,* but after the barbarous Tone and Accent of his Country Befides, neither his Curbs, or his Hair do fpeak him a Freeman.

Timol. But indeed, *Lycinus,* that Drefs of his Hair is the diftinctive Mark of the *Egyptian* Nobility, for there all the Gentlemens Children plait it behind, and our Anceftor did it in *Pallene* (*Tarcho* or *Caniftro*) even till they were grown up to Man's Eftate, who always judg'd it a *decorum* to trim, and curl their Hair, being drefs'd in a Caul tied up under a golden Grafhopper.

Samip. You very readily put me in mind of *Thucydides's* Obfervations of the Luxury of our Forefathers, which at the beginning he charges upon the *Ionians,* when they were fent out to plant a Colony.

Timol. But at laft, *Samippus,* I remember where *Adimantus* left us, 'twas while we ftood gaping up at the Maft, telling the Decks built one over another, wondring at the Seamens climbing up by the Ropes, and running along fo nimbly upon the Sailyard, only by catching at the Arms thereof

Samip.

Samip. That's true; but what shall we do now? Shall we stay for him here? Or shall I go back to see for him?

Timol. No, Let us be jogging on; for it is very likely he is gone before us, and march'd directly Home; or if not, *Adimantus* knows the way well enough, and there is is no Danger of his being lost.

Lycin. But would it not be uncivil to go away and leave him, but yet let us go, if it be *Sanippus*'s Mind.

Samip. Yes, let us go, for we may chance to find him at the *Palæstra*, if it is still open: But as we were saying before, how vast a Ship that was, and the Carpenter told me it was one Hundred and twenty Cubits long, and above Thirty broad, and that from the upper Deck, down by the Pump, into the Hold, 'tis twenty nine: Besides, what a great Mast it has, a mighty Sail-Yard, and how vast a Cable it is fasten'd with, and as the Stern ascends a little bending, bearing a *Golden Goose* for an *Ensign*, the Fore-castle rises proportionably at the other end, extended a great Breadth, the Goddess *Isis*, the Name of the Ship being represented on both sides. But then the rest of the Finery, the Painting, the yellow Streamers at the Sails, and above all, the weighing their Anchor, the Management of all their other Implements, and the large Cabbins at the Stern, are all wonderful to me. And then, for the Number of Seamen, she carries an Army. And I heard she brings as much Corn, at one Voyage, as supplies all *Attica* for a whole Year, and that a little old Fellow took care of all this Charge, guiding the Rudder with a small Pole; I saw the Man, he is very wrinkled and bald, and, as I remember, his Name is *Heron*.

Timol. He is a wonder of his Profession, and more skilful in Sea-Affairs than *Proteus* himself: But have you heard how he brought the Ship hither? What the Sailors suffer'd in their Passage? And how a Star preserved them at last?

Lycin. No, *Timolaus*, but now we gladly would.

Timol. The Master of the Ship, who is a very honest Fellow, and free in Discourse, told me himself, that on the seventh day after he had broke Ground from *Pharos*, bearing sail with a favourable Gale, he got sight of *Cyprus*: Then a West-wind blowing hard in their Teeth, forc'd them to tack about, and cast them upon the Coast of *Sidon*; that being toss'd about by a violent Tempest, he arriv'd on the tenth Day at the Streights of the *Chelidoneæ*, and had like to have been all lost For I remember very well my self, when I have past those Islands, how vast a Sea there runs, and especially with a South-west Wind, for at that place the *Pamphilian* Sea separates its Stream from the *Lycian*, and there the Waves with a swift Current, as if they were interrupted, and stop'd by the Promontory, (for those Rocks are steep and sharp, being continually whetted by the Washes) do sometimes raise very rough and dangerous Storms, with a mighty

Noise of Clashing, and every Wave runs as big as a Rock it self: And the Master told me he was in this Condition, when Night came on with a dark Mist; but that the Gods being mov'd with their Sighs and Prayers, not only discover'd to them a Light from *Lycia,* whereby they knew the Coast, but a bright Star, *viz·* one of the *Dioscuri* fixed upon the Top-Mast, and directed the Ship again into the middle of the Sea, just when she was ready to sink: But once falling out of their way from thence, sailing through the *Egean* Sea, they made our Port Yesterday, in spight of contrary Winds, and being driven backwards and forwards, being the 10th. day after they broke Ground from *Egypt,* being only separated from some at the Stern, who leaving *Crete* on the Right, and doubling the Cape of *Malea,* are by this time arrived in *Italy.*

Lycin. 'Faith, you make this same *Hi-ron* a brave Fellow, and as old in Experience as *Nereus,* who could not have made so long a Voyage, and have gone less out of his way. But who's yonder? Is not that *Adimantus?*

Lycin. Yes, 'tis he, let's call him; So ho, *Adimantus, Adimantus!*

Lycin. 'Tis certain the Fellow's either Deaf, or affronted at us; for 'tis the very *Adimantus,* I see him plain enough, and know him by his Gate, his Cloaths, and shav'd Crown. But let us make haste to overtake him. So, *Adimantus,* have I got you? You can't hear us, unless we pull

you by the Coat, and twirl you about :
But you are in a brown Study Man, and
it does not seem to be about a Trifle neither.

Adim. Truly 'tis about no great matter,
Lycinus, but a strange thought came into
my head, as I was walking along, and I
was wholly wrapt up in it, which made
me I did not hear you.

Lycin. What is it then ! For you need
not stick to tell it, if it be not a secret; But
if it were, you know we can keep Counsel

Adim. But I am asham'd to tell you, you'l
think it such a ridiculous idle fancy.

Lycin. Is any thing of Love in the case ?
For you must confess it to us, who have
been under the same circumstances our
selves, and are as true votaries to his *Deity*,
and enlightened with the same flame.

Adim. Nothing of that I swear, but I
was building Castles in the Air, and head-
ing up abundance of Riches, which most
People call vanity, and you came upon me
just when I was rowling in the midst of
Wealth and Pleasure.

Lycin. Then according to the Proverb,
Share and Share alike, divide it amongst
us, for since we are, *Adimantus*'s Friends, 'tis
but just that we should come in for snacks
with him.

Adim. You all left me when we first came
aboard and as soon, *Lycinus*, as I had hand-
ed you up ; For while I was measuring the
Anchor, you went away from me, I don't
know where. But when I had seen all that
was to be seen, I ask'd one of the Seamen

how much this Ship might generally bring
in to the Owner one year with another;
He told me, at least twelve talents of *A-
thens*. So as I was coming home, I thought
within my self that if any of the Gods
should on a sudden give me such a Ship,
how happy would I be ! and how bleſſedly
would I live ! doing good to all my friends.
Sometimes I'd go on Board to take the Air,
and send my Servants about as I had occaſion; Then besides with these twelve Talents,
I'd build me a fine House in the most publick Place of the City, and leave our ancient
Seat upon the *Iliſus*, and there would I keep
abundance of Servants, several changes of
Clothes, my Coach and Horses, and live
Proportionably every way else. And even
now I was sailing along, looking great a-
mongſt my Seamen, applauded, and call'd
happy by all the Paſſengers, and I thought
my self little leſs than a King. But now
while I was ordering every thing in the Ship,
and seeing the Port a great diſtance off, you,
Lycinus, came and spoil'd all, sunk my Ship,
and ruin'd all my Riches even in the happineſs of the Thought.

Lycin. Then lay hold of me, Sir, carry me
before the Major for a Pirate, since I was the
cauſe of so great a Shipwrack, and that upon the high-way too that leads from the
Port to the City, but to make you some a-
mends, may you poſſeſs five Veſſels if you
please, both much finer, and larger than
this may it not be poſſible to sink them,
and may they five times every year arrive
laden with Corn from *Egypt*. But since, noble

Captain, you carry it so high to us now, how cursedly proud would you be then· For if, when you where Master of this one bottom alone you would not hear us when we call'd after you, if besides this, you were Master of five more well rigg'd, and able to live in the roughest Seas, you'd scorn to look upon your Friends. But however, honest Man, go and set Sail again, while we will sit down by the *Piræum*, and enquire, of the *Egyptian* and *Italian* Mariners, if they know where *Adimantus*'s great Ship the *Isis* lies.

Adim : Now you may see why I was so loth to tell you what I was thinking of, because I knew you would banter, and laugh at me for it. For which reason I will stay till you are all gone and then return to sail in my Ship myself ; for Sailors talk must be more pleasant, than your idle ribaldry

Licin. If you goe, we are resolv'd to follow, and goe aboard along with you.

Adim. But as soon as I am up, I'le haule the Rope after me.

Lycin. If you doe, we will swim after you, for you must not imagine to be Master of so large a Ship, so easily, which you never built nor paid for. Nor need we desire the Protection of the Gods to Swim a great many Leagues without tiring. But heark ye, don't you remember how small a Bark wafted your Friends over to *Ægina*, for two Pence apiece, at *Diana*'s Festival, nor did you take it amiss, that we should sail along with you : But now you are angry, and in a Passion, because we would go

aboard

aboard with you, and as foon as you are in, you fnatch up the Rope to prevent us following. You are reproachful to us, *Adimantus*, and yet favourable to your felf. Neither do you know who you are, altho' you are Mafter of this Ship, the Number of your Servants, and your fine Houfe have made you fo Frenfical. But, honeft Man, I beg of you, by *Ifis*, remember to bring us fome Salt-fifh from the *Nile*, Perfumes from *Canopus*, and fome Snipes from *Memphis*, or if you can ftow it, bring one of the Pyramids too.

Timol. Come, *Lycinus*, you have jok'd upon him enough. You fee you have made him blufh, and have drown'd his Ship in fo many Jefts, it can hardly ever be weigh'd up again, nor can he refift thofe Tides of Ridicule that flow fo faft upon him. But fince we have a great way yet to the City, let every one in his turn pray to Heaven for what pleafes him beft ; fo fhall we deceive the Toil of our Journey, and walk chearfully on, that if we fall into a brown Study, we may fancy the moft pleafant Dreams imaginable, and pleafe our felves with the thoughts of them as long as we will. For let every one wifh what he will, and be it fuppofed that the Gods are ready to grant whatfoever we ask of them, even to Miracles, and things natually impoffible. But firft of all, let this be a *Specimen* of him who would enjoy Riches and Treafure, how he would behave himfelf if he had them.

Samip. That's right, *Timolaus*, and I am of your mind; and when it comes to my turn, I will wish for what I think convenient: But still to please *Adimantus*, we won't ask any more Impertinencies about his Ship, and *Lycinus* ought to consent to it too.

Lycin. But, I say, since I would not seem to covet any common Happiness, let us all be Rich, if you think, that will be a reasonable Satisfaction.

Adim. Who shall begin first?

Lycin. You, *Adimantus*, next *Samippus*, and then *Timolaus*, but I'll perform mine as I run along, and all the half Mile before we come to *Dipylum*.

Adim. Then I won't retreat from my Wishes for the Ship, but if I please, will add something more, for *Mercury* is kind to all. The Ship, and all that's in't shall be mine, the Seamen, Cargoe, Passengers, the Women, and every thing else that is capable to please any Faculty of my Body.

Samip. But you forget *something* in your Ship————

Adim. What that handsome Boy, *Samippus*; no, he's mine too, and may every Grain of Corn, be there never so much, be turn'd to a piece of Gold, and of *Darius*'s Coin.

Lycin. What do you mean, *Adimant.* for your Money at that rate, would be of a larger Bulk, and heavier than your Corn, and consequently would sink your Vessel.

Adim. Don't be envious, *Lycinus*, but when you are to wish, may you turn all *Parnethe* in Gold, if you will, and poffefs it, nor will I grudge it you.

Lycin. But the more fafe you think your felf, the more Care will I take, leaft you are all loft with the Cargoe; may thofe things that are indifferent, in God's Name, be indanger'd, as much as they can. But that poor young Fellow, not knowing how to Swim, will miferably be drown'd.

Timol. Come, be of good Chear, *Lycinus*, for the Dolphins will take care of him, and carry him afhoar; for don't you know a Fidler was once preferv'd by them, as a Recompence or Reward for the Tunes he plaid them, and that a Child was in like manner carried to *Corinth* by them, and why may not *Adimantus's* Boy meet a kind Dolphin to preferve him too.

Adim. What, *Timolaus*, do you ape *Lycinus* too, and caft your Jeers upon me, when you made the firft Profofals againft it.

Timol But fince you have the full Power of your own Wifh, would it not be better to wifh fomething more profitable and convenient, and that you might find all thefe Riches under your Bed, than to be at the trouble to unlade your Ship, and to bring them into the City.

Adim. That's well faid; yes, and I will dig for it under the Stone Statue of *Mercury* that ftands in our Hall; and there I'll find a thoufand Bufhels of ready coin'd Gold; then will I dig under *Hefiod's.* Then

at

at firft I'll take a noble Houfe to live in, and buy up all the Suburbs, befides thofe that ftand upon the *Isthmus*, *Delphos*, and *Eleufine*, and fome few Seats that border upon the Sea, that when I have a mind for Companies-fake, I may remove to the *Ifthmian* Iflands, and *Sicyonian* Fields ; befides, whatever fhady Walks watered with murmuring Brooks, whatfoever is pleafant or delightful in *Greece*, fhall all in a fhort time be mine, nor will I eat or drink but from Golden Veffels, and not fuch light foolifh things as *Echerates*'s are, but pondrous all, and every one of two Talents Weight.

Lycin. But how can your Cup-bearer hand you fo heavy a Bowl, when full of Wine ? And how can you take it without Trouble, when 'tis as heavy as *Sifiphus's* Stone ?

Adim. For God's-fake, Friend, don't thwart my Prayers ; I'll have Tables made of folid Gold, Beds of Gold, and, if you won't be quiet, golden Servants too

Lycin. But take heed, that like *Midas*, your Victuals and Drink don't become Gold too, that you perifh by your Riches, and die with that magnificent Hunger.

Adim. Then, *Lycinus*, do you wifh for fomething more likely to happen, when it comes to your Turn. Next will I be clothed in Purple, Ragoufts, tofs'd up to a Nicety, fhall be my conftant Food, my Sleep delightful, and blefs'd with the moft pleafant Dreams imaginable ; my Friends fhall be always faluting and petitioning me, every
Body

Body refpect and adore me, and Crowds
fhall be waiting every Morning about my
Door, attending upon my Levee ; amongft
them fhall be thofe two great Men, *Clea-
netus* and *Democrates*, who making up, and
crouding to be admitted before any of the
reft, I will have feven Porters, huge lufty
Tartars, that fhall fling the Door upon them,
juft as they ferve others now ; and I, when
I think convenient, will glance down a Look
upon them like the Sun, and turn away,
as if I did not fee them : But if there happens to be a poor Man amongft them, as I
was before I had thefe Riches, him will I
lovingly embrace, and carefs, order him
to be clean'd and drefs'd, and invite him
to Supper.   Then will thofe rich Fellows
be rack'd with Envy, to fee my Golden
Charriots, my fine Horfes, and my charming Boys, of whom I defign to have about
2000, all pick'd and chofen, the Flowers
of every Age.   My Suppers fhall always
be ferv'd up in Gold, (for Silver will be
too mean, and beneath me) I will have
Salt-fifh from *Spain*, and drink *Italian*
Wines; I will have Oil from *Spain* too, all
Nations of the World fhall pay a Tribute
to my Luxury, I'll have the Pheafant from
Colchis, the Peacock from *India*, and Cocks
from *Numidia* : And my Cooks fhall all be
expert at Dainties and *Sophifters* in making
Sauces.   And when I drink to any one, that
has a Mind to the Cup or Tankard, I'll
generoufly let him take it away with him,
and keep it in God's Name.   Then fhall I
bear the Bell from all other rich Men, who
will

will look like Beggars in comparifon of me;
no more fhall *Dionicus* in his Pride produce
his Silver Table and Bowl, efpecially, when
he fhall fee my Domefticks fo full of Money. And thus will I make diftributions
to the Town, every month an hundred
Drachms to the Citizen, and to the Foreigner half as much : For Ornament
fake, I'll erect publick Theatres and Baths,
and cut a long Channel to bring the Sea up
to *Dipylum*, and there fhall be the Port,
that my Ship may come nearer up, and be
feen from *Ceramicus*. But for you, my
Friends, and chiefly to *Samippus*, I will order my Steward to meafure twenty Bufhels of coin'd Gold ; *Timolaus* fhall have a
Peck, and *Lycinus* but a quarter of a Peck,
and that fhall be ftrik'd too, becaufe he is
fo full of his Tongue, and laughs at my
Wifh. Thus would I lead my Life, encreafing and rowling in Riches, and luxurioufly enjoying all the Pleafures of the
World. Now I have done, and may *Mercury* be pleas'd to grant it.

Lycin. But do you know, *Adimantus*, upon how flender a String your Riches hang,
which, if it once breaks, they'll all fly away, and nothing but the Drofs of your
Pleafure will be left.

Adim. Why do you ftill harp upon this
String, *Lycinus* ?

Lycin. Becaufe, honeft Man, you have
no Affurance how long you fhall live and
enjoy your Riches, for who knows but that
after your Golden Table is fpread, before
you fit down, and eat your Peacock and
Numidian

Numidian Fowls, your Soul on a sudden may be snatch'd away, and the Vultures and the Ravens feast upon what you leave? Or shall I tell you of some that have dy'd before they enjoy'd their Estates, and of others living now, that have been bereav'd of all their Possessions by some *Diety*, who thought their Happiness too great? But have you not heard of *Crœsus* and *Polycrates*, who in a short time lost all they were worth, tho' a great deal richer than you? But to speak home to you, do you imagine your Health would be lasting and confirmed? Do you not daily see rich Men living miserably, always tormented with some persecuting Pain; some that are lame, some blind, and others labouring under some inward Distemper? But tho' you have not said it, I know very well that you would willingly undergo all *Phænomacus*'s Sufferings, be full as soft and effeminate, and be equally miserable to enjoy his Riches. I forbear to enlarge upon the many Troubles, which I know are consequent to Riches, besides the continual fear of Robberies, the envy that attends them, and the *Odium* they always draw from the common People; and now you may plainly see what Happiness they will procure you.

Adim. You are resolv'd to thwart me, *Lycinus*, for ever, and now you shan't receive a farthing of the Gratuity I promis'd you, because there is no end of your ridiculing me.

Lycin.

Lycin. Now you follow the Example of most rich Men, very full of Promises, and very dull to the Performance. But now, *Samippus*, 'tis your turn.

Samip. But since, as you know, I am an *Arcadian*, born in *Mantinea*, and living upon the Continent, I need not a Ship to bring me hither, since I can more easily show my self to my Fellow Citizens when I please. Nor will I be a Niggard to restrain my Wish, but give a loose to my Desires, I do not ask so mean a thing as Riches, nor so large a Share of sordid Gold; But (since the Gods are All Mighty, and can perform what we think impossible; and since the Law which *Timolaus* made, bids us to despair of nothing, but to be confident, Heaven will be auspicious to our Prayers, and ready to assent to our most extravagant Wishes) I desire to be a *King*, not such an one as *Philip*'s Son *Alexander*, *Ptolemy*, or *Methridates*, or any other that receiv'd his Sovereignty by Succession. But from the lowest Ebb of Fortune, let me rise to the Command of thirty Confederated Associates, all brave and faithful, by frequent Additions, let them be three hundred, then a thousand, then ten thousand, and at last fifty thousand armed Men, and five hundred thousand on Horseback. Then I being chose, and preferr'd by the free and hearty Votes of all, would endeavour to be the best of Commanders, both in governing my Men with Equity and Justice, and prudently managing my Affairs, and in this I shall be more great and glorious

than all others; that it was my Merit
alone, that qualified and rais'd me, that I
was elected to the Command of the Army,
more for my Bravery and Vertue, than a
bare Title, and that I did not receive my
Crown lazily, by Succession, from some
other, who fought for it, and whose De-
serts justly entitled him to possess it; and
thus far I don't differ from *Adimartus*'s
Mind, in that certainly it must be a more
sensible Joy and Satisfaction to a Man to
obtain a Government by his own Means
alone, and without the least Assistance of
another.

Lycin. Fie, *Samippus*, you said indeed you
would ask no small thing, but you have
cull'd out, and desir'd the very best of all,
in commanding so vast an Army, and by
so many Votes to be adjudg'd the chief and
best. We never could have expected to
have seen so mighty a King, and so brave a
General, to proceed from *Arcadia*, nor
could any of their *Astrologers*, or *Cunning*
Men foresee it. But go on, *Samippus*, reign
on, quietly command your Battalions and
Squadrons, let your Presence adorn and
be a Grace to the Warlike Van. But I
would fain know how you can raise so
many Men in *Arcadia*, and against what
poor miserable People you will make your
first Expedition.

Samip. Hear me, *Lycinus*, and if it be
your pleasure to follow us, I will give you
the Command of five thousand Horse.

Lycin. And for that Honour, *my Liege*, I am obliged to give you my moſt humble Thanks, and according to the *Perſian* manner, fall down at your Feet, and worſhip you, and in all the Actions of a grateful Spirit, I reverence your Turbant, and adore your Crown. But let me beg of your Majeſty to appoint ſome other Commander; for I am wholly a Stranger to thoſe Affairs, and never yet in my Life got up on Horſeback, beſides, I am afraid, that being ſtun'd and confounded with the Warlike Muſick of every Troop, I ſhould fall amongſt the Crowd, and be trampled to Death, or if my Horſe ſhould prove headſtrong, and ſnatch away his Bridle, he might hurry me into the midſt of the Enemy; beſides, I muſt be tied to my Saddle, if you expect I ſhould either keep my Seat, or hold my Bridle.

Adim. I, *Samippus*, will lead up your Horſe, and *Lycinus* ſhall command the Right Wing, for I deſerve your Favour moſt, and merit the greateſt Honour you can beſtow, in that I was ſo liberal to you of my Gold, and endow'd you with ſo large a Fortune.

Samip. But let us ask the Soldiers, *Adimantus*, whether they are willing to be commanded by you : *All ye Horſemen, that are willing to have* Adimantus *your Captain, hold up your Hands* You ſee, *Adimantus*, they all vote for you, therefore you ſhall command them; *Lycinus* ſhall have the Right-Wing, and *Timolaus* the Left, but my ſelf in Perſon will lead up the main Body, according to the Example of the

Persian Kings. And now let us pass over the Mountains to *Corinth*, putting up our Prayers to Heaven to give Success to our Arms; and after we have conquer'd *Greece* (for no Body there can oppose us, or stop the Progress of so great a Multitude, but we shall conquer them like Sheep) let us provide a Fleet, with a sufficient quantity of Provisions at *Conchree*, and having embark'd our Horses, and all other necessaries, we will cross the *Igean Sea*, and land upon *Ionia*; and there having sacrific'd, and perform'd the Holy Rites to *Diana*, surprizing all the Towns in our Passage, and leaving Governours therein, we'll carry on our March thro' *Curia* into *Syria*, then ravage the Countries of *Lycia*, *Pamphilia*, and *Pisidia*, and all the Sea-coasts, and Mountain-part of *Cilicia*, till we come up to the River *Euphrates*

Lycin. For Heaven's sake, if it please your Majesty, leave me Governour in *Greece*, for I am a very timorous Fellow, and a meer Coward, nor do I care to go far from my own Home. Besides, you seem to have a design to turn your Army against the *Armenians* and *Parthians*, bold Warlike Nations, well disciplin'd, and skilful Archers; for which reason, confer the Command of your Right-Wing on some-body else, and leave me your *Viceroy* of *Greece*; least any bold Villain should strike me thro', wounding your poor Captain in some unguarded place of his Body, and leave him to die miserably in a strange Country.

Samip. What, *Lycinus,* will you throw up your Command thro' a flavifh Fear, you know all Deferters muft be hang'd. But fince we are now upon the Banks of *Euphrates,* and have laid a Bridge over the River, and fince we have made all fafe, and Governours of my own appointing are poffefs'd of all the Country behind us, we will invade *Phœnicia, Paleftine,* and *Egypt.* You, *Lycinus,* pafs over firft with your Right-Wing, I'll follow you my felf, then *Timolaus,* and laft of all, *Adimantus,* do you command the Forfe over. We fhall meet no oppofition in *Mefopotamia,* but the Garrifons upon the firft Summons yield up themfelves, and deliver the Fortreffes into our Hands, and as foon as we arrive at *Babylon,* we'll furprize the Town, and maintain the Poffeffion. But the King now keeping his Court at *Ctefiphon,* receives notice of our Progrefs, and immediately pofts to *Seleucia,* and raifes a great Army of Archers and Slingers, my Spies continually bring in News of a hundred Thoufand Men in full March againft me, all bold, lufty Fellows, and twenty Thoufand of them on Horfeback. Neither has he affembled any *Armenians* or *Caffians,* or *Baffrians,* but all within the Frontiers of his own Dominions. It is therefore high time to look about us, and to call a Council of War to refolve upon further Meafures.

Adim. 'Tis then my Opinion, that the Infantry fhould march to *Ctefiphon,* and face the Enemy, in the mean time, I'll ——— here with the Horfe, and Garrifon *Baby-*

Sam ———

Samip. What! are you cowardly too, *A-dimantus*, as the danger grows near us? But what do you think, *Timolaus* ?

Timol. My Advice is, that we all unite into one Body, draw out to meet them, and not stay dully in our Camp to give them an opportunity to grow stronger by continual Supplies, but to meet them on their March, and attack them

Samip You are in the right; but what does *Lycinus* think of it ?

Lycin. Why 'Faith, I'll tell you, since we are almost tired with continual Walking, ever since the morning, and have thirty Paces still to go, thro' all the Fatigue and Heat of the Sun, which now is extreamly hot, let us sit down here under the Olive-Trees, upon the Pedestals, to refresh our selves a little, and then make as much haste home as we can.

Samip. What! *Lycinus*, do'st thou dully imagine your self to be at *Athens* still? When you are before the Walls of *Babylon*, encompassed round with Soldiers, counselling and debating the War, and settling the Fate of Empires.

Lycin. Well you rub me well enough, but I thought my self sufficiently upon my Guard to prevent your catching me

Samip. Come let us go on then, and summon a Presence of Mind, rouze up the Man, nor degenerate from the Spirit and Bravery of your Ancestors But see they fly already, *Enyalius* is the Word. But, you upon the first Sound of the Trumpet, spur up to fall on them at once, shouting and

rattling

ratling your Armour, but halt within Bow-Shot; and maintain a Skirmish. But now *Timolaus* is come up with his left Wing, having put the *Medes* to flight as soon as he encountred them, and wheresoever my Presence is necessary, I share an equal Danger, for now I engage with the *Persians*, and their King is amongst them. now they throw the whole Body of their *Barbarian* Horse upon our Right Wing, Courage, *Lycinus*, lead up your Troops, and encourage them to receive the Assault like Men.

Lycin. Damn'd Fortune! All their Horse at once upon me! And am I the only proper Person to oppose them? But I fancy, if they press too hard upon me, I shall give you the Slip and run home, and leave you to dispute the Empire amongst your selves.

Samip. You need not, for you may easily overcome them. Now you see, I singly encounter the King, for he challenges me, and to refuse it would be dishonorable.

Lycin. By Heaven he'll wound you sweetly presently! But a Wound is great and noble in the dispute for a Kingdom

Samip. That's true, but this has only rais'd my Skin, and not in any visible part of my Body, that will in the least detain me. But you see, by venturing one round, I have struck the Spear out of his Hand, and kill'd both him and his Horse Then cutting off his Head, and taking away his Crown, I place it on mine own Temples, and am adored by all; the very *Barbarians* own me for their Emperor, and worſhip me. Then will I put in force, and command by the *Grecian* Law. Next you may imagine how many Cities I will build, and call them by my own Name, and how many I will demoliſh if they dare reflect on me, or be *Malecontents* to my Government. But above all, will I be revenged on that raſcally Miſer *Cydias*, for that when he liv'd near me, he was the moſt quarrelſome Neighbour, and would never let me walk in his Fields, but immediately thruſt me out.

Lycin. But make an end now, *Samippus*, for it's high time you ſhould be Feaſting and Carrouſing in *Babylon* for ſo conſiderable a Victory ; And now, let *Timolaus* wiſh for what he pleaſes

Samip. But tell me then, *Lycinus*, your Opinion of what I have deſired.

Lycin. Why, moſt excellent King, I think you are more out of the way, more unreaſonable and prepoſtrous than *Adimentus*, for he deſired nothing, but what is natural to all Men, to revel in Delights, to be encompaſſed with Pleaſures, and to entertain his Friends in all imaginable State. But you in every Combate will be wounded, Fears will diſtract you by Day, and Cares will diſturb you by Night. Then you will have a thouſand things to dread beſides your profeſt Enemies, Plots innumerable, the Envy and Hate between your Favourites of Diſtinction, and what is worſe, to be eternally cajoul'd with Paraſites. You'll find none in ſtrict reality your Friends, but all diſguiſing their true inward Sentiments, and diſſembling a Complaiſance, either out of fear of your Power, or hopes of Preferment: You can never get looſe from the Fatigue of your Crown, to unbend your Care, and take a recreating Pleaſure, not ſo much as in your Dreams themſelves, for they will be all broken and diſturbed. You will only poſſeſs the vain-glory and Pomp of the thing, be cloth'd in Purple, ſprig'd with Gold, a Crown upon your Temples, and a Guard continually attending. All the reſt will be Toil and Buſtle, not to be imagin'd, either in giving Audience to Foreign *Ambaſſadors*, adminiſtring Juſtice to your Subjects, or publiſhing your *Edict*. And either ſome part of your Empire will be revolting, or your Enemies making Incurſions, and invading your bordering Country, Fears and Suſpicions of all will continually torment you, and your whole Reign be one uninterrupted Scene of Trouble and Diſtraction. Every Body will eſteem you happier than you really are, which your own Experience will eaſily convince you of. And would you not think it hard, and beneath you to be ſubject to the ſame Diſtempers with the common People, and that a Fever, not regarding you, as a King, ſhould neither make any Diſtinction between your Majeſty and the meaneſt of your Servants, nor Death it ſelf have any dread or concern for your Life-Guard, but whenſoever it pleaſe, will be your Sovereign, and confine you to its Chains, without the leaſt Care of

your

your Crown ? But you, after you have fallen from so high a pitch of Glory, snatch'd from your Throne, and divested of all your Royal Dignities, must tread the same Path with the *Mob*, and herd with the common Flock Perhaps you may leave behind you some vast Mountain for a Tomb, some high Column, or Pyramid inscrib'd with an Epitaph to preserve your Memory, but these are the most vain and foolish Honours , For all those Images and Temples, which your adoring Posterity shall build to your Fame, and that Great Name (tho' they judge you a Deity) will all sink in a little process of time, and be forgot But allow them to be of a longer Duration, that they shall still stand firm, and make you known to many succeeding Ages, and what Advantage or Honour will you reap thereby, since at the same time you are insensible of all Now you may plainly see all the numerous Torments that will attend you while living, and what you are to expect when dead. But now, *Timolaus*, 'tis your turn, and take care by their Example, to wish for those things, as will become a Man of Sense and Experience

Timol. Then hearken, *Lycinus*, and consider whether my Desires are in the least to be cavil'd at, or corrected, for I ask not Gold, such immense Riches, Wars, Kingdoms, or covet to exchange my easy Life for an Empire, all which you justly reprov'd and laugh'd at, for they are frail, inconstant, full of entangling Snares, and procuring more Trouble and Sorrow, then

Plea-

Pleasure or Satisfaction. But I wish, that meeting *Mercury* by the way, he would give me some Rings, which should have these Vertues, *viz.* One, that I might be always well, and enjoy a perpetual Health, invulnerable, and free from all Care and Passion; another like that which *Gyges* had, that when I put it on I might be invisible, Another, to make me stronger, than ten Thousand Men, and that I might easily lift up such a Burthen on my Shoulder, and fly away with it, as they should not be able to move: Another, whereby I might lay asleep whomsoever I would, whereby every Door should fly open at my Access, every Lock, and every Bar be unbolted. But chiefly let me have another, that shall be the most delightful of all, to render me handsome and lovely, always to be surrounded by comely Youths, and beautiful Ladies, and gazed at by every Body, and may there be no Person in the Universe that has seen me, but what has been sensible of the Power of my Face; and the force of Love, no one but to whom I am most desirable; and none but who are continually talking of me; that Multitudes of Women may daily hang themselves for Despair; may our Youth run mad, thro' a vehement desire of me, and think themselves bless'd, if I only glance a Look upon them, and if they perceive the least Contempt or Disdain in my Face, may they die of Grief.

Then should *Hyacinthus*, *Hylas*, and *Phæon*, be all esteem'd but indifferent Beauties in Comparison of me. All these things would I possess and be happy in, not to have a short being here, and only to live the common space of human Life, but to enjoy a perpetual Health for a thousand Years, ever blooming and flourishing, like a Lad of Seventeen, casting off my old Age, and becoming young again like a Serpent. And when I have got these Rings, nothing, should be wanting to make my Happiness every way compleat; for every thing that I lik'd of another Man's, should be mine, since I should have the Power to charm the Watch, to open the Door, and to go in unseen. And if there was any strange Sight in the *Indies*, or the furthermost part of the Earth, any rich, or precious thing, or any Delicacies for Eating or Drinking, not caring to be carry'd, I would immediately fly thither, and enjoy them all to satisfaction: And the *Griffin*, and the *Phænia*, which no body in *India* can see, might I immediately discover, I alone would search out, and know the springing Fountains of the *Nile*, and every unhabited part of the Earth, and sometimes pay a Visit to the *Antipodes*, if there are any such People living on the other side of the Globe. Then would I scrutiny into, and discover the true nature of the Stars, the *Moon*, and the *Sun* it self, since my Ring would preserve me from Fire. And what would be the pleasantest thing of all, I might fly to *Babylon*, and tell them who was Conqueror

ror at the *Olympian* Games the same Day,
and if I happen'd to dine in *Syria*, I'd sup in
Italy. Thus I should be capable to revenge my self on any of my Enemies, by
hovering over their Heads, and letting a
Stone fall that might split their Skulls; and
on the contrary, might do good to all my
Friends, by privately conveying Money
to them, while they were asleep. But for
any proud, haughty Fellow, a Tyrant, or
a niggardly Miser, I would snatch him up
some twenty Miles from the Earth, and
cast him headlong down upon a sharp Rock
And without any Obstacle, I could converse
and keep Company with the Fairies, since
I could be invisible, like them, and lull
every Body else asleep · By the same manner I could freely behold the bloodiest Battle, towring higher, than an Arrows Flight.
And, when I pleas'd, would join the declining Battle, cast the Conquerors asleep,
lead up the vanquish'd against their Pursu-
ers, and recover the Victory. In fine, I
would make the Life of Man, resemble
only a sort of Play, every thing should be
at my disposal, and I should be look'd upon
as a *God*, and this would be the Zenith of
all Happiness, that it should never be im-
bittered with Trouble, never flag, or suffer the least Diminution, and that a perpetual Health should conspire to make
all compleat. And what, *Lycinus*, can you
pick out here, to find fault with?

Lycin. Nothing indeed, *Timolaus*, neither
would it be for me to oppose a Man, furnish'd with such Advantages in his Nature,

as Wings, and the Strength of ten thousand Men. But this let me ask you ferioufly, If in all the Countries you have
flown over, you ever faw an old Fellow fo
far infatuated, that imagin'd by putting on
a Ring, he was able to remove a Mountain, and fo feem lovely to every Body,
and that, after he was bald and flat-nos'd.
And tell me this again, why fhould not
one Ring be fufficient to do you all this
Kindnefs, but you'll wear fuch a Multitude, that every Finger of your Left Hand
will be loaded, and the Number will en-
creafe fo much, you'll find it convenient
your Right fhould bear fome part of the
Fatigue. But one thing, my Friend, you
forgot to wifh for, and which is efpecially
neceffary, that when you put it on, would
reform thefe roving, whimfical Thoughts,
correct your Folly, and rectifie this mad-
ing Humour of your Brain, or perhaps
Hellebore, will be more prevailing to
purge it off.

Timol. But now, *Lycinus*, do you put up
your Wifhes, that we may know what you
defire that is fo perfect, and can admit no
blame, you that are fo ready to calumniate others.

Lycin. But I have no need to wifh for
any thing ; for we are already come to
Dipylum ; and this honeft *Samippus* with his
fighting before *Babylon*, and you *Timolaeus*,
with dining in *Syria*, and fupping in *Italy*,
have taken up all the time that belong'd
to me, and have done very well in't, efpecially fince I don't defire to grow rich fo
suddenly,

suddenly, and afterwards to mourn and repine at my volatile Plenty, and return to my old poor Diet of Bread and Water, which in a short time will be your Cases, after your Happiness and Treasure has left you in the Lurch, and after you are dispossess'd of your Crowns and Riches, as if you awaked from a delightful Dream, you will find every thing of a contrary Appearance at Home ; just like *Tragedians*, that have been personating the Actions of Kings, coming off the Stage, lay aside all their Pomp and Majesty, retire to an humble Brandy Shop, and sometimes many of them perish with Hunger, when a little before they were all *Agamemnon's* and *Creons*, Then, as is probable, will you not be almost rack'd to Death with Grief, when every thing at Home will be too mean, and displeasing to you, and you, especially, *Timolaus*, when you shall suffer the same Fate with *Icarus* of old, when your Wings begin to melt, and you fall from the Heaven of your Happiness, and walk upon the Ground like other Men, without any of your Rings, which of themselves will fall from your Fingers But this shall be satisfaction enough to me, that instead of all your Riches, and even *Babylon* it self, i shall have the Pleasure to laugh at every thing you wish'd for, how glorious or excellent soever, and that at a time when you your selves shall applaud my Philosophy.

H A R-

HARMONIDES.

By S. Atkinson, *Esq,*

The Argument.

*The Author here justifies himself by the Ex-
ample of* Harmonides, *in that he addresses
to the* Nobles, *and most eminent Persons of his
Country to get their Approbation. For upon
their Judgments depend all the Voices of the
inferiour Sort.*

Harmonides an accurate Player upon the
Flute, once asked his Master *Timotheus* this Question, Tell me, *said he,* how
I may raise my self by my Art, and what I
shall do to render my self famous amongst
the *Greeks,* for you have shown me all the
secrets of *Musick,* the Mechanical part of
forming Instruments to soften, to relish and
humour the Notes, the Measure and proportion of Time, the Symmetry to be observed in *Chorus's,* the Nature and Propriety of every particular Consort, as the
Divine Fury of the *Phrygian* Mood, the
Dolefulness of the *Lydian,* the *solemn Gravity*
of the *Doric,* and the *Sweetness* of the *Io-
ic.* That I have thus far succeeded in my
Undertaking, is principally owing to you:
But

But what is most material, and the greatest Inducement to this Study, I don't perceive how I shall obtain so much Honour hereby, and so singuar a Reputation in every Bodies Opinion, as to be pointed at for my Excellencies; that whenever I appear in Publick, I may be look'd upon and admired by all, expressing their Esteem of me in this manner · *This is that famous Minstrel* H A R M O N I D E S : As when you, *Timotheus*, first left *Baotia*, you played in *Pandionis*, and when you got the Victory in the *Raging Ajax*, tho' your Adversary usurped your Title to set off his Lesson, every Corner, at that time, was so filled with your Name, that there was none, that had not heard of *Timotheus*, that incomparable *Musician* of *Thebes*, and now at your first Appearance, the People flock to you from all Parts, as the small Birds about an Owl.

These were my Motives for the Undertaking, and for this end did I endeavour so much at Perfection, for *Musick* considered in its self, without the Addition of *Fame* and *Renown*, is a thing of so little moment, that few, or none would encourage it. And what signifies it to be as great a Master, as *Marsyas*, or *Olympus*, if no Glory may be acquired by it. For 'tis with *Musick*, as with all Sciences, if concealed and unknown, are useless, and worth nothing. But instruct me, *said he*, how I shall employ my self and Art to the best Advantage, and I shall be doubly engaged to you. First, in that I have arrived to the

Height

height in Musick, and chiefly for the Glory which I shall reap from it.

Timotheus moved with this Petition, made this Answer.

Harmonides, said he, you well know, that what you search after, is of very great Importance, *viz.* that Satisfaction which is derived from Fame, to be conspicuous, and noted in the World. But if you mean to compass this by charming Crouds, and *Multitudes* of People, you would be so far out of the way, that it is impossible you should ever effect it. For where is there a Theatre so spacious, that at once will afford you an Audience of all the *Greeks?* But let me advise you in this case, in order to an Accomplishment of your Wishes; shew a Master-piece sometimes in publick Places, but strive not then to win upon the Affections of the Multitude, for the shortest and surest way of arriving at Glory, is to take the Opportunity of the publick Rendezvouse, and Assembly of all the great Men of *Greece*, who exceed all others in Dignity and Authority, and are in reality Men of Candour, Worth and Quality, and who are beyond Controversy the heads and Leaders of all the rest, and Men of try'd Impartiality and Truth: If, I say, you give such Men as these an extraordinary Proof of your Skill and Art, and perform with their Applause, you may assure your self, that their Fame will quickly o'erspread all *Greece*; and thus I have drawn your Desires into a very narrow Compass. In those, who are known, reverenced, and

K k   had

had in Veneration by all, upon Experience, allow you to be an Artift, you have no need of the Votes of the Commons, who always truft in others, as more competent Judges in fuch matters. For that illiterate part of Mankind, which is employed wholly in Mechannical Operations, are unacquainted with Things fo much above their Sphere: But to whom their Rulers have vouchfafed their Commendations, they conclude it no rafh Action, fo they extol him too. As in Plays many Spectators applaud and explode the Actors, but few adjudge the Victory.

Harmonides was not fo happy, as to profit by this Advice, for when firft he played for a Prize, he ambitioufly ftriving at too high a Note, breath'd his laft in his Flute, and died in Emulation, without being crown'd upon Stage. His firft and laft Mufical Performance, was in Honour of *Bacbus* This Counfel, *Timotheus*, was not directed folely to *Harmonides*, and thofe of his Profeffion, but to all, that thirft after Honour, and by fome fignal Acts purfue popular Applaufe. This occafioned the like Thoughts in me, thereupon I fought an Opportunity of publifhing my felf to the World; fo venturing on *Timotheus's* Advice, I confidered with my felf, who was chief Magiftrate of the City, to whom a Truft and Secrefy was committed, and who could fuffice for all. You fhould have been prefented as a Perfon qualified to our purpofe, for you are indeed reckon'd a Pattern of Vertue, a Standard, and infallible Rule for all others.   Nor

Now, if my Productions upon Perusal, should so affect you, as to move you into a Protection of them, thro' your Patronage, they would have so popular a Reception, that my Desires would then be fulfilled, and I should have all the Voices compriz'd in one. What if in my Election I had preferred some other ' then I should have plaid the Fool, but according to the Proverb, *In one Man we will run the Risque of all.* for 'tis in a manner the same, as if I should expose it to all the World, for it is plain, that you excel all others, whether separately, or jointly considered. The Kings of *Lacedemon* had each of them two Voices in their Council, others only one, but you, above the Magistrates, and Elders, have all in point of Learning, in that yours are always, clear and wholsome, which gives me great Encouragement at present, else I might with reason, have feared for the greatness of the Attempt Nay, this too emboldens me in my Design, in that you are no Stranger to my Concerns, for I am of that City, upon which you have heaped your Favours both publick and particular But if the Scale should turn, and I should lose the Majority of Votes, do you add that Suffrage of *Minerva*, and of your self make up the Defect, and you'll have the Honour of the Amendments. Nor is that Satisfaction enough to me, that I've been in great Repute formerly, or that my Fame is still of as large an Extent, or that my Discourses are daily applauded by the Auditory ; for these are vain, airy Dreams,

and only Types and Shadows of what is
real.

But to difcover the whole truth of the
matter, this was the particular Scope of
my Endeavours, and now 'tis beyond all
queftion, nor can any one with Reafon
doubt, but what bears the Signet of your
Approbation, is to be received as the beft
of all, yet it is requifite for a Man, who
is to engage in fo great an Encounter, to
ominate, and petition for Succefs. Wherefore we addrefs our felves to the Gods for
a Confirmation of that Praife which Men
will give us, that for the future we may
with greater Confidence appear upon the
Stage, for he need fear no Cirque, or Place
of Exercife, who has been crowned Victor
at the *Olympick* Games.

P H 2

PHALARIS I.

The Argument.

Phalaris *was a famous Tyrant of* Agrigentum, *one of the principal Cities of* Sicily, *to this Tyrant* Perillus, *or* Perilaus, *a Statuary, presents a brasen Bull, so contriv'd, that when the enclos'd Malefactor was broiling with the Fire, that was plac'd under it ; his Groans and Outcries resembl'd exactly the Bellowing of a Bull. In this Discourse* Phalaris *is suppos'd to send this Brazen Bull to* Delphos, *to be placed among the other Offerings, and consecrated to* Apollo *But being sensible that he lay under a general Imputation of being the most cruel, barbarous, and inhuman Tyrant in the World, and fearing, that, on that very Account, the Priests of* Delphos *would reject the Offering, as coming from a wicked and impious Person, by his Embassador, in the following Oration, he endeavours to clear himself from so odious an Imputation, which arose only from the Errors of Vulgar Fame. The Word* Tyrant *is often us'd in this Discourse, but it is of a good and bad Signification in the*

Kk 3   Greek

Greek, *but here it is us'd always simply in the best Sense.*

PHalaris our Sovereign Lord (O ye *Delphians*) has sent us his Ambassadors to conduct this Brazen Bull to *Apollo*, and to trouble you with a few words, not unworthy your Attention, both on our Prince himself, and the Gift he has offer'd. These therefore are the Heads of our Instruction, and the Purport of our Commission to this Place, is to inform you of the particulars in his own words.

It is above all things my desire, O ye *Delphians* (says *Phalaris*) to remove the Prejudice I lie under, and that all the *Grecians* shou'd form their Opinion and Esteem of me, by what I really am, and not by that lying Fame and Rumour, which has been unjustly rais'd and spread among those, that are intirely ignorant of me, by my Enemies, and those envious of my Dignity and Power. But of all the *Grecians*, it is the first of my wishes, to establish this Opinion with you, who excel all others in Sanctity and Holiness, are the Counsellors and Associates of the *Pythian Apollo*, and I may almost say, the familiar Friends and Companions of the glorious God himself. For I am fully perswaded, that I shall clear my self to all the rest of the World, if I can but convince you, by plainly demonstrating how unjustly I have been dealt with, and how little I deserve this Odium of *Cruelty*, which has been thrown upon me. To give a just Weight to my Word

]

I invoke the awful Majesty of that bright
Deity your selves, whom I cannot deceive
or impose on by any Falacy, or Sophistry
of Argument, or artful turn of Discourse,
to witness the truth of all, that I shall deliver to you.   It may, perhaps, be no hard
matter to impose on Men, but it is impossible to banter and deceive a God, especially this God *Apollo*, who sees all things.
My Ancestors were of no obscure Condition in *Agrigentum*, but I was born of as illustrious Parents as any one, and being
qualify'd with a liberal Education, and instructed in all sorts of ingenuous Literature and Arts, I was not negligent of ren-
dring my self popular with my Fellow Citizens   I always took care to observe both
Modesty and Equity with all those, who
were concern'd with me in the Commonwealth ; nor did any one ever pretend to
accuse the early years of my Life of Violence, Injuries offer'd to others, of Con-
tumely or rash Judgment.   But when I had
undoubted Proofs of the secret Machinations of those, who differ'd with me in the
Administration of Affairs, against my Life,
and that they were extreamly industrious
to hunt for and find out means of putting
an end to my Days, and that our whole
City was in a Ferment, and perfectly di-
stracted with Factions, and partly turbulent
and irreconcileable.   I cou'd find no way
of Escape, or Security to my self, or to
the Commonwealth, in times of such Difficulty and Confusion, but a forcible
Seizure of the Sovereignty and absolute
                  K k 4   Adm

Administration of the publick Affairs, that
I might thus restrain their Rancour, and
quash that Lust of Treachery and Plots a
gainst my Life, to which they were with
so much Study and Application enclin'd,
and by the same means to reduce the City
to that peaceable and quiet State, of which
the heat and violence of popular Parties
deny'd the Enjoyment. Nor did I presume
on so great an Undertaking, without the
Approbation of many of the most sober,
moderate Citizens, and who were faithful
Lovers of the good of the Commonwealth,
from whom it was impossible for me to
conceal my Opinion and fixt Design. By
the help of both the Advice and Assistance
of those Gentlemen, I found it no hard
matter to obtain my Desire. From this
time all Factions ceas'd, nor were they any
longer busied with the Study of Novelties
and innovations, or stirring up Tumults
and seditions, or quarrelling, or falling
out among themselves, but all were united
in a perfect Obedience to my Commands.
The Sum and Head, therefore, of my
Crime, was, that I had seiz'd the Sove
reignty, and that the City was depriv'd of
its Liberty. But I never sought out, or put
in Execution any Proscriptions, Prosecut-
ons against so much, as those very Men, who
had often treacherously laid Plots against
me. But it will be worth your while (O
ye *Delphians*) to hear the principal Methods
and Means which I made use of for the defence of my Sovereignty. I flatter'd my
self into a perfect Confidence, that by

Len*g*

I enity, Affability, Mildneſs, and Equality of Honour and Dignity, I ſhould win
all to a full Obedience.   To this end, laying aſide all Reſentment, I reconcil'd my
ſelf to all my Enemies, without regard to
any thing paſt, I admitted moſt of them to
my Converſation, and my Counſels. Beſides, when I had obſerv'd, that by the
ſupinity and neglect of a very corrupt
Magiſtracy, ſpoilers of many publick Ornaments, and Robbers of the common
Treaſure of the State, the City was much
in Decay, I repair'd the *Aquaducts*, and
adorn'd the Streets with magnificent Buildings, and ſecur'd the City, by ſurrounding
it with a Wall; and made no ſmall Addition to that Revenue, which the care of
the Magiſtrates had left common to the
Publick I had a particular care of the E-
ducation of Youth, and paid the utmoſt
deference to old Age. But I retain'd the
Hearts of the People by Shows, Largeſſes,
ſolemn Entertainments and publick Feaſts.
Such was the averſion I had to the infamous deflouring of Virgins, the abominа-
ble and impious Corruption of Pupils, the
injurious ſending of Soldiers into the Houſes
of the Citizens, and Tyrannical Threats,
that I thought the very Name of them
ſcarce lawful to be heard And now,
having deriv'd ſo great Benefits to my
Country, by my Adminiſtration, I began
to conſider with my ſelf, and to entertain
thoughts of quitting the Sovereignty, if I
cou'd but find out any way of having a
ſecure Retreat, where I might live without

out Danger, and free from the Turmoiles
and Tempefts of Cares, in Peace and
Tranquillity. For I cou'd not but reflect
that to act the Prince, and to adminifter all
things, fo that they be done with Equity,
Care, and Wifdom, is a Task of the greateft Odium, and envy'd, tho' laborious
and uneafie. But that which now employ'd
my Thoughts, was how to leave the Ad-
miniftration in Hands, as equitable and juft,
on my Abdication. While I yet was bu-
fied with thofe Thoughts, and my Mind
wholly taken up with their Importance,
my Citizens had Recourfe to Sedition, and
rofe up againft me, and were now deliberating of affaulting my Perfon, and a total
Defertion. Befides, they entred into fecret Confpiracies, provided Arms, and
from private Contributions, rais'd a Sum
of Money, invited the adjacent Cities to
fend them Auxiliary Forces, and had dif-
patched Ambaff.dors, or rather Meffen-
gers, into *Greece*, to *Lacedemon* and *Athens*,
to beg for Help To this end, they had
firft contriv'd and agreed, what Crimes to
lay to my Charge, and then they feverely
threatned fome certain Method they had to
oblidge me to kill my felf Neither did
they conceal their Intentions, as to what
Punifhment they were to undergo, whom
they devoted for publick Sacrifices. That
all their Threats prov'd vain, and that I
underwent none of thofe Evils they defign
ed me, is due to the immortal Gods, whofe
Goodnefs I muft always acknowledge, in
difcovering to me thofe Confpiracies and
                        Contrivance

Contrivances againſt me.   But of all the Gods, my Thanks are moſt due to *Apollo*, by whoſe peculiar favour I had Viſions, and thoſe ſent to me, by whoſe Diſcovery I was inform'd of all their Contrivances, and with a great deal of Cunning I found and apprehended them. I deſire (O ye *Delphians*) your Advice on this very Juncture, and in theſe very Streights, what wou'd you have had me done, in the midſt of ſuch a Surprize, and in the very point of ſuch an Apprehenſion, the Grief of which, how much it touch'd me, you may perceive, by what I utter, I deſire, I ſay, to know what Advice you your ſelves wou'd have given me in the moment of theſe Tranſactions, and thoſe Diſcoveries, now almoſt Captive in the Hands of the Conſpirators, and ſeeking Safety, without any Guards to defend me? I beg you, in your Minds, for a little while to take a ſmall tour towards *Agrigentum*, and to me, beholding their preparations, and hearing their Threats and inſolent Menaces, tell me what Courſe cou'd I ſteer? What wou'd you have me to do? Wou'd you have me ſtill to have gone on with Humanity and Mildneſs, that I ſhou'd have paſs'd an Act of Oblivion, and forgiven the Malice and Traiterous Endeavours of thoſe abandon'd Citizens, and that I ſhou'd have diſſembled my Reſentment, and bore their Wickedneſs, altho' I was immediately to periſh? Was it moſt adviſeable, that naked and unarmed, I ſhou'd ſuffer a barbarous Death from the bloody Citizens, and ſee my my dearest Friends cruelly executed before my Face? Or won'd this not rather have been look'd on, as the tame suffering of a Man without Sense, and perfectly out of his Wits? It was more agreeable to a Person of Generosity, and more worthy a Man of Resolution and Prudence, of a Man that had receiv'd an Injury, to prosecute them with the utmost Indignation, and so escaping these Dangers to fortifie my self for the future, and arm my self with Security against any farther Attempts? This Course without doubt you would have advis'd me to take Give me leave therefore to let you know the Measures I took upon this Discovery: I sent for all those who were engag'd in this Conspiracy, and giving them full leave to answer for themselves, and make their own Defence, I produc'd my Proofs and Witnesses, and having fairly and clearly discover'd every one of them, and fully convicted them of their Guilt, when they had now nothing left to urge in their own Vindication, I punished them as they justly deserv'd, being extreamly angry with them, not for their Attempts on my Life, but because they had now render'd it impractical for me to pursue that course and manner of my Administration, which from my first Assumption of my Authority, I had proposed to my self, and hitherto observ'd. For from this Plot discover'd, I have been oblig'd to secure my self with the Attendance of a perpetual Life-Guard, and continue to punish whomsoever I find contriving or

carrying

carrying on any fecret and dangerous Defigns againſt me. Thus Men lay Cruelty
to my Charge, not much confideiing who
were the firſt Introducers of this neceſſary
Evil; with too much Negligence, and too
little Juſtice, reflecting on the cauſe of
thoſe Puniſhments inflicted on theſe wicked Citizens, but impute all thoſe Rewards
of their Villany, as Crimes to me, and the
Executions they fee, they falſly call Cruel-
ties. Give me leave to make it your Caſe,
upon your throwing any Sacrilegious Robber down your Precipice, ſhould any one,
without regard to the Guilt of the Criminal, only take notice of the puniſhment,
and not reflecting on the Robbers entring
the Holy Temple at Midnight, carrying
off the moſt precious Gifts and Sacred Offerings, and ſpoiling this moſt religious
Fane, attacking the moſt Holy Statues
themſelves with their Sacrilegious, and impious Hands, ſhou'd however accuſe you
of Cruelty, becauſe being both *Grecians*,
and Holy Men, fet apart to the Worſhip
of the Gods, you inflict a Puniſhment on a
Grecian, ſo near the Temple it ſelf, for
I have heard, that adjoining to this Sacred
Place there is a Rock deſtin'd to theſe Executions. But certainly, ſhou'd any Man
be ſo very filly, as to urge any thing of
this nature againſt you in theſe Circumſtances, you wou'd think him worthy nothing but your Laughter; for all Men beſide wou'd give your neceſſary Severity a-
gainſt the impious Criminals, the higheſt
and juſteſt Praiſe. In ſhort, the Thought-
leſs

lefs People, not at all confidering the Qualities, the Vertues, or Vices of the Perfon,
who is at the head of Affairs, nor diftinguifhing whether it be juft or unjuft, hate
the very Name of Tyranny, and are to the
laft degree difgufted at the Tyrant himfelf,
and tho' *Æacus, Minos,* or *Radamanthus* were at
the Helm, wou'd run on headlong to cut them
off, and lofe the Confideration of the Good,
and involving the Innocent in the Guilt of
the Wicked, by fixing them only before
their Eyes, as the Fuel and Food of their
Refentment. But I have heard, that there
have been many wife Tyrants among you
in *Greece,* who, under this odious and in-
vidious Name, have fhown themfelves
ufeful and mild to all; and that your Sacred Temple has receiv'd and preferv'd the
fuccinct and pithy Prayers, Statues, and
Gifts to the *Pythian Apollo.* I defire you alfo to caft your Eyes on the Aim and Infti-
tutions of the Legiflators, who have attributed very much in Government to the
Reafon and Cuftom of eftablifhing of Pe-
nal Laws, as if there were very little to
be expected from whatever they propofe to
themfelves in their Political Syftems, unlefs they had fet up Fear and Terror to evil
Doers, and a certain view of unavoidable
Punifhment for their Crimes.

But there is vaftly a greater Neceffity
impos'd on us Tyrants, of having recourfe
to thefe Sanguinary punifhments, both becaufe our Sovereignty over others is forc'd
neceffarily on us, and becaufe we live with,
and are furrounded by thofe, who purfue *"*

with an envious Hate, and are always plot-
ting our Deſtruction ; where even in Diſ-
guiſe we reap no Benefit of our Caution,
and are never ſenſible of any Security ;
but all our Tranſactions are like the Fable of *Hydra*, for the more Occaſions of
puniſhing we cut off, ſo many the more
burge up in their Places.   But this we muſt
undergo, and perpetually lop off thoſe
Heads that ſpring up, and burn them, according to the Inſtitution of *Iolaus*, if we
deſign to enjoy our Empire in Safety.   For
he that is once compell'd by neceſſity into
this State, he muſt either be of a piece
with the Office he has aſſum'd, or by a
fooliſh Clemency to wicked and rebellious
Citizens, entirely periſh himſelf.   in fine,
can you imagine, that Man of ſo ſa-
vage a Nature, and ſo abſolute Inhumani-
ty, that can take any pleaſure in condemning others of the ſame nature to Whips
and Scourges, or in hearing the Groans of
the tormented, or in beholding the Slaughter and Gibbets, and places of Execution,
if he was not forc'd by an unavoidable
Cauſe to ſo rigorous a Courſe ? How often
have the Tears flow'd like a Torrent from
my Eyes, when Criminals have been whipt
with Scourges ? How often am I oblig'd to
deplore and lament my own Fortune, un-
dergoing a much more grievous Puniſhment in my ſelf ? For to a Man of a human Temper, and tender Nature, it is
much harder to be compell'd by a cruel
neceſſity to puniſh others, than to ſuffer
himſelf.   But if you will permit me to
ſpeak

ſpeak my Thoughts freely, if I was to chuſe whether I wou'd put the Innocent to Death, or die my ſelf, aſſure your ſelves, moſt holy *Delphians*, I wou'd much ſooner die with all the Alacrity and Satisfaction in the World, than puniſh any Man, who has not juſtly incurr'd the Cenſure of the Law.

But ſome may perhaps demand of me, whether I wou'd rather periſh unjuſtly my ſelf, than on very juſt Grounds to puniſh Conſpirators againſt me? To make an Anſwer to this Query, I ſhall again appeal to your Advice (O ye ſage *Delphians*) and aſk you, whether you think it more excellent and eligible to ſeek an unjuſt Death, or unjuſtly to preſerve a Traytor, who had conſpir'd that Death? Sure there can be no Man ſo mad, ſo void of common Senſe, who wou'd not rather chuſe Life, than to preſerve his mortal Enemies by his own Death. But how many have I forgiven, and preſerv'd from my Reſentment, who have endeavour'd to take away my Life (as *Acanthus, Timocrates,* and *Legoras*) in conſideration of that Familiarity and Friendſhip I had formerly had with them.

But if you have a mind and deſire to make a more ſtrict Enquiry into my Manners, Temper, and Principles, conſult thoſe Travellers, who frequently come to *Agrigentum*, and aſk of them my Conduct to them, whether I am hoſpitable and generous to thoſe that viſit me, who have my Spies and Auditors in the Ports, to inquire whence, and who the Paſſengers that I may treat every one according to his Dignity and Merit. Some there are who voluntarily, and of their own accord, come hither to fee me, and thofe not only *Grecians*, but the wifeft of *Grecians*, who refufe not our Friendfhip, or fly from our Careffes. Among thefe lately *Pythagoras*, cou'd not be deterr'd from vifiting me, by the injurious Reports he heard of me. But after he found all things fo different, and contrary to vulgar Fame, he left me with no fmall Praife, for my Ignorance of thofe Evils, and very much pittying me for the Neceffity I lay under of being obliged to have Recourfe to Cruelty

Laftly, Can you imagine, that he who is Mafter of fo much Humanity to meer ftrangers, cou'd ufe fo great Severity to his own Domefticks, his own Family, if the Injuries he receiv'd did not exceed all Bounds?

Thefe are fome of thofe tnings which I had to fay, and which I perfwade my felf have abundantly clear'd my Reputation with you, fince they are true and juft, and much more worthy, in my Opinion, of Praife, than Hatred.

It is now time to fay fomething of the Gift I have fent you, that you may know how I came by this Bull, the Work of a Statuary that was not employ'd by me. For I am not fo mad, as to defire the Poffeffion of any fuch things. But there was a very ingenious Artift of our City, by Name *Perilaus*, as perverfe and barbarous in his Temper, as excellent in his Art.

This Man being infinitely miftaken in my Inclinations, and making a very falfe Judgment of the Severities I'm oblig'd to ufe, imagin'd that he cou'd not more ingratiate himfelf with me, than by furnifhing me with a new and unheard of manner of Punifhment, as if the greateft Pleafure I was capable of taking, was in the Execution of the Criminal. This *Perilaus* having now form'd this Bull, brings it to me, adorn'd with all the Perfection of Art, and to the Eye compleatly reprefenting the living Animal, fo that there feem'd nothing wanting to the Life but Motion, and Bellowing. I no fooner beheld this Statue, but I prefently cry'd out, *This is a Prefent worthy Phœbus, this Bull muft be fent to* Apollo *Perilaus* ftanding by interpos'd, and faid, *Will you pleafe to hear the Excellence, that is within him, and know for what Ufe and End it was made?* And then immediately open'd a little Door in his Back. *If you have a Man to torture any one,* faid he, *having caft him into this Machine, and clos'd the Back upon, apply thefe Pipes to the Noftrils of the Bull, command Fire to be kindled under it, and the Wretch enclos'd will Groan, and cry out, fuffering unufual and ineffable Torments, but the Noife he makes paffing thofe Pipes, will convey a very fhrill Sound to your Ears, and warble a fort of melancholly Ditty; befides, as the Torment continues, it will raife a moft doleful and plaintive Bellowing, and yield you moft new and fingular Pleafure.*

Having

Having heard this from *Perilaus*, the utmost Averfion ftruck me for the cruel Machine, and detefting the barbarous Genius of the Inventor of it, I inflicted on him a Punifhment anfwerable and due to the Work. *Perilaus*, faid I, *that we may be fatisfy'd that your Promife is not vain, and a meer Boaft, get you into the Bull, and imitat ng the Cries of the tormented, give us a Proof that we fhall hear this Mufick thro' the Pipes, as you have pretended.* Perilaus, without farther Delay, obeys my Commands, and enters the Bull. But caufing the Back to be faften'd when he was enter'd, I order'd a Fire to be lighted under it. *Receive*, faid I, *the Reward due to your wonderful Art, that you being the Mafter of this Mufick, fing firft your felf.* Thus did he meet with a Fate equal to his Merits, and the highest Juftice, enjoying the Fruit of his own excellent Induftry. But I commanded him to be taken out before he expir'd, leaft that by dying in the Bull, he fhou'd contaminate the Prefent I defign'd, but commanded him to be thrown down the Rocks, and left unburyed But have fent the Bull, after its being purify'd by Expiations, to be dedicated to the God, commanding all the Story to be written, that is, the Name of me the Dedicator; of *Perilaus* the Artificer of the Bull, his cruel Sentence, my Juftice and Equity in punifhing Malefactors, the Punifhment anfwerable to the Crime, the firft Song and Modulation, being the firft Experiment of his own Mufick

But you (O *Delphians*) will fhow your
Juftice, by joining with my Ambaffadors in
Sacrifices for me ; and dedicate the Bull in
the beautiful Temple, to your God ; that
my Conduct with Evil-doers may be made
known to all Men, and with what fingular
Severity I punifh the abounding Lufts of
malicious Defigns. This Fact alone, therefore, fufficiently demonftrates my Principles and my Manners, *Perilaus* being punifh'd, and the Bull made an immediate
Offering, and not referv'd for renewing
the Barbarous Mufick, by the Tortures of
the Malefactor, which has given no other
Sound, I folemnly aver, but thofe of the
wicked Artificer himfelf ; that I made no
other Experiment of his Art, but immediately filenc'd the favage and inhuman Mufick.

This was what I had at prefent to make
an Offering of to the God. But I fhall
make far more frequent and magnificent
Prefents, when by his Bounty I fhall attain
the Happinefs to have no further need of
ufing Severity and Cruelty to Offenders.

Thus (O ye *Delphians*) have we given
you a faithful Account of all the Actions
and Principles of *Phalaris*, our Sovereign
Lord : And we prefume, that we have fully difcharg'd our Truft, if we have brought
nothing but the Truth in his Vindication,
and to your Conviction , being neither ignorant of the matter of Fact, and under
no Occafion or Temptation of offering you
a Lye.

But if we muſt likewiſe become Suppli-
ants for one, whom too many have injuri-
ouſly and falſly looked on, as a wicked Man,
becauſe againſt his Will, and contrary to
his natural Temper and Inclination, he is
compell'd to puniſh the wicked Malefactors; behold we Citizens of *Agrigentum*,
who are both *Grecians*, and deſcended from
the ancient *Dorians*, do ſupplicate you;
embrace, embrace the Man that deſires to
enter into Friendſhip with you, and who
makes it his Study to be extreamly bene-
ficial and ſerviceable to you, to every one
of you, both publickly and privately. Take
you, therefore, take and receive this Bull,
dedicate it to your God, and offer up your
Vows for the *Agrigentines*, and the Health
and Safety of *Phalaris* himſelf.   And do not
diſmiſs us from *Delphos*, without ſucceeding
in our Embaſſie, leaſt by a Conduct ſo unjuſt, you affront him, and at the ſame time
rob your God of the moſt juſt, and moſt
elegant Gift, that can be offer'd him.

PHAL

PHALARIS II.

The Argument

One of the Delphian *Priests is by this Oration suppos'd to perswade the Reception of the Bull offer'd them in the foregoing Speech, for the* Pagan *Priests were not willing to lose any Offering, tho sent by one more profligate, than* Phalaris *was reported to be.*

SInce before this very Moment (O ye *Delphians*) I have never had any Correspondence and Affairs with the Citizens of *Agrigentum*, nor secretly contracted any particular Familiarity and Alliance with *Phalaris* himself, and that I have not any more singular and peculiar Cause of present Intimacy, or mutual Engagements, or hopes of entring into any future Friendship with him, but have only heard those Ambassadors he has delegated to *Delphos*, offering to us nothing in their Speech but what was equitable and modest, I cautiously and nicely consider'd both what you might do with Piety, and what wou'd be conducive to the publick Benefit, and chiefly what the *Delphians* might do, without infringing their Honour and Dignity. I rise up to offer my Reasons to perswade you neither to put an Affront on a Sovereign Prince, when he acts with so much Piety, nor that you reject and deprive your selves

of a magnificent Prefent, which is already
offer'd and dedicated to *Our God*, efpecially fince it will be a perpetual Monument
and Record of three things, firft of the
Mafter-piece and Perfection of Art, next of *a
moft cruel Defign*, and thirdly of a *juft Punifhment*.

I muft therefore confefs, and freely declare, that even this Meeting of ours on
this very Debate, does not feem to me
over Religious, that is, that you fhou'd
make the leaft Hefitation or Doubt of what
you are to do in this matter, or that the
Magiftrates have left to your Confideration and Decifion, whether this Offering be
to be receiv'd, or return'd back again to
the Perfon, who fent it. At this rate
there will be no room left for Piety, for
this will be neither better nor worfe, than
moft wicked Sacriledge, whofe blackne s
fo exceeds that of all other Crimes whatfoever. Nor will it be a lefs impious Deed,
to deny any the Power and Liberty of
making their Offerings to the God, when
they have a defire to do it, than to commit a Robbery on the Temple, and fpoil
him of thofe Gifts, of which he is already
in poffeffion

I beg you, fince I am my felf one of the
Delphians, and equally a Partaker of the
Glory of my Country, if it be preferv'd,
and obnoxious to the contrary, if we do
any thing unjuftifiable and ignominious,
and derogatory to our Reputation, I beg
you, I fay, not to fhut up the Gates of the
Temple againft Pious and Religious People ;

nor expofe this our City to the Obloquy
and Contempt of all Men, as if we fat here
to judge of and make a deceitful Scrutiny
into the Gifts and Offerings made to our
God, by falfe Accufations, or nice Tryals
of their Value and Validity. Shou'd we
do thus, for the future, no Man will prefume to make any Offering, being affur'd,
that it is very probable, that the God will
not accept, or become propitious on any
Gift, which has not been view'd, fearch'd
and judg'd by the *Delphians*.

But, Gentlemen, the God himfelf feems
to me to have already decided this matter,
as to this Gift fent him by *Phalaris*. For if
Phalaris had been odious, and an Enemy to
the God ; if *Apollo* had contemn'd, and
been averfe to his Offering, how eafie had
it been for him to have funk both that and
the Ship, that brought it, in the midft of
the *Ionian* Waves, in its Paffage hither ?
But he, your God, (O ye *Delphians*) has declar'd himfelf of much a contrary Opinion to you, fince (as they pofitively affure
us) he granted them a Serene Sky, and a
profperous Gale thro' the *Ionian* Sea , and
brought them fafe even to the Harbour of
Cirra, which is a fufficient and clear Demonftration, that he does not diflike or
difapprove the Piety of this Monarch. But
you ought to fubmit and join your Judgments to the Sentence of the Deity, and
fo add this Brazen Bull to the other Ornaments of the Temple. For without doubt
it wou'd be the moft abfurd thing in Nature, if any one, who brings an Offering

so excellent in its kind, and so magnificent, should be forbid entrance into the Temple, and be sent away with the Doom of the Impious, that is, be adjudg'd unworthy to make an Offering to *Apollo*.

But he, who differs from my Opinion, as if he were just brought in the Ship from *Agrigentum*, relates to us certain Slaughters, Injustice, Rapines, and Depredations made by the Tyrant, and thunder'd them out in a too Tragical Tone and Outcry, telling us, that he almost saw all things with his own Eyes, when we know, that the Extent of his Travels never reach'd beyond the Harbour in this Life. But indeed, I think it no way disagreeable to Reason to suspend our Belief of these things, from the Mouth even of such, as say they have suffer'd them themselves. For we must be in the dark, whether what they tell us be true or not; and therefore we shou'd be cautious, least we rashly, in things of which we have no certainty, accuse those unjustly of Crimes, of which they may be innocent.

But supposing that some of these things may be done in *Sicily*, what have we *Delphians* to do to be curious about the matter, unless we design instead of the Office of Priests, preposterously to usurp that of Judges. It is our Duty to Sacrifice, and the Duty of others to adore the Gods ; and if any Presents were sent, it was our Office to dedicate them to our Deity. Is it any Business of ours to sit here and examine, whether any of those Princes cross

the

the *Ionian* Sea, difcharge the Adminiftrati-
on of his Goverment, as he ought or not ?
I think it is no matter at all to us how o-
ther People manage their Affairs. But we
ought to look to it, that we are not ignorant of our own, both as to their ancient
State, and prefent Condition, and what
farther we ought to do for their Benefit and
Advantage. For we have no occafion of
waiting for *Homer* to make it plain to us,
that we live on fteep Rocks and Piecipices,
or that we have nothing to cultivate but
barren Stones, but this we e'ery day beheld with our own Eyes ; nor are we to
feek in our Obfervation, that we daily fub-
fift in a Country, whofe Port is very deep
But the *Temple* it felf, *Apollo*, and his *Oracle*, the *Sacrificers*, and *Servants* to the
Works of Piety, are the Fields of Corn,
the Paftures, the Stores of the *Delphians*
Thence fpiings our Abundance, thence
flows the plentiful Tyde of Provifions in
upon us. For it is but juft, that I pafs nothing in filence, or with an injurious diffi-
mulation flur over any Truth, that I know
and fhou'd urge ; and as the Poet fays,
without plowing or fowing our felves, our
Husband-man the God brings us in all
that we want ; who is not content to give
us all the good things, which other People
enjoy, with a plentiful Hand, and meafure
over-heap'd ; but every one ftrives to bring
to *Delphos*, every thing, that is rare or precious, either among the *Phrygians*, or the
Lydians, or the *Perfians*, or the *Affyrians*, or
the *Phænicians*, or the *Italians*, or laftly, a-
mong

mong the extreameſt and moſt northerly
People of the World And even we our ſelves
are in a wonderful manner, and next, and
in the ſecond place to the God worſhipped
by all Men, and being provided with all
Affluence, lead the moſt happy and fortunate Lives. But theſe are things you all
know, as well as my ſelf. But to come to
the preſent Debate, we muſt make it our
endeavour to perſevere with Conſtancy in
preſerving the ſame Inſtitution of Life
which we have once begun. It is my O-
pinion that there has never yet been ſo
much as one Precedent in any time, or in
the memory of Man, of our paſſing our
Judgment on any Gift, that was brought to
Apollo, or of the prohibition of any Man
from ſacrificing or dedicating any Gift that
was brought; and this, without doubt,
is the reaſon that the Temple of *Apollo* is
ſo repleniſh'd with Gifts and Preſents beyond Meaſure.

We ought not, therefore, to be raſhly
guilty of any Innovation, or to ordain any
thing different from thoſe Ways, Means,
and Conſtitutions we have received from
our Forefathers. Nor muſt we judge of
the Offerings, by the Bribe of Inclination,
nor eſteem them according to their ſort
and kind, or conſider whence, or from
whom they are ſent to this Place. But we
ought to receive the Gifts, and conſecrate
them to the God; and we ought with all
our Will and Ability to ſerve the God, and
thoſe who come hither, in obedience to the
Call of Piety it ſelf.

                                    You

You will in my Opinion (O ye *Delphians*)
do moſt judiciouſly in thoſe things, which
you have now made the ſubject of your
preſent Debate, if you firſt of all take into your ſerious Conſideration, the Importance and great Weight, and Conſequence
of what you are deliberating about. Remember therefore in tht firſt place, that
you ſit here upon the *God* himſelf, and his
Temple, next upon the Sacrifices and Offerings, upon the Rites and ancient Manners,
Cuſtoms, and Laws, and the Glory of
Prophecy, and ſo upon the whole City, and
upon thoſe things, which privately or publickly are conducive to the uſe and behoof
of every *Delphian* Citizen. Beſides all theſe
weighty Conſiderations of your Debate,
it is no contemptible Hazard you run
in the Opinion of all Mankind, either
of arriving at Glory, or falling into Infamy I think (if you are Maſters at all of
Reaſon) you will think nothing greater
or more neceſſary, than what I have urg'd
The ſum therefore, of our Debate, is not
Phalaris alone, or his famous Bull, or the
Braſs of which it is made; but all Kings
and Princes, and every one, who applies
himſelf to our Temple Beſides this, the
Gold, Silver, and whatever other more
precious things, which in great Numbers,
and frequently, come to us to be dedicated to the God. For firſt we ought to
weigh things according to the Counſel of
the God himſelf. What ſhall be therefore
our Motive, in conſideration of what ſhall
we decide of the Conſecration of Offering

if not on that which was our most ancient
and long us'd Custom? Or what fault do
we find in those Customs made reverend
by their Antiquity, that we give our Minds
to Innovations? And design to do what
was never done since this City was inhabited, or *Apollo* deliver'd Oracles, or the
Tripos spoke, or the Priestess was possess'd
by the Divine Afflatus of the Deity, that
is, sit in Judgment on those, and examining
and putting them under a Scrutiny, who
send Gifts to *Apollo*.

But rather lay close to your Thoughts
the venerable old Custom and Institution
which never excluded any one from the
Power and Liberty of making what Offerings, they pleas'd; how much the Temple
was replenish'd with Gifts, when all were
suffer'd to offer, and every one according
to his Abilities, to bring his Presents to
the God. But if once we assume and
usurp the Right of judging and censuring
the Gifts, that are sent, I am afraid, that
we shall soon labour under a Penury of those
things, on which we are to pass our Judgment, since no Man will ever suffer himself to be plac'd as a Culprit, and to be at
the expence and charge of the Tryal to receive his Sentence, and put all upon a hazard, that he might avoid. But who do
you think will bear the Judgment with
Patience, if he be adjudged unworthy of
making his Offerings?

HER-

HERMOTIMUS:

Or of the

Sects of PHILOSOPHERS.

By Colonel Henry Blount.

Lucian. YOur Book, and hasty walking, *Hermotimus*, make me believe, that you are going to your Philosophical Lecture. I'm sure that your Mind seem'd to be taken up with some serious Meditation, your Hands and Lips mov'd, as if you were disposing some Oration, or conning some difficult Question, or finding out some Sophistical Speculation, that you might lose no time in Idleness, without doing something conducive to the improvement of these Precepts you learn.

Hermotimus. You have guest pretty near the truth, *Lucian,* for I was running over e'ery particular, that our Master yesterday deliver'd to us in the School. I do not think we ought indeed to lose any time, since the truth of that Maxim of *Hippocrates,* that *Life is short, but Art long,* is too evident. This he affirm'd of Physick, which is an Art attain'd with much lefs Difficulty than Philofophy, to the Maftery of which, length of time, without an entire Application of all the Faculties of the Mind, muft be ineffectual. Nor is this a thing of finall confequence; for we muft either miferably perifh among the dregs of Mankind, or gain the Prize of a happy Life, by the help and precepts of Philofophy

Lucian The Rewards you propofe, I confefs, *Hermotimus*, are of the laft import. But, I prefume, you are not far diftant from the enjoyment of 'em, if we may guefs by the time, that you have dedicated to this Study, or the pains and indefatigable induftry with which you have thus long purfu'd it; for if I miftake not I have now known you for near thefe twenty years, a daily hearer of fome Mafter or other, and fo entirely devoted to your Book, that you are grown as pale and lean as a Ghoft with your Cares; for my part, I've thought you fo wholly involv'd in this Affair, that even your Slumbers cou'd not have force enough to unbend your Mind from the agreeable Contemplation Thefe Confiderations make me fuppofe, that you will fuddenly arrive at this diftant Land of *Happinefs*, if you are not got thither already, without our Knowledge.

Hermot. How can you imagine that, when I am but now, as it were, fet out on my Journey, ———— Whereas Virtue, as *Hefiod* affures us, dwells in a far remote Country, the way to which is long, difficul.

cult, and steep, not to be pass'd without a-
bundance of Toil and Sweat.

Lucian Have you not toil'd and sweat
enough yet, then, made a sufficient progress in this fatiguing Voyage?

Hermo Oh, Sir, far from it——For had
I reach'd the end of this Journey, I shou'd
be entirely happy in all things, but alas!
my *Lucian*, I am yet but setting out

Luci But *Hesiod* you know says, that
the Beginning is half the whole, so that we
may truly say, you are now half way up
the steep Ascent.

Hermo Oh, Sir, far short of that, tho'
I have made a considerable Progress toward
it.

Lucian. How far in your Journey then
may we say you are reach'd?

Hermo Alas, dear *Lucian*, I am yet but
at the foot of this Mountain, endeavouring to clamber up. But the Ascent is steep,
and slippery, and to mount it, I want the
careful hand of some Guide.

Lucian. And none so qualified as your
Master, who sitting on the loftiest point,
like the *Jupiter* of *Homer*, lifts you up
with the Golden Chain of his Precepts and
Maxims, to that height to which himself
is long since arriv'd.

Hermo. You have touch'd the very point,
my *Lucian*, for his Labour and Pains have
not been wanting to raise me up aloft, and
set me among 'em, tho' my own Defects
keep me still below.

Lucian. Well, but you muft take heart, when you behold the end of our Journey, and Happinefs, feated at the end, efpecially by the Encouragements that he continually affords you. But pray, Sir, inform me what hopes does he give you, and when will that wifh'd for minute come, that you fhall find your felf arriv'd to that bleft abode ? Does he believe another year will do the Bufinefs ?

Hermo. Oh, Sir, you allow too fhort a time.

Lucian. Well, what think you of five years more ?

Hermo. Alas ! even this is too narrow a fpace of time to arrive at the Excercife of *Virtue*, and the poffeffion of *Happinefs*

Lucian. Ten years will certainly be enough——Elfe the malicious World may accufe you of great Sloth and Lazinefs, if you can't get thither in the fame time that a Man may go three times with eafe, from *Gibralter* to the *Indies*, and back again, tho' he view the Countries he pafs thro', and do not make a direct and continu'd Voyage of it. But how much fteeper, and more difficult of Afcent muft we fuppofe this Mountain, where your *Virtue* dwells, than that of *Aorna*, which *Alexander the Great* pafs'd, and became Mafter of in a few days.

Hermo. Alas, good *Lucian*, there is no parallel in the Cafe, nor is this a Bufinefs of that eafe you imagine, to be pafs'd and taken in a fhort time, tho' fix Hundred *Alexanders* fhou'd join and unite all their

M m   Force

Force to attempt it. For many have endeavoured to afcend, and even now, not a few that are fortify'd with the firmeft Refolution and Courage, do furmount the fteep Afcent, and make fome Progrefs; fome more, fome lefs, but meeting with many Difficulties and Perplexities, tir'd with the Fatigue, in the midft of their Journey, they return out of Breath, all in a Sweat, and unable to fupport the Labour. But thofe who perfevere to the end, gain the higheft Summit, and from that time forward, they poffefs *Happinefs*, and the remainder of their Lives, is a Life full of unutterable Wonder and Tranquillity, and then they look down from on high, on the reft of Mankind, as fo many little bufy Emmets.

Lucian Ha, *Hermotimus*, to what a degree do you diminifh us, when you allow us not fo much as the Magnitude of Pigmies, but reduce us to a Similitude of fuch little Reptile Animals, and not without Caufe, I confefs, for you even from your firft fetting out are full of fublime Wifdom. But we poor Rable of Mankind, who creep along the Ground, will adore you, who are mounted higher, than the Clouds with Prayer and Incenfe, like the Gods.

Hermo Ah! my dear *Lucian*, I wifh it were fo well with me. Oh that I had but the power to afcend——For alas! yet is there a great deal of my Journey to come

Lucian. But you are not particular as to the quantity, so that one might guess how much time wou'd be requir'd to arrive at the end of it

Hermo. That I do not very well know my self, yet I do suppose, that twenty years will be the longest time, after which I shall have ga'n'd the very highest point of all the Mountain

Lucian. Ah, *Hermotimus,* you've taken a great while

Hermo. Great things are not to be found without Labour.

Lucian. That's very true, but has your Master assur'd you, that you shall live twenty years, being skilful, not in Wisdom alone, but in Futurity also, or is he one of those that are learned in the *Chaldean* Doctrines, for the knowledge of these things is attributed to such For it does by no means seem reasonable to me, that you shou'd undergo all these Labours, Cares and Fatigues, Day and Night, when you are uncertain, whether or no you shall live till you arrive at *Virtue,* or when you know not but the Fates may ravish you from your imperfect hopes, the minute before you reach that wish'd for Height.

Hermo. No more of that——for 'tis maliciously spoken——Yet would to God I might live to reach the Goal of Virtue, that I might enjoy Happiness but for one whole day.

Lucian. And shou'd you think one day reward enough for so many, and so great Pains and Labours?

Hermo.

Hermo. Yes, even the ſhorteſt moment

Lucian. But prithee, my good Friend, how came you to know, that there is ſuch Happineſs in Supernal things, that is woꝛth the expence of all this Pain and Fatigue? For as I take it, you never yet were up among 'em.

Hermo. True, Sir, but I believe my Maſter, who aſſuꝛes me of it, and who is now at the veꝛy higheſt Point.

Lucian Very good, and what ſoꝛt of Happineſs, I pray, do's he tell you is theꝛe? Aꝛe there moderate Riches, Glo-ry, and incredible Pleaſuꝛes?

Heꝛmo Hold a little, Sir, —— for thoſe are things not at all conducive to a Life, that is under the Guidance and Govern-ment of Virtue.

Lucian. Well, if I am miſtaken in 'em, Pꝛay wnat aꝛe thoſe *Goods* and Benefits ne pꝛopoſes to thoſe, that arꝛive to the end of this difficult Diſcipline.

Hermo Wiſdom, Fortitude, Virtue it ſelf, *Juſtice,* and a ceꝛtain Knowledge of all things as they are in their own Natuꝛe But leaving Rꝛiches, Glory, Pleaſures, and all other *Goods* of the Body here below, he aſcends, free fꝛom that Clog, like *Her-cules,* to the Number of the Gods, in the Flames of Mount *Oeta* , for he having put off all that human Natuꝛe, which he had aſ-ſum'd from his Mother, and having now a pure and incoꝛrupt Divinity, that, being ſeparated by the Fire, mounted up aloft to the Gods. In this manner theſe Seekeꝛs of Vertue, being purg'd by Philoſophy, as

by

by a kind of Fire, from all those Trifles
which the foolish World admires; having
gain'd the Summit of the Hill, live happily, without ever troubling themselves
with the thoughts of *Riches*, Glory and
Pleasure, but laugh at those wretched
Fools, that can think them of any Value

Lucian. Nay, by the *Oetean Hercules* himfelf, *Hermotimus*, these things, which you
relate of 'em make a Happiness indeed,
and worthy of the choice of Men But
pray answer one Question——Do they never descend from this height, if they have
a mind to it, to make use of those things,
that they have thus left below, or are
they of necessity oblig'd, when once they
are got up, always to converse with *Virtue*,
by laughing at Riches, Glory and Pleasure?

Hermo. Not only that, but whenever a
Man has attain'd a Perfection in Virtue, he
is no longer affected with Anger, Fear,
Desire, Grief, or any other Passion

Lucian Well, might I but speak truth,
——But I must be silent, ror, as I take it,
the Actions of the *Wise* are not to be
look'd into, so I say no more.

Hermo. Oh, pray speak your mind freely

Lucian. You see, my dear Friend, how
extreamly I'm affraid to do it.

Hermo. Out with it noble Sir, never
fear to speak it to me alone.

Lucian. I agreed with you in some of
the Advantages you gave 'em, and believ'd
em Masters of Wisdom, Fortitude, Ju-

stice,

ſtice, &c. and was prettily amus'd with your Diſcourſe ; but when you wou'd have perſwaded me, that they contemn'd Riches, Glory, and Pleaſure ; and that they were inſenſible of Anger and Grief, here, I confeſs, I was preſently ſtop, (no Body hears us) by the memory of what I had ſeen one of them do, ſhall I tell you the Man ? Or can you without his Name find him out ?

Hermo. No, pray name him.

Lucian. Why your very Maſter, who, a-part, is a venerable Man, and now very old.

Hermo. Well, and what did you ſee him do ?

Lucian. You know that yellow, contentious *Heraclean*, that lives with him, and has for a long time been his Scholar, theſe Philoſophical Studies ?

Hermo. You mean *Dion*

Lucian The ſame——This Man did I ſee your Maſter t'other day hale away to the Pretor, for not paying his Quarteridge, full of Noiſe and Indignation, and had not ſome of his Friends happpen'd to've come in and reſcu'd the young Man from him the old Gentleman was in ſo violent a Paſſion, he wou'd certainly have bit his Noſe off.

Hermo. Ah, my *Lucian*, he deſerv'd it all, for he's certainly ingrateful, and an ill Pay-Maſter, for he never did ſo much to any other, who have Monies of his at Uſe and keep their times of Payment.

Lucian. Well——but my Friend, what fhou'd they pay Intereft to him for? Shall he, whom Philofophy has purg'd, and who has no occafion, or need for that Lumber he quitted on Mount *Oeta,* trouble himfelf about that

Hermo Why, d'ye think he troubles himfelf about thefe Affairs for his own fake? No, no, he takes all this care to make Provifion for his little Children, that they may not be reduc'd to a neceffitous Life.

Lucian Why, methinks *Hermotimus,* it had been worth his while to've rais'd them up to the poffeffion of this *Virtue* you fpeak of, that fo they might fhare with him in the fame Happinefs, by a Contempt of Riches.

Hermo Sir, I muft beg your pardon, I vow, for I am not at this time at Leizure to difcourfe of thefe Matters, for I muft now make all the hafte I can to hear him, that I may not lofe all, that he fhall deliver.

Lucian Oh, Sir, let not that trouble you, for this Day is a Play-day, fo that you need go no farther on that account

Hermo How fay you, Sir?

Lucian. That you will fcarce fee him this bout, if we may credit his publick Advertifement, for over his Door hung a Bill, with this infcrib'd in great Letters——

TO DAY WE SHALL HAVE NO PHILOSOPHICAL LECTURES.

Befide, they fay, that he fupt yefterday with *Eucrates,* who folemiz'd his Daughter's Birth-day, and that he was in a Paffion at

Euthydemus

Euthydemus the *Peripatiete*, on a dispute he had with him on this Subject, which is indeed the perpetual Fuel of Contention betwixt the Stoicks and Peripatieticks · That he made the Head ach with too much bawling, and prolonging the Discourse till midnight put himself into a great Sweat. Nay, I believe to pledge all the Healths that were drank to him, he swallow'd more Wine, than he cou'd bear, and eat more than his old Stomach cou'd digest; which made him, as the report runs, disembogue as soon as he came home; and having taken for his Servant, the Victuals he had filch'd from the Table, and convey'd to him behind his back, and seen that he had not defrauded him of any part, he soak'd 'em up, and went to his repose, ordering none to be admitted to disturb him This I heard his Servant *Midas* tell a great many of his Disciples, whom I saw in it returning to their several homes

Hermo. Well, But who had the better of the dispute, good *Lucian*, my Master or *Euthydemus?*

Lucian. Why truly, Sir, I'm inform'd that the Battle was pretty equally fought at first, but Sir, Victory at last declar'd herself of your side, and that the old Genteman was much of superior force, nor did *Euthydemus* draw off without Bloodshed, but with a mighty Wound in his Head. for he being very positive and contentious, not easily admitting of any perswasion, or allowing himself to be convinced, your most excellent Master lifted up a great old

fashioned

fashioned Goblet which he had in his Hands, and laid it over his Pate as he sat by him; and thus he came off victorious.

Her. He did very well, for there is no other way to deal with those who will not yield to their Betters.

Lucian Ay indeed, *Hermotimus*, he had a great deal of reason, for why should *Euty mus* go to provoke a Man of his Age, a Man averse to Anger, and of more Sence than himself, at a time when he had such a swinging Cup in his Hand? Well, but since we are now at Leisure, why will not you show me, who am your Friend, in what manner you first apply'd your self to the Study of *Philosophy*, that if possible, I may now beginning, make the Journey along with you? For I hope your Friendship to me is such, that you will not exclude me your Company.

Hermo. If you please, *Lucian*, you shall in a short time see how much you will go beyond others, be assur'd that you will have so much greater a share of Understanding, than the generality of the World, that you will look on them, as so many Boys, when compar'd with your self

Lucian. I should be satisfied, if after twenty years I could be such a one, as you now are.

Hermo For my part, truly at your Age (which I take to be about forty years) I I first began to study *Philosoply*

Lucian.

Lucian. That is juſt my Age, *Hermot. mus*, therefore lead me on the ſame way it is reaſonable I ſhould tread your Foot ſteps, and firſt tell me, do you give Lear ners the liberty of contradicting, if they diſlike any thing, which is ſpoken? Or is that a Freedom you deny to young Peo ple?

Hermo. Not at all, but for your part, I give you free leave to ask Queſtions, and contradict whenever you pleaſe, for ſo you will learn much the more eaſily.

Lucian. Now, by *Mercury*, I conjure thee (to whom thou art almoſt like in name) tell me one thing, is there only one way to *Philoſophy*, which is that of you Stoicks, or is there (as I have been told a great many more?

Hermo. Oh ſeveral others: as of the *Peripateticks*, *Epicureans*, *Platoniſts*; beſide the Followers of *Diogenes* and *Antiſthenes* the *Pythagoreans*, and a great many more.

Hermo. True, *Hermotius*, there are ſeve ral of them, but do they all tell us the ſame thing, or have they different Opini ons?

Hermo. Quite different

Lucian. But in my Judgment, there can be only one of them in the right, and not all, ſince they differ from each other

Hermo. Moſt certainly.

Lucian. Well then, my Friend, pray tell when firſt you undertook the Study of *Philoſophy*, whoſe Advice did you that whilſt ſo many Doors were open you, you ſhould pitch upon that of

Stoicks, as the only one, which could give you accefs to Virtue, and put you into the right way, paffing by the reft, as leading you aftray, and befide the Mark? By what reafon did you make this Choice? Nor ought you here to confider your felf, as the Man you are at prefent, (whether it be perfectly wife, or but half wife) who can diftinguifh what is really good, fo much better, than many of us   But anfwer me, as a Perfon wholly ignorant, fuch as you your felf was, and I now am.

Hermo. I don't underftand, *Lucian*, what you would be at by this Difcourfe of yours.

Lucian. My Queftion is plain enough, for fince there are fo many Philofophers, who are Followers of *Plato*, *Ariftotle*, *Antifthenes*, and your Predeceffors *Chryfippus*, *Zeno*, and others, I ask which of all thofe you have believ'd before the reft, and which, of all the above-mention'd Seats you have chofen to follow the Study of *Philofophy*. Has *Apollo* made you, as he did *Chærephon*, to embrace the Doctrine of the *Stoicks*, by telling you they are the beft of all others? For he ufes to exhort one to one fort of *Philofophy*, and another to another, whilft (I fuppofe) he thinks *Philofophy* alike neceffary to them all.

Hermo. But, *Lucian*, I never ask'd the God any fuch Queftions

Lucian. What then, did you think this Affair not of Importance enough to confult the Gods about, or did you believe your felf capable enough of chufing what was
beft

beft for you, without the Advice of a
Deity ?

Hermo. Truly, fo I thought.

Lucian. Therefore, firft of all, fhow me
how I may at the very beginning difcern,
which is the beft and trueft *Philofophy,* and
which above all others a Man ought to
chufe.

Hermo I'll tell you how; that Sect
which I faw had the moft Followers, I im
mediately judg'd to be the beft.

Lucian. Which then was the moft numerous Tribe, that of the *Epicureans, Plato-*
nifts, or *Peripateticks?* For you have reckon'd them all, as if you had been polling,
or taking their Votes

Hermo. I did not count them, I only
went by guefs.

Lucian. Why then you do not inftruct,
but would rather impofe upon me, if you
conceal the truth, and tell me you judged
both by number and by guefs.

Hermo. Not only that, *Lucian,* but I
heard from every Body, that the *Epicu-*
reans minded nothing but to live voluptuouf-
ly, that the *Peripateticks* were great lovers
of Riches, and very much addicted to
wrangling, and alfo, that the *Platonifts*
were proud and vain-glorious ; but for the
Stoicks, many agreed, they were a manly
fort of People, who know every thing,
and that he only who follow'd their Steps,
was Rich, a King, had Wifdom, and at
once all things that were defirable.

Lucian. To be fure other People gave
you this account of them, for you would

not have believ'd them if they praised themselves.

Hermo. You say true, but it was others told me.

Lucian. 'Tis probable those, who were of a contrary Opinion did not tell you, by those, I mean such as were already engag'd in other Doctrines

Hermo No

Lucian. Were they then unskilful, ignorant People who told you so?

Hermo. Yes

Lucian. Do but see again how unfairly you deal with me, and how you disguise the Truth. Sure you think you have to do with a Fool, to make me believe that *Hermotimus,* a Man of such a consummate Prudence, and forty years old, should so far pin his Faith concerning Philosophers and Philosophy it self upon the opinion of ignorant People, as to be by them directed in the choice of the best Sect When you tell me this, I can't believe you.

Hermo But know, *Lucian,* that I have not only given faith to others in this case, but also to my self. For I observed them always to walk with a decent Gravity, to be frugally clad, meditating continually, their Aspect coarse and homely, for the most part shav'd close, allowing nothing, that was in either extream, of Slovenliness or Luxury, but keeping that middle State which all People hold to be the best.

Lucian. Did you never observe in those things, which I just now told you I had seen your Philosophical Master do? (*viz*)

putting

putting out Money to ufe, violently demanding it back again, arguing with much Heat and Vehemence, and feveral other Tokens they give of the Difpofition of their Mind? Or do you look on all this, as nothing, provided the Habit be plain, the Beard long, and the Hair fhaved clofe to the Head? Wherefore, according to *Hermotimus*, let this be for the future our certain Rule, our Touch-ftone, by which we muft examine thefe things. Thus by the Habit, the Gate, and the Shaving, we are to judge who are beft. But whoever has not all thefe Accomplifhments together with a fevere and contemplative Look, he muft be rejected. But pray take care you don't cheat me again, purely to try whether I can't perceive my felf to be impos'd upon.

Hermo. Why do you fay this?

Luc. Becaufe the Knowledge we may receive from the Habit, is applicable not only to Men, but alfo to Statues, for thofe which *Phidias*, or *Alcamenes*, or a *Myron* have form'd in Imitation of fome beautiful Original are certainly of a neater Habit, and more becoming Drefs, than ours. But if you will argue from fuch things, as thefe, pray what muft a blind Man do, that fhould have a fancy to ftudy Philofophy? How can he diftinguifh who is of the beft Sect, fince he is uncapable of obferving either the Habit, or the Gate?

Hermo. But, Sir, I don't fpeak of the Blind, I have nothing to fay to thofe fort of People.

Lucian. With your pardon (good Sir) in a matter of this Importance, and of so general a use, an Instruction ought to be universal to all Mankind. But since 'tis so, we will if you please, exclude all blind People from the Study of *Philosophy*, because they can't see, (tho' they had need to be thoroughly Philosophers, that they might the better support their Affliction) But tho' a Man have his Eye-sight perfectly good, pray how can he see thro' this external Habit, and be able to distinguish the Qualities of the Mind? What I would say, in short, is this, when you went first to these Men, you were not only in love with their Wisdom, but had your self also a design to edify and grow wiser by their Company.

Hermo. Very true.

Lucian. How then could you by those Tokens you have mention'd, discern which of these Philosophers reason'd right, and which otherwise? For those things are not to be seen, but are in their own Nature so obscure, that they are scarce to be found out, even by a long Converse, by Disputations, or by any such ways. I suppose you have heard in what *Momus* found fault with *Vulcan*, if not, I'll tell you. As the Story goes, there happen'd a Dispute between *Minerva*, *Neptune*, and *Vulcan*, who was the greatest Artist amongst them. *Neptune* made a Bull, *Minerva* built a House, but *Vulcan* framed a Man. Now when it came to *Momus*, whom they had chosen for their Judge, to pass Sentence, he having
                                    consider'd

consider'd every ones Work, (not to mention what Faults he found with the rest)
did very much blame *Vulcan*, for that in
the Breast of his Man he had not made
certain little Doors, which being open'd,
all People might see his most secret
Thoughts and Desires, as also, whether he
lyed or spoke Truth.

But you have Eyes more piercing than
Lynceus himself, who can see so clearly within the Breast, as not only to discover what
we wish, and what we think, but even
which of us is better, and which is worse.

Hermo. Well, *Lucian*, I see you banter me,
but however, I chose by the Gods Direct-
on, nor do I repent my Choice, and that's
enough for me.

Lucian. Prithee, my dear Friend, instruct me in another manner, but do not
despise me, and leave me for ever to herd
with the ignorant Vulgar

Hermo. Why nothing, that I can say will
please you.

Lucian Rather, you will say nothing
that shall please me ; but since I see you so
industriously strive to keep me in Ignorance, and have a sort of envious Jealousy, least I should grow equal to you in
the Study of *Philosophy*, I am resolv'd to try
my self, and find out the surest and most
exact way of tasting and chusing right.
Therefore now pray do you hear me ?

Hermo. That I will with all my heart,
Lucian, for it may be you'll say something
very extraordinary.

Lucian But you muſt not laugh at me, if I ſhould go a little awkardly to work; ſince there is a neceſſity for my doing this, if you know better and will not explain your ſelf more intelligibly.

Let Virtue then be a City (as your Maſter who has been there can tell you) inhabited by none but happy Citizens, ſuch, as are perfectly wiſe, valiant, juſt, temperate, not much inferiour even to the Gods themſelves. Let thoſe Crimes too common amongſt us, as Rapine, Violence, Avarice, &c be not ſo much as heard of in that City, but let every one peaceably execute his Function in the Service of the Republick, and all this not without a great deal of reaſon, ſince thoſe things, which in other Cities cauſe Diſpute, and Seditions, make People lay Snares one for another, are not here to be found; for Pleaſures, Gold, and Honours are not here ſo much regarded, as to make the leaſt Diviſion amongſt them, but have been long ſince baniſhed the City, as things unneceſſary to a civil Society. So they lead an eaſie ſort of a quiet Life, perfectly happy, bleſs'd with good Laws, Equality, Liberty, and whatever elſe is deſirable.

Hermo. Well then, *Lucian,* pray is it not reaſonable, that all People ſhould deſire to become Inhabitants of ſuch a City, without deſponding, either thro' the length of Time, or of the Road, till they can arrive at the wiſhed for Haven, and being enrolled amongſt the number of the Citizens, enjoy all the Rights and Privileges of the Place?

N n

Lucian.

Lucian. By *Jove, Hermotimus,* this is a-
bove all things to be endeavoured, without any other Confideration, nor ought
any one to be here detained, either by an
Affection to his Country, or by the Entrea-
ties of his Children and Relations, but
thofe he muft exhort to go along with him,
whom if he finds either incapable or unwilling, he muft even fhake them off,
and go himfelf to that Seat of perfect
Happinefs, nay, tho' they caught hold of
his Cloak he muft leave it and break from
them, fince you need not fear any Body
fhould exclude you for coming naked, for
heretofore I once heard an old Gentleman
give an account of the Place, and he
prefs'd me very much to accompany him
thither, telling me, that he would go before, and when we came thither wou'd
make me a Freeman of the City, as alfo
give me the Honour of being his Companion, that I might be happy like the reft
of them. But I (fuch was the folly of my
Youth) being not then fifteen years old
would not take his Advice, which, if I
had done, I might perhaps have now been
in the Suburbs, or at the very Gates. Yet,
if I do not miftake, he told us, amongft
other things, that in this City there was
no fuch thing as a Native of the Place, but
that all were Strangers, nay, that in it
there dwelt many barbarians, Slaves,
alfo many little, deformed, and poor People, in fhort, that whofoever pleas'd
might be made free, it being a Law
amongft them, when they beftow the

Freedom of their City, not to have any confideration either for Riches, Habit, Stature, Beauty, Family, or illuftrious Anceftors, fince all thefe things are with them of no account. But he faid, that whoever did pretend to be a Citizen of the Place, muft be a Man of very good Sence, muft be ambitious of all things, that are good and honourable, and muft not fhrink at any fort of Fatigue, or be difcouraged at the many Difficulties, he may meet with in the way, and that when he had once done thefe things, and was arrived at the City, he was then immediately allowed to be a Citizen, and as good as the beft of them, fince better or worfe, noble or ignoble, Bondman or Free, were Names not fo much as heard off amongft them.

Hermo. Well, *Lucian,* you fee I don't trifle away my time, whilft I endeavour to become a Citizen of fo happy a Manfion.

Lucian. 'Tis true, *Hermotimus,* and I love the very fame things, which you do ; nor is there any thing I could fooner wifh to attain ; nay, had that City been near, or eminent, and vifible to all the World, I fhould have been there long fince. If therefore, as you, and the Poet *Hefiod* tell us, 'tis fituate in a very remote Country, we lie under a neceffity of enquiring the way thither, as well as the beft and fureft Guide. Are not you of this Opinion ?

Hermo. How elfe is it poffible for us ever to arrive at it ?

Lucian. Very well, now an innumerable Company of Guides prefent themfelves to

you, and affure you, that they will conduct you the direct way, for there are a-
bundance who pretend themfelves Natives
of this Place, and ply as it were for their
Fare. Again, the ways that they would
perfwade you lead to this City, are many,
various, and quite different, that have no
Correfpondence with each other, for th
feems directly to the Weft, that to the Eaft,
this to the North, and that to the South
This leads you thro' Meadows, green
Herbs, thro' fhady Groves, Springs, and
pleafant Profpects, in which you meet with
no rugged uneafie way. Whilft another
offers you nothing but Rocky, and fcarce
paffable Roads, with the unpleafant Fatigue of being expos'd to the Sun's Heat,
Thirft, Hunger, and great Labour and
Pain Yet thefe Men would perfwade you,
that all thefe various and different way
lead to this one City, tho' they terminate
in contrary Places This it is involves me
in the moft perplexing Doubts For le
me come into which you pleafe, th
Gurde, that waits in the very entrance of
each way, and whofe Affurance merits of
Belief, immediately offers you his Head,
and urges you with a great deal of earneft-
nefs, to chufe his Road, which he affirms
he only knows to be the right, and that the
the reft deviate into erroneous Paths, and
as they never have been there themfelves,
fo they are utterly incapable of conducting
any other thither. The fame I find his
Neighbour affert of his way, and detract
from all others, and fo thro' all the Tribe

T h

This number and diversity of these ways, embarass me extreamly, and fix me in a perpetual Uncertainty, to which nothing contributes more, than the Guides themselves, who oppose each other with the highest Obstinacy, each extolling their own with a thousand extravagant Eulogies. For I am not able to judge which to follow, nor by whose Conduct I shall be sure arrive at this City.

Hermo. But I can deliver you from all this Doubt, for if you follow him that has already been there, you cannot mistake nor lose your way.

Lucian. Whom should I follow? Or the Guides of what Path? For here again recurs the same Doubt, tho' it assume another Form, by passing from things to Men.

Hermo. How so, good *Lucian.*

Lucian. Why here, that Man that has follow'd the Way and Conduct of *Plato* for Example, will praise and extol that above all others; whilst the Follower of *Epicure* will do as much for his Leader, and the way he has gne, and so the rest, thus you would prefer yours *Hermotimus*, for how can it be otherwise?

Hermo. And why not?

Lucian. Why, as yet you have not remov'd my Doubt, being still ignorant which of these Travellers I must believe; for I find e'ry one of 'em, and e'en their Leaders, have try'd one way, which they praise and affirm to be the only Path, that can bring you to that City; but I have no means left me to discover whether he

speaks

speaks Truth, or no. But perhaps I may follow him, that has arriv'd at some end of his Journey, and has it may be, seen some City or other, but I cannot be certain, that this City, which he has seen, is the same, that he ought to have seen, in which you and I have so great a desire to live. As for Example, he was to have gone to *Corinth*, and having mistaken his way, and reach'd *Babylon*, shou'd return, and think that he had seen *Corinth*. For since there are more Cities in the World, than *Corinth*, it cannot be said, that he who has seen a City, must of necessity have seen *Corinth*. And that which gives me the greatest perplexity and doubt is, that I know, that of necessity there is but one true way, as there is but one *Corinth*; and that all other Roads carry us sooner to any Place in the Universe, than to *Corinth*; unless any Man should be so mad and whimsical, as to imagine, that Roads that go directly to *Norway*, or the *Indies*, wou'd yet bring him to *Corinth*?

Hermo. But how is that possible, for those Roads go quite contrary.

Lucian. For which Reason, worthy Sir, there is as much caution to be us'd in the choice of our Way, as Guides. Nor must we presently do what they persuade us, nor go whither soever our Feet wou'd carry us, for by that means we shou'd ignorantly follow the Road, that leads to *Bachtri*, or *Babylon*, not to *Corinth*. Again, it wou'd be very imprudent to trust to Fortune, which might at last convey us to some Port or other, when we hop'd and de-

　　　　　　　　　　　　　　　　　　sire-

figned only the beft. For this may be, and has perhaps been done in fo long a fpace of time   Nor fhould we caft away all, or retain but fmall hopes, the Source of our Induftry, like Men expos'd to Tempeftuous Seas, in a leaky and fhatter'd Veffel ; fince we can neither juftly blame Fortune, if fhooting the Arrow, and cafting the Dart, fhe hit not the white Spot of Tiuth, which is but fingle, and one among a multiplicity of Falfhood and Errors, which even *Homer*'s Archei, whofe Name I think was *Tucei*, cou'd not obtain, when inftead of the Dove, which he aim'd at, he cut the String that ty'd it to the Pole. But, I think we have more reafon to fear, that our random Shot fhou'd pierce a Thoufand other things, fooner than the Maik I have, if I don't deceive my felf, expreffed to you, that there is no fmall Hazaid, if by committing the juftnefs of our Choice to Fortune, we mifs the right, and light by miftake upon one of the devious and erroneous Ways. For whoever his once put himfelf out to Sea, cannot fo eafily return into the Poit, but muft undergo the feveral Fatigues of a ftormy Paffage, which he might by a little forefight have prevented, by taking a view of the Sea before he fet out, and confider'd whether it was then Navigable, and the Wind fair to convey him fafe to *Corinth*, to pafs fuch turbulent Seas, he ought to have chofe the beft Pilot, and a Veffel wellbuilt, and in good Geer.

Hermo. Thefe Cautions, *Lucian*, I confefs wou'd contribute much better to the
fuccefs of his Voyage. But I can affure
you, that when you have try'd and examin'd all, you will not, nay cannot provide your felf with better Guides, and
more skilful Pilots, than the *Stoicks*, and
whenever you defign to arrive at this *Corinth*, you can never compafs it, but by
following them in the Track of *Chryfippus*
and *Zeno*.

Lucian. In this, *Hermotimus*, you tell me
no more, than the reft weu'd do; for thus
wou'd the *Platonift*, *Epicurean*, and the Dif-
ciples of any other Philofpher perfwade
me, that I can never come to *Corinth* but by
the Conduct of each of them. So that I
muft either believe them all to be in the
right, which wou'd be very ridiculous ; or
elfe believe none of 'em, which is much
the fafeft way, till we can find one in
whofe Promifes there is nothing but Truth
But put the cafe, that I now, who am
yet ignorant whom I fhou'd take for a
Guide, fhou'd follow your Party, being
influenc'd by you, my Friend, who yet
are acquainted with no Difcipline but that
of the *Stoicks*, nor ever purfu'd any other
Road ; and fuppofe then that fome one of
the Gods fhou'd reftore to Life, *Plato*, *Pythagoras*, *Ariftotle*, and the reft, who fur-
rounding me, fhou'd each of them find me
guilty of Contempt of them, accufing me
in this manner. What reafon, what Motive prevail'd with you, O *Lucian*, to prefer a fort of upftart, modern Gentlemen,
one

one *Chryſippus* and *Zeno* to us, who have by
ſo much the Advantage of them, in the
hoary and venerable Honours of Antiquity, eſpecially, without either conſulting
us, or making any Experiment of what
we have left in writing for your Inſtructi-
on. Shou'd they thus upbraid me, what
reaſonable Anſwer cou'd I make 'em?
Will it, d'ye think, be enough for me to
alledge, that I truſted my Aquaintance,
and very good Friend, *Hermotimus?* They
would without doubt reply, We know
nothing of this *Hermotimus*, nor he of us,
ſo that there was no Equity in condemning all us, without ſo much, as hearing
what we had to ſay for our ſelves, and
truſting to one Man, who was acquainted
with one only Path of Philoſophy, and
perhaps had no exquiſite knowledge of that.
All Lawgivers have ordain'd another me-
tod to Judges, than to hear only the one
ſide, and deny the other leave to ſay
what they can for their Cauſe; but oblige
'em to hear fairly both Parties, that both
their Pleadings being conſider'd, and thoroughly examin'd, they might, with the
more eaſe, find out and diſtinguiſh the
right from the wrong, and if one Judge
fail in this, the Law empowers them to
appeal from him to ſome other Court,
where he ſhall have a more fair and equal
Hearing. Or ſuppoſe one of them ſhou'd
queſtion me in this manner————Shou'd
any Man among the *Æthiopians*, who had
never been a Foot out of his own Native
Country, nor ever ſeen any Men of our
Colour,

Colour, affirm, among any of his Countrymen, that there were no Men in the World,
white or tawny, but all Black, like them,
d'ye imagine, that he wou'd be believ'd?
Certainly, some one of the graver and
more ancient *Æthiopians* wou'd contradict
him, and say, Thou impudent Fellow,
how cam'st thou by this Knowledge, for
thou haft never travell'd, nor dost thou
know what other Countries and People afford of variety from what thou seest at
Home. Shall we not agree that this Rebuke
is very just and reasonable? What think
you *Hermotimus* of it?

Hermo. I am of the same Opinion, and
think the old Gentleman wou'd very reasonably reprimand so bold an Affertor.

Lucian. I agree with you too; but I fear
you'll scarce be of my Opinion in the consequence, which I assure you I firmly believe.

Hermo. And pray, Sir, what is that?

Lucian. Why thus wou'd he pursue his
Discourse——There is as little Reason and
Justice in proposing to us any one Man, as
your Friend *Hermotimus* by Name, who is
skill'd in the *Stoick* Discipline only, and
who never ventured abroad from their
Precepts, to the *Platonic* Academy, to *Epicure*, or in short, to any other of the Philosophers, so that he must be look'd on as
a vain, rash Man, to assert, that no other
Sect taught any thing so delightful or true,
as the Doctrines of the *Stoicks*, when he is
ignorant of all but what they teach themselves, and never has been a step out of his

O 2

own Native *Æthiopia*. What wou'd you have me anſwer him?

Hermo. Why this is evident Truth—— That 'tis true we learn the Precepts of the *Stoicks*, but are not ignorant of what others teach; for our Maſter in his Lecture propoſes and refutes them.

Lucian. Well, and d'ye think this a ſufficient Anſwer to Silence the *Platoniſts*, *Epicureans*, and the reſt. Don't you rather expect they ſhou'd burſt out into a Laughter, and cry to me, Why *Lucian*, is not your Friend and Companion *Hermotimus*, a pleaſant ſort of a Gentleman, to think it reaſonable to believe our Adverſaries Account of Affairs, and take our Doctrines as they are pleas'd to repreſent 'em, either thro' Ignorance or Deſign. Shou'd we ſee a Wreſtler ſtrugling with the Wind, and toſſing his Legs about in the Air, and boxing with his Fiſts, as if he was engaging his Adverſary, ſhou'd we from thence immediately conclude, that he was the Cock of the Ring, and bore the Bell away from all the reſt? Or ſhou'd we not rather think this was a cheap and ſafe Oſtentation of his Force, without an Opponent, and that the Victory ſhou'd not be given on his ſide, till he had indeed abſolutely vanquiſh'd his Adverſary himſelf? In like manner, *Hermotimus* ought not to think his Maſters Conquerors, for fighting againſt Shadows, and by their Contempt or Refutation of our Opinions in our Abſence, or that they are with ſo little difficulty to be refuted, for that is like the little Houſe

buſlt

built by Boys with the Cards, which they
themselves with more ease through down,
or by *Jove*, like those, who make a large
thin Straw But, and fix it into the Ground
very near them, and when they shoot into
and transfix it Huzza, as if they had perform'd some mighty Deed.   But your *Per-
fian* and *Scythian* Archers take another
Course; but shoot whilst themselves are in
Motion on Horseback, nor will they have
the Mark they aim at fix'd in a place, and
wait, as it were for the Arrow to pierce it,
but they let fly at a Mark, in motion, as
well as themselves, and one, that shall endeavour, as much as possible to escape their
Shot   For they generally shoot at wild
Beasts, and often at Birds on the Wing,
or if ever they shoot at a Butt, they transfix a solid piece of Timber, or a Shield
made of raw Bull-Hides, not Bull-Rush-
es; and from thence assure themselves,
that their Arrows will hereafter penetrate
their Enemies Coats of Armour.   Therefore, let me desire you in our Name, to
tell your *Hermotimus*, that his Masters set
up those flight Marks of Straw to shoot at,
and then wou'd persuade 'em, that they
have vanquish'd armed Men; and that
they darted their Arrows into our Pictures,
which having overcome, as they well
might, they imagine they have destroy'd
us.   But each of us may say to them, as
Achilles did of *Hector*————*The very sight
of my Helmet frights 'em.*

And this they might all say one after a-
nother.   And *Plato* in all likelihood, wou'd
tell me one adventure of many that happen'd in *Sicily*, for 'tis said, that *Gelon* the
Tyrant of *Syracusa* had   stinking Breath,
which he was a long time ignorant of, because none of his Subjects durst tell the
King of such a Defect, till having an In-
trigue with a Foreign Lady, she ventur'd
to inform him of it, upon which he went
to his Wife in a great Rage, that she, whose
Duty it chiefly was, had not let him know
it   But she pleaded, that never having
had to do with any other Man, nor so
much as discours'd with 'em near enough,
her Ignorance ought to excuse her, if she
thought that all Mens Breath had the same
Smell; thus *Hermotimus*, who had never
had an Intimacy with any but the *Stoicks*,
says *Plato*, is ignorant of the sweetness of
others Breaths?

Thus much I shou'd hear from *Chrysippus*,
and more too, shou'd I follow any of *Plato*'s Disciples, without examining and hearing his Doctrines   In short, I shall sum up
the whole difficulty in one word; that
since we're uncertain which Sect of the
Philosophers is in the right, we ought to
make choice of none of 'em, since that
wou'd be to affront the rest.

Hermo   For God's sake, *Lucian*, let us
have no more of *Plato*, *Aristotle*, *Epicure*,
or the rest of 'em, nor can I presume to
contend with them.   But let us, I mean
you and I, examine whether the subject
matter of Philosophy be what I affirm or
not.

not But what occasion have we to fetch
the *Æthiopians*, or the wise *Gelon* into
our Discourse?

Lucian. Nay, if they seem nothing to
our purpose, e'en let 'em go say I, and
pray now take your turn of speaking,
since you now look as if you wou'd offer
something of Moment, and to the purpose.

Hermo. I am of Opinion, that a Man
may gather the Truth from the Doctrine
of the *Stoicks* alone, tho' he has not taken
the Pains to learn the Precepts of the rest
of the Philosphers. For consider, should
any one tell you that two times two make
four, must you needs run about to all the
Arithmeticians, to know if any of them
maintain, that twice two made five or seven? Wou'd you not rather, without any
doubt or delay give your Assent to the
Position, as an evident Truth?

Lucian. Without doubt, *Hermotimus*

Hermo. Very good, Sir, why therefore
do you think that a Man may not acqui-
esce in those Truths which he hears in the
Schools of the *Stoicks*, without any need of
consulting others, since he's satisfy'd, that
four can never be five, tho' a thousand *Plato's*, and *Pythagoras* shou'd affirm it.

Lucian. You're quite wide of the matter
good *Hermotimus*, for you endeavour to
make a parallel betwixt Doubts and Cer-
tainties, which have a wonderful Difference and Distinction; else what is't you
say? For have you ever met with any of
those other Philosophers, asserting that

two times two makes Seven or Eleven?

Hermo Not I indeed, for nothing but a Madman cou'd ever make more, than four of 'em.

Lucian. But have you ever in your Life (I beg you good Sir to do me the Favour, to endeavour to tell me the Truth) find a *Stoick* and *Epicurean* that did not disagree in their Principles and End?

Hermo. Never.

Lucian. I beg you, Sir, be not so ungenerous to impose on your good Friend; for when we are enquiring whose Philosophy proposes to us the Truth, you immediately take it as granted in favour of the *Stoicks*, telling me, That these are the Men who propose Truths, as evident as twice two makes four; when all the while 'tis that very point that is controverted and uncertain; for the *Epicureans* and *Platonists* may as well affirm, that they only make that just Number of twice two, and that the *Stoicks* would have them to be seven or five. Do you not perceive, that this is the case, when you affert, that the *Summum Bonum* is purely and simply Virtue, when they add Pleasure to it; You affirm, that all things are Corporeal; and *Plato* holds that there are some Things, in Nature that are incorporeal? But as I said, comprizing the question in one Point, that you attribute that, as undeniable, and peculiarly to the *Stoicks* alone, when others put in as loud a Claim to it as they, and positively declare, that it belongs to them only:

wi

and in this particular I think is the chief, and most important ufe of Judgment requir'd, for if it were evident to all the World, that the *Stoicks* alone affirmed, that twice two made four, all other Pretenders to it wou'd be immediately put to Silence, but as long as e'ery one contends for this very point, they muft all be heard, or it will be very evident, that we are very partial in our Judgment.

Hermo. You feem not, *Lucian*, to apprehend what I wou'd fay.

Lucian. You muft then fpeak plainer, if you fay, or mean otherwife, than I have taken it.

Hermo I'll foon convince you of what I intend, fuppofe then, for Explanation of the matter, that two Men went into the Temple of *Efculapius*, or *Bacchus*, and during their being there, there is a facred Goblet of the Temple loft, both are to be fearch'd, to find if either of 'em has it about him.

Lucian. Right Sir.

Hermo. One of them muft have it?

Lucian. Without doubt, for 'tis loft you fuppofe.

Hermo. But if you find it on the firft, there is no need of fearching the other, for 'tis evident that he has it not.

Lucian. Very right, Sir.

Hermo. Again, if it is not found on the firft, then there is no need of fearching the other, for he muft have it.

Lucian. Very well.

Hermo. **Thus** we who have formed the Sacred Goblet among the *Stoicks*, will not be at the trouble of fearching elfe-where, having already in our Poffeffion, what we fought for; for to what end fhou'd we be at the expence of all that Supererrogatory Pains.

Lucian. To none at all, certainly; if you have found it, and can know when you have found it, that it is that very Numerical Goblet, that was loft. But *firft*, my good Friend, in this Cafe your parallel won't hold, for there were more, than two that entred the Temple, fo that there is no Confequence to be drawn from the firft's not having the Goblet, that the next muft have it, for there are Numbers prefent. *Secondly*, 'tis uncertain what it is that is loft, that is, whether it be a Goblet, or Cup, or a Crown; for e'ery Prieft (and there are many of them) is of a different Mind, fome will have it one thing, others another; nay, they do not agree of what Materials 'twas made, for one fays 'twas Brafs, another of Silver, athird of Gold, a fourth of Tin, and fo on, fo that there's an abfolute neceffity to fearch all the Company, if you intend to find the loft Goods; and tho' you find on the firft a golden Goblet, yet you muft go on and examine the reft.

Hermo, Why fo?

Lucian, Becaufe 'tis not agreed whether 'tis a Goblet, or no, that is left, but were that granted by all fides, yet they don't all fay 'tis a *golden* Goblet. Nay farther, it 'twere evident that 'twas a golden Goblet that was loft, and you had found fuch a one in the firft; yet that fhou'd not ftop your fearch of the reft; becaufe you are not certain whether that be it, which belongs to the God, for there are more Golden Goblets, than one.

Hermo. True.

Lucian. You muft therefore fearch the whole Company, and having placed all their Goblets together, you may guefs which of 'em is the Sacred Offering. For hence will arife a very perplexing Doubt, fince e'ery one of the Company has fomething about 'em, one a Beaker, another a Goblet, a third a Crown, *&c.* This has one of Brafs, a fecond of Gold, and a third of Silver. Nor do we yet difcover whether any, or which of them is the Sacred Veffel of the Gods. So that yet you are to feek which of 'em is the Sacrilegious Perfon, fince tho' all their things were alike, you cou'd not tell which had ftoln the Offering from the Temple, for all thefe things may belong to private Perfons; but I fuppofe one caufe of this Difficulty, is the want of an Infcription on the loft Goblet, for if we fuppofe, that it had either the Name of the Votary that offer'd it, or the God to whom it was made an Offering we fhou'd have much lefs Pains in finding out the Theft, and having found that with the Infcription, we fhou'd have no need of fearching the reft of the Company ; fuppofe *Hermotimus,* you have feen the Wreftling Games often before this time

He 2

Hermotimus. You're in the right, Sir, for I have often, and in many Places seen 'em.

Lucian And have you never sat near the Judges of the Games?

Hermo. Yes, lately at the *Olympian* I sate at the Left Hand of the Judges, when *Evandra,* the Son of *Eleus,* took me a convenient Place for my seeing the Sight, for I had a mind to observe all that the Judges did.

Lucian. Well, and d'ye know the Method they take, when they appoint, by Lot, who shall wrestle with one another?

Hermo. I know it very well

Lucian You therefore, who have seen it so near, can give the best Account of it

Hermo. Of old, when *Hercules* was Judge, they took Laurel Leaves.]

Lucian. Tell not me, *Hermotimus,* of those ancient matters, but what you your self saw done.

Hermo There was placed in the midst of 'em a Silver Urn, Sacred to the God, into which they put little Lots, with Letters inscrib'd on 'em, each, as big, as a Bean Each two were mark'd with the same Letter as *Alpha* for Example, on two, *Beta* on two more; *Gamma* on two others, and so thro' the whole Alphabet, if the Number of Wrestlers were great; then the Wrestlers approach'd the Urn, and having invok'd *Jupiter,* each singly pats in his Hand, and draws his Lot, another succeeds him, till they were all drawn; and by each of them stands a Fellow, that bears a Whip in his Hand, to hinder him from

reading

reading the Letter he had drawn. But now, when they are all drawn, the Prieſt of the God of thoſe Games, or one of the Judges (for I don't remember well that particular) going round, as they ſtand in a Ring, ſees what Letter each of 'em has drawn, and ſo appoints them that have the ſame Letter, to Wreſtle, or Box with each other   This is the Method, if the Wreſtlers are even in Number, as four, ſix, eight, or twelve; but if they are odd, as five, ſeven, or nine, then there's one Lot put in with one Letter, that has none to anſwer it, and whoever draws it, wait to encounter the Victor; nor is it a ſmall Advantage and Happineſs to that Wreſtler that gets it, ſince he is to engage freſh and robuſt, with thoſe, that are fatigu'd, and tyr'd already

    Lucian Enough——for this is what I chiefly drove at. Well, here are nine Wreſtlers, who have now each drawn a Lot. Now do you go round 'em (for of a Spectator I make you a Judge, and view the Letters, I ſuppoſe you will not be able to tell the Man, that is to engage the Conqueror, till you have coupl'd the reſt, and found the odd Letter

    Hermo How ſay you, *Lucian*.

    Lucian I ſay, that you cannot immediately find out that Letter, that marks or the Wreſtler that is to engage him, that worſts the reſt, or if at firſt you light on that Letter, you cannot diſtinguiſh, or know for certain, that 'tis that, which we ſeek, for before you ſee 'em all, know not whether it be *Cappa*, or *My*, or *Iota*: But when you've found *Alpha*, you go on till you find another *Alpha*, and then you fet them together for the Ring; thus when you've found *Beta*, you feek another *Beta* for its Opponent, and thus you do with all, till he is left, who has got the folitary Letter without a Fellow.

Hermo. But what wou'd you do if you met with this folitary Letter at firft, or in the fecond place?

Lucian. Who I? Nothing at all; but I wou'd know of you, that are now conftituted the Juge, what wou'd you do? whether you wou'd immediately decide the matter, and fix him, that draws that Letter for the Opponent of the Victor, or going round the Ring, examine if you cou'd find in any of their Hands, a Letter, that did anfwer it, which you can't tell, unlefs you look on all their Lots.

Hermo. But in Nine at leaft, I fhou'd eafily diftinguifh the odd one, for if the firft or fecond had *Epfilon*, he muft be the Man.

Lucian. How fo, *Hermotimus*?

Hermo. Why thus——Two of 'em have the Letter *Alpha*, two *Beta*, two have *Gamma*, and the other two *Delta*, and thus Eight Wreftlers have drawn four Letters, fo that there only now remains the Letter *Epfilon*, and who ever has that, muft be the frefh Man, to engage the Vanquifher of the reft

Lucian. Well, I know which I shall do, *Hermotimus*, praise the singular Industry, and Perspicatiousness of your Wit, or make those Objections I think of Moment to what you have said?

Hermo. Oh Sir, your Objections by all means, for I long to know of consequence what you have to object to what I have advanc'd

Lucian. You have by the order of the Letters, that denote the fresh Man, that is to attack the conquering Wrestler, and I confess this to be the Method in the *Olympick* Games. But suppose we confusedly take five Letters out of the Alphabet, as *Chi, Sigma, Zeta, Ro, Cappa,* and *Theta,* and write four of 'em on the eight Lots, and *Zeta* for the odd one; how wou'd you without a Scrutiny thro' all, find that to be the odd Letter, and that by consequence the greatest Advantage to him that draws on it if the first you look'd on had drawn *Zeta* for here the order of the Letter wou'd not help you.

Hermo. You ask a Question of some difficulty, *Lucian*

Lucian. Well, let us consider this after another manner; suppose we shou'd not inscribe the Letters of our Alphabet, but certain Characters, like the *Egyptian* Hieroglyphicks, as Mens Bodies, with the Heads of Dogs, or Lyons? Or if we use those exotick Figures alone, and make the Figures of Men on two of 'em, on Horse on two more, Cocks on other two, and on the last two Dogs; but upon the Ninth the

Picture of a Lyon, which muſt denote the
Man that is to contend with the Victor; if
you meet with that Lot at firſt, which has
the Lion, how can you tell for certain that
this is the odd, till you have examined all
the reſt, to ſee whether any other has a Fellow to it or no.

Hermo. To this I can anſwer not one
Word.

Lucian. Not a Word, I'm ſure that
bears any plauſible Appearance of an
Anſwer So that if we will find out him,
that ſtole the holy Viol, or a ſure Guide to
that *Corinth* Virtue mentioned, we muſt of
neceſſity examine them all, and with a
nice and ſevere Scrutiny, enquire and
ſearch into 'em all; nor after we have done
all this, we ſhall ſcarce be able to fear the
Truth at laſt. But if there be any Man
that I wou'd truſt in Matters of Philoſophy, he muſt be one, who thoroughly
knows every Sect, and all things, that relate to 'em, for all other Adviſers in this
Affair, are but Triflers, nor wou'd I even
credit him, if he were ignorant but of one,
for that might happen to be the beſt of all;
for ſhou'd any Man bring me a very handſome Man, and aſſure me, that he was the
moſt beautiful Youth in the Univerſe, I
ſhould never believe him, unleſs I knew
he had ſeen all the Men in the World. For
tho' this might be a very handſome Man,
yet unleſs he had ſeen all others, he cannot
juſtly affirm him to be the moſt handſome:
And as for us, we're enquiring not for one,
that has his ſhare of Beauty, but him, that

has

has the moft, which if we mifs, we have labour'd to no purpofe ; for we fhall not be fatisfy'd to have found any one handfome Man, but we feek him, who has all that Symetry of Parts, and Elegance of Form and Shape, which compofes that Sov'reign Beauty, which is but one, and fupream.

Hermo. You are in the right, *Lucian.*

Lucian. Have you therefore any one to propofe to me, that has experienc'd any fort of Philofophy, who knows all the Precepts of *Pythagoras, Plato, Ariftotle, Chryfippus, Epicurus,* and the reft ; in fhort, who has from all of 'em found out a way, which by his Experience and ftudious Obfervation he has prov'd, and found to be the only true and direct Path, that leads to Sov'reign Happinefs ; for cou'd we find out any fuch Man, moft of our Difficulties would be remov'd.

Hermo. 'Tis no eafy matter to find fuch a Man.

Lucian. What can we do then, *Hermotimus?* We muft not defpair, becaufe we cannot yet meet with any fuch Guide. Is it not more fafe for us, from the beginning of our Studies, to perufe and thoroughly examine all, that each of the feveral Sects advance ?

Hermo. That indeed feems the Confequence of your Argument, unlefs what you faid before oppofe it, *viz.* that he, that has once left the Port, and committed himfelf to the open Sea, and hoifted all his Sail, cannot fo eafily recover the Harbour, for how

how can he travel every way, who will be detain'd in the firft he enters.

Lucian. I fhall make that a little more plain. We fhall imitate that Fable of *Thefeus*, and having gain'd a Clew from *Ariadne*, that will eafily bring us out of any Labarinth we fhall enter.

Hermo. But who fhall be our *Ariadne* ? or where fhall we get this Clew of Thred.

Lucian. Oh never defpair, my good Friend, for if I miftake not, I have found one, which will lead us out of thefe perplexing Turnings.

Hermo. And what is that ?

Lucian. Nay, 'tis nothing of my own, but a Saying of one of the wife Men, *Be fober and diffident* ; for if we were not over credulous, and believ'd not all that we heard, but like Judges, gave each fide the liberty of fpeaking, we fhou'd perhaps eafily get out of thefe Labarinths

Hermo. You are in the right, my Friend *Lucian*, let us therefore purfue this courfe.

Lucian. Agreed,——but whom fhall we near firft, or is that a matter of Confequence, if we begin but with any one of 'em, as with *Pythagoras* for Example, if it be his luck to chance firft ? How much Time muft we expend in the Learning his Doctrines ? I bate thofe Years of Silence

Hermo. I believe with them, about five and thirty years will do, without 'em about twenty.

Lucian. Well, well, fuppofe this to be fo, then we muft allow as many to *Plato*, and after him, no fewer to *Ariftotle*.

Hermo.

Hermo. Not a Day lefs.

Lucian. I fhall not any more afk you how many *Chryfippus* requires, fince you have already told me, that forty will fcarce fuffice.

Hermo. Very true.

Lucian. Then to *Epicurus,* and the reft I name no more, becaufe you may obferve, that there are abundance of *Stoicks*, *Platonifts*, *Epicureans*, fourfcore years of Age, who all agree in this, that neither of them know all the Rules of his own Sect fo perfectly to be infallible in their Precepts. But did they not confefs this Ignorance, yet *Plato, Chryfippus, Ariftotle,* and before this, *Socrates* (a Man of no lefs excellence than them) openly profefs'd before all the World, that he was fo far from knowing all things, that he knew nothing, only this, that *he did know nothing* But in fhort, let us now fumm them up We allow'd *Pythagoras* twenty years, *Plato* as many, and fo to the reft, fo that, fuppofe only ten Sects, what wou'd the Summ total of them be ?

Hermo. More than two hundred.

Lucian. Shall we then fubract the fourth Part, fo that fifteen years, or even ten be only allow'd to each ?

Hermo You may do in that as you think fit, but I find already, that very few will never be able to run through all the Sects though he fhould apply his firft Studies to em.

I 4

Lucian. If it be so, *Hermotimus*, what shall a Man do ? must we destroy our own Maxim we have already establish'd, that *chuse the best, we must know all,* and that he who light on the best by any other means, owes his Advantage to Fortune, not Judgment. Was not this the sum of our Discourse ?

Hermo. Ev'n so, *Lucian.*

Lucian. Then 'tis absolutely necessary, that our Life should be of a very long and lasting Date, if we must make Choice of the best Philosophy, by trying e'ery Sect, and arrive by our Knowledge of it, to the *Summum Bonum,* or the Happiness we seek But before we can do this, we shall dance in the dark, as they say, stumbling on what-ever we find, and imagine, by our Ignorance of the Truth, that the first thing that offers it self to us, is that which we were in pursuit of; and if by an extraordinary hit of Fortune we chance to find it in some Place or other, we have no certainty, that it is what we were in search of; for there are many things, that are like these, and which all affirm themselves to be that one Truth we follow.

Hermo. I know not, *Lucian,* how probable what you say is, but I'm very sure, to confess the Truth, your Arguments, and too nice Disquisitions in what requires 'em not, give me no small Pain Nay, perhaps I came abroad with an unlucky Omen, in meeting with you, who have thrown me from the very Borders of Hope, into the Abbyss of Despair, by making appear the
impossibility

impossibility of my finding out the Truth, when so many years are requir'd to the effecting.

Lucian. You have much more reason to quarrel with your Father *Menecrates*, and your Mother (by what Name soever dignify'd, for that I don't know) or rather indeed with Nature, that has not given you the Age, and numerous years of *Tithonus*, but extends not the Life of Man beyond an hundred years at the longest. But as for me, I have done no more, than by your help, and weighing the matter with you, found those Consequences of our Disquisitions.

Hermo. No, no,——you are always a Scoffer, and I know not for what reason you hate Philosophy, and ridicule the Professors of it.

Lucian. You that are wise, *Hermotimus*, as your Master and you, can give a better Account of *Truth*. But for my part, all that I know of her is, that she is not very pleasant and easy, but generally obscur'd with Falsity, which being the more plausible, proves the more agreeable Company. But Truth, not conscious to her self of any Blemish, takes a great deal of Liberty in her Discourse with Mankind, and by that means becomes very troublesome and unwelcome to 'em. And see you your self are a proof of this, for you're angry with me, who having with you found out the Truth of these things, we enquir'd about, let you see, how difficult it was to discover those things, which we both meru-

ally had an extraordinary Paffion for. Which
Ufage, is fully as unreafonable, as if, when
I perceived you in love with a Statue, and
imagining you cou'd enjoy it, fince you
believ'd it human, I fhou'd, perceiving
your Error, and finding it to be Stone, or
Brafs, out of pure good-Will, or Friendfhip,
let you know, that what you were fo fond
of, was incapable of giving you Satisfaction by poffeffion, you fhou'd immediately
be angry with me for undeceiving you,
and not permitting you to be abfurdly impos'd on, by an Appearance, to hope what
cou'd not be hop'd, or ever obtain'd.

Hermo. You therefore affert, that we
ought not to apply our felves to Philofophy,
but give our felves up to Sloath in a private Life, without any Figure?

Lucian. Where did you hear me affert
any fuch matter? For I never faid, that we
ought not to apply our felves to Philofophy. But fince we are to do fo, and that
there are many and various Paths, each of
which pretends to be the right, I only affirmed, that we ought to ufe an extream
Caution in the choice of that Way. For I
thought, we cou'd not make choice of the
beft, out of many, unlefs I've try'd all
Upon which we found this Tryal would
be of a great length, and take up a prodigious fpace of time. This was my Opinion, but pray, Sir, what think you of the
matter? For I fhall demand of you again,
whether you wou'd take up with the firft
Guide you meet to follow him through
the Study of Philofophy?

Hermo.

Hermo. What farther Answer can I make you, who assert, that none can make a true Judgment of the matter, unless he can live the Age of a Phænix, and try and examine all the several Opinions of the World; and who think, that we ought not to credit those, who having experienc'd it themselves, recommend it to us, with their Assurances of its Truth.

Lucian. Who are those numerous Gentlemen, I pray, whom you pretend, by their Experience of all, are capable of giving a true Judgment; find me but one such, and I'm satisfy'd, without seeking after a greater Number. But if you urge the unlearned, 'tis not their Multitude, that shall engage my Belief, till they make it appear, that they either know nothing, or else, that they alone, of all the rest, are skill'd in these things.

Hermo. You alone therefore, have found out the Truth, and all others, that have given themselves to the Study of Philosophy, are Fools?

Lucian. You accuse me of an Arrogance I'm not guilty of *Hermotimus,* in saying, that I prefer my self to all others, and you have forgot what I said, but now, when I, with more earnestness, than any else, asserted, that I knew not the Truth, but own'd, that we were all ignorant of it.

Hermo. Nay, I confess, *Lucian,* that it seems agreeable enough to Reason, that we shou'd have recourse to all, and examine all their Doctrines, and that there is no other way of chusing the best. But then 'tis ftrangely ridiculous to oblige us to fpend fo many Years in our Examination of each, as if we might not know the whole by fome little Sample of their Precepts; this being fo evident to me, I can't ever fuppofe fo tedious a Scrutiny at all neceffary. There goes a Report of a certain Statuary: If I miftake not, it was *Phidias*, who by feeing a Lyon's Nail, drew thence the Proportion of the whole Beaft; and fhould any Man fhow you only the Hand of a Man, with the reft of his Body covered from your Sight, you wou'd have no doubt but that, which was hid, was the Body of a Man, and of no other Creature, altho' you did not fee the whole Body; thus a little part of the day, is fufficient to run over the Heads of all they teach; nor is this tedious Enquiry fo abfolutely neceffary to our choice of that which is beft; but we may form our Judgment from thofe heads I've inftanc'd.

Lucian. Alas! *Hermotimus*, how weak are the Conclufions you wou'd make, when you wou'd have us know the whole only from a part, fo contrary to the known Maxim, receiv'd by e'ery one, that is, *He that knows the whole, knows the Parts, but he that knows only a part, does not know the whole.* Pray anfwer me this, had *Phidias* known it to be a Lyon's Nail, if he had never before feen a whole Lyon? Or cou'd you from the firft fight of a Man's Hand, have known it to've been a Mans, if you had never before feen a Man? Why are you filent? Wou'd you have me give no Anfwer to the

purpofe

purpofe, fince you can't ? Why, 'tis ten
to one but *Phidias* is difappointed in this
intended Lyon. For your Inftance holds
no proportion to the thing in hand : Or in
what does their Likenefs confift, for neither you nor *Phidias* had any other means
of knowing the Parts, but by the Fore-
knowledge of the *Whole*, I mean in your
Inftances of the *Man* and *Lyon.* Thus alfo in Philofophy, as in the Sky for Example, how can you underftand the Whole
by a Part ? Or how can you demonftrate that
the Doctrines that contain that Virtue they
propofe ? For you know not the feveral
Parts that compofe their Syftem. Then
as for your Affertion, that a little part of
of one day is fufficient to run over the
Heads of all Philofophy ; 'tis true, we may
eafily demonftrate, that we may without
much difficulty confider, what Principles
and Ends of things they propofe, their
Opinions of the Gods, and of the Soul,
who of 'em are for making Pleafure their
Summum Bonum and fupream Happinefs,
others *Virtue,* and fo on through the reft ,
but pray a little more ferioufly reflect,
whether you will not only have need of
your little part of one day, but many
whole days to find out who of 'em are in
the right , or to what purpofe have each of
thefe Sects written a hundred and a thoufand Volumes a-piece ? but to demonftrate
the Truth of thofe very few things, which
you would have fo eafily underftood. Thus
you find, you muft either have a Prieft to
chufe that which is beft for you, unlef
you

you admit that difquifition I propofe, that when you have perus'd all and every one of 'em entirely, you may make a judicious Election. I confefs it wou'd indeed be a very compendious method to procure a Prieft, and offer a Sacrifice at e'ery particular Head, as 'tis read, for then the God, by difcovering the beft and moft eligible in the facred Liver, wou'd free you from an infinite deal of pains and trouble, but if you pleafe, I'll tell you a more compendious way than this, and of lefs expence, in which you fhall not be oblig'd to purchafe, at a vaft price, any of the tribe of the Priefts to affift you, take the Names of the feveral fects of Philofophy, and write 'em on feveral pieces of Paper, and put 'em all into an Urn, that done, take a young Boy, both whofe Parents are living, and make him draw the firft, that comes to his Hands, and what ever it be, make choice of that fect for ever after

Hermo. This is fcurrilous, nor can it be the natural Product of your Nature, *Lucian.* But pray tell me, have you bought any Wine your felf?

Lucian. O, very often, Sir

Hermo. And did you trouble your felf to run to e'ery Tavern in the Town to tafte, compare, and examine all their Wines?

Lucian. O, Sir, by no means.

Hermo. And yet I fuppofe you wou'd willingly have the beft.

Lucian. Yes, by *Jove*, wou'd I.

Hermo. And yet you cou'd tell by that

little

little tafte that you drank, how good the whole Veflel was.

Lucian. Without doubt.

Hermo. But if you fhould go to the Vintners, and fay, *Gentlemen, I want to buy half a dozen Flasks of Wine, pray therefore, let me drink your Cellar dry for a tafte, that I may, n I n I've drank all, know where to purchafe the l i' Wine :* Shou'd you harangue 'em in th , manner, don't you think they wou'd laugh at you, or on your more earneft preffing, wafh your hot Head with a Bucket of cool Water, into your fober fenfes again ?

Lucian. Without doubt I fhould richly defeeve it

Hermo. This fame thing will hold in Philofophy , where is the need of drinking of whole Hogfhead, when a Glafs or two will inform the Palate as well, what the whole Veflel is.

Lucian. How flippery a Spark you have nown, *Hermotimus,* that you may get out of my Hands, and yet you have gain'd but little advantage by it, for when you think your felf efcap'd, you fall into the fame Ne again.

Hermo Your meaning, good Sir, W fay you fo ?

Lucian Becaufe you compare Wine, thing very well known to all People, with what has no parts or likenefs to it, and which all Men doubt as of things that are obfcure and uncertain , nor can I imagine how you'll find any one thing in which Wine and Philofophy agree, but this alone, that the Philofophers give us Precepts as the Vintners Wine, by mixing, adulterating and bad meafure. But let us confider what you fay, as you have laid it down. You tell me that the Wine that's in the Hogfhead is all the fame, nor is there any abfurdity in that farther than that by drinking never fo little, one may know what the whole is. Thus far you're in the right, but then confider, does Philofophy and Philofophers, as your Mafter, for example, propofe to you the fame things, and e'ery day treat of the fame matters, or e'ery day furnifh him with new difcourfe on different fubjects? For 'tis granted, my Friend, that the fubjects are various and many. But do you not ftill perfift in hearing, as you ought indeed, wandring to and fro like *Ulyffes*, whereas, if he always faid the fame things, wou'd it have been fufficient for you to've heard him but once.

Hermo. Why not?

Lucian. How therefore, fince he daily produces fomething new, cou'd you, by the firft draught, know all that he had to fay, nor like Wine, was he always the fame, fo that unlefs you had drank of the whole Veffel, you cou'd not have gotten your load, for the God of Philofophy feems plainly to have plac'd the *fummum bonum* in the bottom under the very Lees, fo that you muft drink it off to the laft drop, or you'll never come to that heavenly draught, after which you feem thus long to thirft for with fo great a vehemence. Again do you imagine Philofophy to be fo potent a Li-

quor

quoi, that the tafting the leaft drop of it, is
enough to give you immediately, the very
heighth and zenith of Wifdom ; as the Story of the Delphic Prophetefs, who as foon
as fhe had drank of the facred River, immediately, full of the God, gave out Oracles
to thofe, who came to confult her.   But 'tis
very probable that our Affair is not of this
Nature, which made you but now, when
you   had   drank almoft half the Veflel
oil, fay, that you had but as yet begun.   So
that I believe you'll find Philofophy rather
like this I fhall now maintain, I'll yet keep
the Veflel and the Chapmen to difpofe of it,
but inftead of Wine, fill it with all forts of
Seeds, larger and larger , Wheat on top,
Beans under that, then Meflin under that,
then Vetches, Lentils, and fo on, now
you come to buy fome Seed, the Chap-
man gives you   a fample in your Hand
of Wheat, can you, by that, difcover the
goodnefs of the reft that lye out of your
fight ?

 Hermo. By no means.

 Lucian. Nor can you, by the firft thing
you hear, judge of any whole Body of Ph-
lofophy, for 'tis not compos'd of fingle
Parts, like Wine, with which you compar'd it, imagining the whole like the tafte
but of various and many fold, which require more than a hafty furvey, for the lofs
is not much if we buy ill Wine, but to be
ftifl'd in the Lees, is an evil of fome confequence   Again, he that drinks off a Veflel
to buy half a dozen Flasks, injures the Vintner by fo large a tafte , but nothing like

this can happen to Philofophy; for 'drink and fwill as long as you pleafe, the Veffel is ne'er the emptier, nor the Vintner damag'd, *for here,* as the Proverb fays, *Labour has an inexhauftible Spring, and is quite contrary to the* Damaid's *Sieve, for that holds not what is put into it, but here, what ever you take out, you ftill leave more behind you* But I'll give you another inftance, that is like your Philofophical draught, but I defire you not to fuppofe that I intend any fcurrilous reflection againft Philofophers, when I compare it with fome poifonous Dregs, as Hemlock, or the like, nor will thofe, tho deadly Poifon, kill a Man, if he take but a little off with his Nail, and tafte it, but they will if you have no regard to Quality and Manners, with its mixture with fuch and fuch things, but you wou'd needs have it, that the very leaft, minuteft part, wou'd fufficiently inform us of the knowledge of the whole

Hermo Well, *Lucian,* be thefe things as you will To what purpofe therefore fhou'd we live an Hundred years, and undergo fo many troublefome Affairs? Can we have no other way of Philofophizing?

Lucian. By no means, *Hermotimus,* not that fo great a grievance, if what you faid at firft is true, that *Life is fhort,* and, *Art long* but I know not how or by what ftrange change, you are very angry, and diffatisfy'd that you can't, in a day, become a *Plato, Chryfippus,* or *Pythagoras*

Hermo. You perfectly befiege me, *Lucian,* and without any juft provocation, prefs me on e'ery fide, and rob me of all defence;

P p 3

out of envy to be fure, becaufe I have made
fome progrefs in Philofophy, and you e'en
at this Age, neglect your own Improvement.

Lucian. Well then, take my advice,
take no notice of what is faid by fuch a
Madman as I am, but leave me to my own
folly, and purfue the way you've already
enter'd, till you arrive at the end you defign'd.

Hermo Nay, but you are fo hard and fevere upon me, that you'll not allow me to
make any choice till I have experienc'd
all

Lucian Nor fhall I ever fay otherwife,
and when you accufe me of feverity, you
feem to accufe the Innocent, unlefs what
has been faid for you, have at all leffen'd
the feverity of the inftance, that have been
already produc'd, for Reafon will propofe
things yet much more fevere, but perhaps
I have faid enough already to provoke your
Accufation, without proceeding to this.

Hermo. What have you of Reafon more
to urge? Is it poffible that any thing is
omitted that can be faid on this Particular

Lucian Reafon will tell you that it is not
fufficient to make the beft and moft jufti-
able Choice, to have feen, and perus'd all
Parties, but that the greateft thing is yet
wanting.

Hermo. And what was that, good Sir

Lucian A certain fharpnefs and ftreng
of Judgement, and fkill in trying and e-
xamining, an induftrious Mind, and a Ge-
and Wit, that is piercing and unco
rupted

rupted, as that ought to be, which is to judge of things of so great Moment. Nay, it will have it, that it is not a small time that is required to a thing of this nature, and that having set all before us, we chuse him who delays the assent to the first appearances, but weighs 'em by Contemplation and Reflection, and who regards not the *Habit* or *Age* of any Teacher, who has gain'd the opinion of Wisdom, but imitates the *Areopagites*, who judge by night and in the dark, that they may not mind who speaks, but what is spoken, and then, when you have follow'd certainly in your choice, you may begin to play the Philosopher.

Hermo That is after this Life, for the consequence is plain, that no Man can live long enough to view all Parties, to examine each of 'em accurately, having done that, make his judgement of 'em, and then his choice, and after all this, begin to Philosophize. For this you contend can be attain'd by nothing but Reason.

Lucian. I'm very loth, *Hermotimus*, to tell you, that all this is not yet sufficient, for we yet seem to deceive our selves, when having found nothing so, we persuade our selves that we have found something certain, like Fishermen, who often draw their Nets, hoping e'ery weight they find in 'em, to be a good draught of Fish, and when they have dragg'd their Net out, find nothing but some ponderous Stone, or some Vessel fill'd with Sand, let us take care we do not do some such thing ourselve

Hermo. I do not underſtand what you mean by your Nets, for you evidently hold me faſt in 'em

Lucian. Endeavour therefore to eſcape out of 'em, for by the help of ſome God, you may ſwim if any elſe do, for tho we experimentally examine all Parties, and live long enough to finiſh our Inquiries, yet even then in particular, whether any of 'em gain what we ſeem to aim at, or whether they are all equally ignorant of it.

Hermo What ſay you? have none of them any thing of the matter?

Lucian. We do not perceive 'tis not evident to us, that they have Do you think that 'tis not poſſible but that they may all lye, and that Truth is ſome other ſort of a thing, which none of 'em have found out?

Hermo. How is that poſſible?

Lucian. Even thus, let us ſuppoſe the true number twenty, as for example, let a Man take in his Hand, twenty Beans, and ſhut 'em cloſe, then let any one aſk ten Men the number he holds in his Hand, in their Gueſſes one will ſay, perhaps, ſeven, another thirty, another ten or fifteen, and ſo one one number, another another; it happens that by chance ſome of 'em hit right

Hermo. Yes.

Lucian. So 'tis not impoſſible but that they all be falſe, and neither of 'em gueſ that this Man has but twenty Beans in his Hand. What ſay you, Sir?

Hermo. That is not impoſſible.

Lucian. Thus all your Philoſophers enquire what is Happineſs ; and one is of one
Opinion, another of a contrary ; one will
have it be *Pleaſure*, a ſecond, *Virtue*, and
ſo each forms his particular Idea of it, ſo
that it may be likely, that none of them
may hit upon *Happineſs*, nor is it abſur'd to
ſuppoſe, that Happineſs is ſomething elſe
different from them all, that they have
thought it, and we ſeem to act contrary to what
we ought to do to haſten to our end, before
we have found out yet the Principles or
firſt Footings , but, whereas in my Opinion,
it ought firſt to be evident what Truth is
and to be abſolutely in the cuſtody of ſome
one of the Philoſophers, who knows it ;
and after this, to enquire through their
ſeveral Claſſes in their order, whom we
muſt believe

Hermo What you ſay therefore, *Lucian,*
amounts to this, that tho we ſhou'd peruſe
all the ſeveral ſects of Phyloſophy, we
ſhou'd yet never furniſh our ſelves with
Power and Means of finding out the Truth.

Lucian. Nay, good Sir, ask not me but
the Words that I have ſaid, and the Reaſons I have advanc'd, and perhaps theſe
may anſwer you that as long as this is uncertain, whether any one of thoſe things
the Philoſophers expoſe for it, be it or no,
that it is no where to be found

Hermo So that by what you have ſaid, I
conclude we ſhall never find it, and therefore we ought not to apply our ſelves to the
ſtudy of Philoſophy, but quitting thoſe

ſuit-fruitleſs Speculations, and ſit down in the common Track of a private Life.

Lucian. What you ſay happens to be true, that 'tis not convenient to apply our ſelves wholly to Philoſophy, which yet no Man is able to attain, for firſt you direct him that is betaking himſelf to that Study, to chuſe the beſt Sect ; and a juſt choice ſeems to conſiſt in this, after our examination of e'ery particular Sect, we chuſe that which is the trueſt, and then by a computation of the time, that each one of them requires to a perfect knowledge of it, we proceed ſo far that we make it the work of future Ages, ſo that the time that is neceſſary to find out the Truth, exceeds e'ery Man's Life, and after all, you e'en make this doubtful, whether or no any of the ancient Philoſophers ever found it out ; for can you, *Hermotimus,* affirm on Oath, that any of 'em has found it ? for my part, I aſſure you, I ſhou'd not venture on ſo raſh an Oath. Beſides, how many things do I paſs by, which require a long and tedious enquiry.

Hermo. What are thoſe ?

Lucian. Do you not obſerve, that the *Stoicks,* the *Epecureans,* or *Platoniſts* ſay, that each one of them have the Reaſons of all things, excluſive of all the reſt, altho' the others ſeem to merit equal credit ?

Hermo. This I confeſs is true.

Lucian. Again, does it not ſeem to you a Work full of fatigue and difficulties, to diſtinguiſh the ſkilful from the unſkilful, who yet boaſt themſelves to be ſkilfull too.

Hermo. It is ſo.

Luci.

Lucian. If you therefore find out the best of the *Stoicks*, you must, at least, hear the greatest part, if not all of them, and having try'd 'em, you chuse the best Master, who shall first instruct and enable you to judge of them, lest by your ignorance, you make choice of the worst. But do you confider your self how much time this will take up, for I omitted that confideration on purpose, lest I shou'd make you angry, tho' I think that this one thing is of the greatest confequence and neceffity, at leaft, in things of this nature, which are obfcure and uncertain. You have only lent you, a firm and certain hope of difcovering the Truth, and nothing elfe, by which you may diftinguish between Truth and Faifhood, and like Goldfmiths, with their Touch-ftone, difcern the true and uncorrupted Metal from the falfe and adulterated. But having, at laft, got this Art and faculty, you can then apply your felf to a difcovery of thofe things that each delivers; But if you are defective in this knowledge, you have nothing to fecure you from being led by the Nofe, as they fay, by every one, and like Sheep, follow the Bough, that is fhew'd before you, or you will rather be like the Water fet on the Table, eafily with the tip of their Finger, drawn to what fide of the Table they pleafe, or before, like a Rufh growing by the Water-fide, bent to and fro by every lighter blaft of Air. Thus if you find out a Mafter that does underftand any Art by which he can teach you the Rules and Methods of De-

mon

monftration, and judging of things that are doubtful, you will be eas'd of your greateft fatigue ; for that, which is moft eligible will appear fo to to you, and by the help of this Art of Demonftration, Truth and Falfhood will be evidently difcern'd, and having follow'd Certainty in your Choice, and join'd with it a ftabillity of Judgement, you may then Philofophize, and having gain'd poffeffion of the moft defireable and amiable beauties of Happinefs, fhall lead the moft pleafing Life, having in her all the Goods you can wifh

Hermo. Now you fay fomething, my *Lucian,* for what you now offer is more agreeable, than what you urg'd before, and give me no fmall hopes And I'm convinc'd I ought immediately to make it my bufinefs to find out fome fuch Man, who may inftruct me in the faculty of knowing, diftinguifhing, and what is moft valuable of all, of demonftrating, fo that what remains, may for the future, afford me no great trouble or pains, and require no great matter of Exercife and Application , and I think my felf extreamly oblig'd to you for difcovering this admirable and compendious way for me.

Lucian. Hold, Sir, I affure you I have no right to your thanks, nor have I found out any thing by my Invention, that fhould fet you near to hope, but we are yet farther off, than ever, and we are e'en where we were before all this trouble and difquifition.

Her.

Hermo. How's this? For you look as if you were going to utter fome dreadful unforefeen misfortune.

Lucian. I was going to fay, my Friend, that tho' we fhou'd meet with a Man that profeft himfelf skilful in demonftration, and capable and willing to inftruct any other, I think we ought not immediately to believe him, but we muft feek fome body who is able to judge, whether what he fays of himfelf be true or no ; and tho we fhou'd find this Man, we are yet to feek whether he that is to difcover the excellence or defect of the Profeffor, knows how to make a juft and adequate judgement of him or no, and fo it feems neceffary that we fhou'd find out fome other to difcover his Abillities, or how fhou'd we defcern who is capable of making the beft judgement in things we do not underftand our felves? D'ye obferve how far the difficulty ftretches it felf, and to what an immenfe extent our fufpenfion of Affent reaches, and how diftant we are from comprehending 'em, for all thofe numerous Demonftrations, you will perceive, are controverted, and without any thing of certainty, for moft of thefe force usby other doubts to perfwade us, that we know; others comprehending the moft obfcure things, with the moft evident, that have nothing common with 'em, affert, that they are the Demonftrations of 'em, juft, as if any one fhould go to prove, that there are Gods becaufe Men fet up Altars to them Thus *Hermotimus,* like thofe, that run in a Lttle,

we return again to thofe doubts where we
fet out.

Hermo. Lucian, what an injury have you
done me, fhewing me dead Coals for Treafure; and deftroy, in all liklihood, the
pains and labour of fo many ftudious years
as I have paft.

Lucian. But 'twill be no fmall comfort to
you, *Hermotimus*, to reflect that you are
not the only Man excluded from your hop'd
for Benefits, but that all the Philofophers
quarrel about the Affes fhaddow, as the
Proverb has it. Is there any Man can go
through all, that I have propos'd, you have
confefs'd already that they cannot, and
therefore you feem to me to do as prepofteroufly, as he, that fhou'd weep and rail at
form, becaufe he cou'd not mount up into
the Heav'n, or like a Bird born aloft in the
Air, we cou'd not pafs from *Greece* to the
Indies in a day, or fwim through the Ocean
from *Sicily* to *Cyprus*. But the caufe of this
Man's Grief is the entertaining fuch a chy-
merical Hope, becaufe in his Dreams, he
has fome time, or other feen fome Image of
fuch a thing, or fram'd it perhaps to himfelf, without confidering whether his
Wifhes were capable of being fatisfy'd, or
agreeable to the Power and Nature of Mankind; thus, my Friend, my Difcourfe finding you entertain'd with many gaudy and
pleafant Dreams prick'd you, makes you ftart
out of them, and not well yet awake, and
your Eyes fcarce yet open, nor eafily roufing
from a fleep that gave you fuch Amufements,

you quarrel and are angry with your felf. The fame happens to them, who frame to themfelves an empty and groundlefs Happinefs; if their Boy interrupt 'em, whilft they are building Caftles in the Air, and in their minds heaping up Wealth, digging up hidden Treafures, act Kings and Princes, and are wonderful happy in all other things (all which the Goddefs *Euche*, that is, Defire, eafily performs, magnificent in her Gifts, nor contradicting 'em in any thing, whether her Devotes would be fwift of Foot, or of a *Collofean* bignefs, or have whole Mountains of Gold) if I fay their Boy fhould interrupt them in thefe whymfical Meditations, and fhou'd ask about any thing of ufe in this Life, as how he might buy fome Bread; or how he fhou'd put off his Landlord for the Rent, that is due for his Houfe, which he has a long time and often demanded, they are full of as great Indignation as if he that had interrupted them had, in reality, robb'd them of all thofe Advantages, and 'tis ten to one but they go near to bite off the poor Boy's Nofe for his neceffary prefumption. But, my good Friend, let me defire you not to ufe me after that manner, If I interrupt your thoughts that are digging of hidden Treafures, flying aloft in the Air, and forming extraordinary Imaginations, and hoping things that will never come to pafs, if, I fay, your Friend, have not fuffer'd you all your Life long, to be converfant with nothing but a Dream, tho perhaps a pleafant one; but wou'd have you employ your felf, being now awake, in things that

are

are of ufe, and which will not forfake you
all your Life, whilft things, that are of
common ufe of Life are the object of your
Thoughts ; for thofe things, that but now
engrofs'd your Thoughts and Contemplation, differ not at all from the *Hippocentaur*,
Chymeras and *Tergons*, and thofe various
Dreams, which Poets and Painters feign e ery
day with a great deal of liberty, which ne
ver had, or can have a Being in Nature, wn ch
yet the Vulgar believe, and is pleas'd with
fuch Stories and Sights, becaufe they ae
new and monftious, and you upon heaing
fome fabulous Romancer defcribing fome
fovereignly beautiful Woman, more chaim-
ing than the Graces, or *Urania* her felf, full
of love with hei before you examine whether, or no, there be any fuch Woman in
the World, as they fay *Medea* did with *Ja-
fon* in her Dream. But if I am not out in my
conjecture, that which chiefly contributed
to your Love, as well as that of the icft
who were in love with her Image, was that
you believ'd the Peifon, that told you of this
Woman, for you believ'd he told you truth
t fiift, made all his defcription of a piece
and coheient ; for that was the only thing
you minded, and having thus put youi Note
into his hand, he will eafily lead you about by
it afterward, and lead you by that way which
he told you went directly to your beloved,
for all, after this, I fuppofe were of no great
difficulty, nor was theie any of you, who
examin'd the entiance of the Road, to fee
whether he, thiough neglect or forgetful-
nefs, perfu'd a path, that he ought to have

divided

divided; but he follow'd the Tracks of those, that went before him, as the Sheep do their Shepherd, whereas the business had been to consider at the very Entrance of the Road, whether that was the Path, they were to take. But what I say will be more evident, if we compare it with something not altogether unlike it; for shou'd one of the most impudent of the Poets, tell you, that there was formerly a Man with three Heads and six Hands, and you, at first admit this, as a Truth without any difficulty, or examining whether such a thing can possibly be, or no; with as strong a reason he might infer, that he had also six Eyes and, as many Ears; that he spoke with three Tongues at once, and eat with three Mouths that he had thirty Fingers, not like us, ten on both our Hands, that when he fought, he held in each of his three Hands, a Shield, in each of the three others, a battle Axe, a Spear, and a Sword; cou'd any one, that admitted the first deny all this? For granting the first foundation of the discription, which ought to've been controverted, he must of consequence yield all the rest to be so; granting the Premises, the rest necessarily follows, nor can he deny the rest, that are consentaneous and agreeable to the first granted Principle. The same happens to you, for your Love and Sprightliness is so great, that you never examine what is first offer'd to you, you proceed on your way, drawn on by the Chain of Consequences, nor do you so much, as think, or consider whether that, which is agreea-

Q q   ble,

ble to that, which went before be true, or
falſe , as if, for example, any one ſhou'd
tell you, that twice five make ſeven, and
without computing it, you believe him,
he immediately infers, that four times
five make fourteen : And ſo he might do to
the end of the Chapter. Such likewiſe are
the wonders of Geometry ; for that pro
poſing to the young Beginners, in the Art,
ſome abſurd Poſtulata, peremptorily demanding their aſſent to 'em, altho they are
inconſiſtent, as individual Points and Lines
without Lattitude , and ſo builds on the
falſe Foundation, and will needs perſwade
you, that it produces from falſe Principles
wherewithal to give you true Demonſtra
tions. In like manner you Philoſophers
having your Principles of each Sect granted
you, believe all, that follows from 'em, a
eſteem their Conſequences, tho falſe, as t
Mark and diſcovery of Truth   Then m
of you dye in the midſt of your conce,
hopes before you have diſcovered the Tr
and found out the Impoſtors , and part t
they find themſelves deceiv'd, yet ber
now old, fear to go back, being aſham
to own, that they knew not at that age
that they buſied themſelves with Boy
Trifles. That Shame makes them perſever
in the ſame Studies, and praiſe their preſer
Condition, and perſwade all they can i
the ſame Circumſtances, that they ma
be deceiv'd without Company, but have th
comfort, that many others ſhare in th
common evils for they ſee plainly, that
they ſhou'd confeſs the Truth, they wo

no longer as they are now, be above the People, or have so much honour and respect paid them. Wherefore they are never willing to confess this Truth, since they are very sensible, that if they shou'd quit this pretence, they wou'd be thought like other People, and so esteem'd. But you shall find, that there are very few, who have Courage enough to own, that they have been impos'd on, and to dissuade others from making so fruitless an Experiment, but if you can find any such Man, you may give him the glorious appellation of a Lover of Truth, of a good and just Man, and if you please of a Philosopher; for to him alone I shall not regret that Title. But for the rest, either they know nothing of the Truth, tho they imagine they do, or if they do, they, out of Fear, or Shame conceal it, that they may be honour'd above the rest of Mankind. Well, let us forget all, that I have advanc'd, and let us grant, that the *Stoick*'s Philosophy is the best of all others, and let us examine whether 'tis possible for any one to arrive at perfection in that, or whether all that burn with a desire of it, give themselves a pain and fatigue to no purpose; for we are promised wonderful things, when we get to the top of this Philosophical Hill, and that we shall possess the most absolute Happiness, and that these alone shall enjoy all the unexperienc'd Benefits there But you can best tell whether you have ever met with any *Stoick* of that perfection, that was neither touch'd with grief, nor inveigl'd by Pleasure, or transported by Anger, above

the

the power of Envy to disturb, a Contemner of Riches, and was on all sides and in e'ery thing so serene and happy, as the Rule and Mark of that Life ought to be, that is regulated absolutely by Vertue. For where there is the least thing wanting, that is imperfect, tho it abound with all things besides, nor is he happy as yet, who has not obtain'd ev'n that

Hermo. I never yet saw any such Man

Lucian. You do well, *Hermotimus*, to speak a voluntary Truth. To what end and purpose then do you apply your self to Philosophy, when you see that neither your Master, nor his, nor any, if you proceed to the tenth preceding generation, is, or have been perfectly wise, and in that absolutely happy? Nor will it suffice, as you've rightly observ'd, if any one become next Neighbour to that Wisdom and Happiness, since he reaps no Advantage from thence; so notwithstanding that, we are still out of our way, and he, that stands at the Door, as well as he, that is at some distance from it, are equally in the open Air, yet they differ in this alone, that he, that is nearest suffers the greater pain to want what he is separated from by so little a distance. And then as you make your nearest approaches to Happyness (for that I'll grant you too) you overcome with so much pains, and wearing your self out with fruitless Labours, and lose so much of your Life in fatigues, labour and watching, and lastly, as you say, you must spend at least twenty years more in these painful endeavours, till you

have

arrive at four score years of Age Who
has enfur'd your Life to that time ? However, you'll be of their number, who are
not yet capable of Happyne(s, unlefs you
vainly fuppofe, that you alone fhall obtain
this, or by your purfuit catch that, which
many others before you, both ftronger and
more fwift, cou'd not with all their hafte
and dilligence overtake. But if you think
fit, take it, and poffefs it entirely. I cannot fee any thing of that moment, as to
deferve fo many pains and fatigues, and
then how long will you enjoy this, when you
are now in the clofe of your Life, now under
the extreamity of old Age, and unfit for
Pleafures of any fort, with one Foot, as
they fay, in the Grave ? Unlefs you, good
Sir, prepare your felf by this Exercife for
fome other Life, that when you come thither, you may live more comfortably according to the Rules you have learn'd here,
as if any one fhou'd prepofteroufly prepare
himfelf with various Exercifes for his Supper till he perifh'd with hunger nor have
you, as I think, obferv'd that Virtue confifts in Actions, as juft, wife, and valiant
Deeds. But you (when I fay *you* I mean
thofe fupreamly accomplifh'd Philofophers)
flighting the ftudy and endeavours after
thefe, confider only a wretched Company
of Words, Syllogifms, and Doubts, and
trifle away the greateft part of your Lives
in them; in which the Conqueror feems to
you a very fine Fellow. Under which capacity, if I'm not miftaken, you admire
your Mafter, a Man of extream old age,

that he can perplex those, with whom he has to do with Doubts, and knows what Question, to ask them, and invelope them in Sophisms, to deal deceitfully, and cast them into inevitable snares; and thus evidently losing the fruit, that is usualy gathered from our labour, you busy your selves about the Berk, only casting Leaves at one another in your disputation. Do you do any thing else, *Hermotimus,* all day long, from Morntill Night?

Hermo. Nothing else in the World.

Lucian. Might not any one, therefore, justly say, that you neglect the Substance and pursue the Shadow? Or do like any one that shou'd put Water into a Mortar, and pound it up and down with a Pestle, and believe, that he is doing some necessary thing, or what was of use and advantage, when he is not ignorant, that Water will still be Water tho he pound his Heart out. Give me leave to ask you one Question. Whether (excepting his Learning) you be, in all things, like your Master, that, so cholerick, so contentious, so selfish, so great a voluptuary, altho he does not seem so to many

Hermo. To whom?

Lucian. Shall I tell you, *Hermotimus,* what I very lately heard from an old reverend Gentleman, almost worn out with age, who had many young Men resorted to him to learn the prescripts of Wisdom? For when, in a great passion, he demanded of one of his Scholars his Quarterige, which he said was long since due, that is, for seventee venteen days; that is on the thirtieth day of the Month, for that was the agreement, which was the motive of his Indignation Upon which, the Uncle of the Youth being by, a Man of a plain Courtly appearance, and, in comparison of you Philosophers, a meer Ignoramus, no more complain, said he, that we have injur'd you in not yet paying you a reward for the empty Words we bought of you; for as yet you have all you sold by you, nor is your stock of Precepts one jot diminished. But that which I desired and hop'd, when I put this Youth to you, I am far from obtaining, for he is not the least bette'd for all your Instruction, for he has since ravish'd my Neighbour Echerate's Daughter, and had held up his Hand at the Bar for the Rope, had not the poverty of *Echerates* enabled me to buy off the trespass for a Talent, and t'other day he beat his Mother, for taking him in the Fact of stealing a Vessel of Wine, to make merry with his Gang I suppose, for he was much better before he came to you, than now as to turbulent Passions, Anger, Impudence, saucy Boldness and Lying, and I had much rather he should have made some progress in the correcting these notorious defects under you, than in those out of the way, Whims, that he is teizing us e'ery day at Supper with, that is, *That there was a certain Crocodil, that took away a certain Boy, whom he said he wou'd return again on condition his Father cou'd answer such a question*, or what's all one, *if it be day 'tis not night*. And he, now and then, wou'd perswade us, that we have

Hornes

Baines, by joyning his words together after a set sort of way, which we do nothing
but ... ... but chiefly when stopping his
E... and designs within him-
self ... Habits and Dispositions, Com-
prehensions and Imaginations, repeating
abundance of such odd sort of Words. Besides we have heard him say, that there was
no God in the Heavens above, but that he was
in and past thro' all things, Wood, Stone Mi-
nerals, nay the most inconsiderable and vi-
lest things in the World, and when his Mother asks him why he plays the Fool so, he
laughs at her, and says he, if I do but
with diligence learn these Trifles, there is
nothing in my way to Riches and Power,
which none but I shall obtain, and without
which, I shall think all Men else in comparison of me, to be Slaves and Victims
When he had said all this, behold, my
Hermotimus, what an Answer that old Gentleman gave him, how worthy a Philosopher? But reply'd he, don't you think he
wou'd 'a' been guilty of more hainous
Offences? if he had not been under my Di-
rection perhaps he had been hang'd before
this But since he has been check'd by the
Precepts of Philosophy, he is become
much more modest and pliable, and it
is to my Instructions and Care, you are
to ascribe the alteration you may observe in his Manners and Deportment,
which are pretty tolerable at present, because he is asham'd to be thought unworthy of the Name and Qualifications of
a Philosopher; so those Doctrines he carried

ried away with him when he left me, are
such as detain him at least in the Rules of
Discipline, so that you can't charge me
with doing you Injustice if I expect to be
rewarded for my Labour, even tho he
proves not much the better Man for it ;
tho, at the same time, 'tis the Respect he
bears to Philosophy, that has made him a-
void those Enormities and Crimes, he would
doubtless have otherwise been guilty of.
This is a thing so well known, that nothing
is more frequently heard even among
Nurses, when they say that unlucky Boys
must be sent to School , for I protest to you,
there is no other Place in the World, where
they have the same Conveniency of being
instructed in what is good, and in avoiding
of what is evil, that they remain under the
School-master's Tuition.   For my Part, as I
am sure I have, in all respects. discharged
my Duty in making this young Man a
compleat Scholar, so to convince you of it,
I desire you to get some Friend of yours,
who knows what belongs to a good Scholar,
and bring him along with you to my House ;
there you will see how promptly and acute-
ly he will propose his Questions to some of
his Fellow Philosophers , and with how
much nicety and ingenuity he will answer
theirs.   You will then be satisfyed what
pains I have taken to make him a good Profi-
cient in Learning , when you hear him
discourse of Books, and reading of Maxims, Syllogisms of various Constitutions,
Duties, and a Thousand other Niceties. For
the rest, if he beat his Mother, if he ravish'd

vish'd a young Virgin, what is that to me?
For you know I was not made to be his Pedagogue.   Thus the old Man concluded
his Harrangue concerning Philosophy. Now
perhaps, *Hermotimus,* you will tell me, that
according to your own Opinion, it is sufficient if we apply our selves to the Study of
Philosophy with an intention to avoid ill and
vicious Actions, but I desire you to remember whether the only end we proposed to
ourselves at first in the Study of Philosophy,
did not reach beyond seeing ourselves scarce
one degree above the vulgar Sort? Thirdly, Will you not vouchsafe to return me
an Answer to this Question?

Hermot. what Answer would you have
me give you, but that your Relation
makes me ready to weep for Grief, that I
should be such a Wretch, as to misspend
and squander away so much of my precious
time and good Money, as I have done upon those Vanities; I assure you, I am at
this time, like one, who having been inebriated by the force of strong Liquors, is
fully recovered from his Drunkenness, sees
without disguise, and in their own Colours,
those things he was so fond of before,
regretting both his time and the pains
and troubles he has suffered for those trifles

Lucian, What signify Tears, my *Hermotimus,* what good will weeping do you? You
will act a better and much wiser Part to follow the Advice of *Æsop's* Fox, mentioned
in his Fables He tells you of a certain
Person, who having taken a Whimsey to

count the Waves of the Sea, as they run to the Shore, placed himfelf fo near (to make his Obfervation the better) that in a little time he had enough to do to fave himfelf from drowning; whilft he was bemoaning his Mifhap, by comes a cunning Fox, who feeing him in this Pickle, and being told by him, that nothing vex'd him fo much as to be difappointed in his aim, becaufe the Waves were beaten with fo much violence by the Wind upon that Point of the Shore, he told him, what makes thee trouble thy Head about thofe Waves, that are paft, get thy felf into a more convenient ftation, and try whether thou canft number thofe thou wilt fee there. So *Hermotimus*, would I have you apply your Thoughts to what is to come, and what will prove moft ufeful to you, to live like other People, do not fhew the Converfation of your Fellow Subjects, without filling your Head with Vanities, Pride and falfe Imaginations I would not have you in the leaft be afham'd, becaufe you did not begin to grow wife till after you had fpent a great part of your Days in Follys, and therefore, dear Friend, don't imagine what I have faid to be on purpofe againft the Sect of the *Stoicks* only, as if I bore a peculiar grutch to them, but you muft interpret my words as directed againft them all, without diftinction I can affure you, I fhould have faid the fame thing, had you been a Follower either of *Plato* or *Ariftotle*, without taking any notice of the reft ; but knowing you to prefer the

Stoicks

Stoicks to all the other Sects, I levell'd in a more particular manner, my Arguments against them, without declaring any further Enmity, or Aversion to them.

Hermot. You say very well, and I am just now ready to change my former course of Life and my Cloaths together, in a very little time, you see me no more (as you do at present) with a long frightful Beard, you will see me no more lead an austere and doleful Life, but to seek for my Enjoyments in such things as are worthy the Care and Satisfaction of Men of a liberal Education; nay, perhaps you may see me appear in Purple, to convince the World, that I have laid aside all my former trifling notions, and I wish it were in my Power to find a Vomit, that would clear my Head of all, that ever I heard them say; and, that you may not call the Truth of my real Sentiments in question, I assure you, I would even not refuse to take a good dose of Hellebore (contrary to *Chrysippus* his Opinion) provided I was sure, that none of their Notions would ever recur to my remembrance. But to draw to a conclusion, my Dear *Lucian,* I ought to return you my hearty Thanks for the trouble you have given your self to pull me out of these Whirlpools, wherein I had plunged my self, as I was driving along with the Current, without reflecting whether I was a-going, so that I must look upon you no otherwise, than one of those Gods, the *Tragick Poets* used to bring unexpectedly upon the Stage out of the Clouds for relief, when all seem to be lost to humane Aid, I think also it would not be very improper for me to have my Head shaved, as it is a custom among Mariners, after they have escaped the manifest danger of a Shipwreck ; if I judge right I ought to celebrate this day like a Festival, seeing it has proved so salubrious and fortunate to me, in dispersing those Clouds, which hitherto had darkened my Eyesight ; and I will further tell you, that for the future I shall be so much terrify'd at the sight of a Philosopher, that whenever I happen to meet any one of them in the Street, I will be sure to get out of his way, as fast as people are used to run away from a mad Dog.

THE

THE

King-Fisher:

A Dialogue between

Chærephon and Socrates.

From the Story of the King-Fisher, *he takes an Opportunity of discoursing of the wonderful Power of divine Providence*

Chær. HArk! What melodious Sound is that? It comes from the point of the Promontory, on that side of the Shore. What harmonious Creature can it be? The very Fishes are silent; and yet marine Fowl are rarely any thing of Songsters.

Socr. This is a Sea Bird, however; and its Name is the *King Fisher*; by the sadness of its Ditty, you may see, she consists of nothing but Lamentation and Sadness The general Story, that goes of her, is, that being in times past, one of the fair Sex, and Daughter to *Æolus*, having lost her Husband *Ceyx*, the charming Son of a no less charming Father, *Phosphorus*, tho she was then but a Girl, yet loving him entirely, he.

ex-

exceſſive Grief and continued Anguiſh for his Loſs, brought her into a deep Conſumption; the Gods, out of meere Compaſſion to her, have cloath'd her in Feathers, and ever ſince, in the Figure of a Bird, ſhe has rov'd about the Seas in purſuit of him, whom ſhe has ſought for ſo long in vain on Shore.

Char. I never heard this ſame *King-Fiſher* er before as I remember, that made me take it for ſome exotic Creature; there is ſomething wonderfully languiſhing in her Notes. What ſort of a Bird pray is it?

Socr. Her Body is but little, tho her Beauty is great, yet her Honour is more remarkably ſo; for the Winds, in token of her Affection, ſtop their Breath from the time ſhe begins to build her Neſt, till ſhe has hatch'd her Young; the Sea it ſelf is ſo indulgent, even in the hardeſt Winter, to be all calm, This here is one of them they call generally, *Halcyon* days How ſerene are the Skies, and the Ocean' how without the leaſt frowning Surges, all is as ſmooth as Glaſs.

Char. Right, and yeſterday was ſo too But pray, *Socrates* give me to underſtand, what our Fore-fathers meant, by tranſmitting to Poſterity ſuch Tales, that are equally ridiculous and impoſſible

Socr. 'Tis no eaſie matter, *Chærephon*, to determine what is poſſible or impoſſible; for that were to meaſure the infinite Power of Divinity, by our feeble and narrow Capacities. Man compared to the *Firſt Cauſe*, is but a meer Infant when he has liv'd never

fo long, and his Life is lefs, than a moment
in comparifon with Eternity. You took
notice what a violent Tempeft we had three
days ago ; how Thunder and Lightning,
and fuch Frets of Wind rattled and roar'd,
as if Heaven and Earth had come together
Which do you think the more unlikely or
miraculous, to affwage fuch a Hurrican into a perfect Calm, or transform a Woman
into a Bird. You fee daily what various
figures and forms of Things the very little
Children fafhion and fhape out of Wax,
Dough, or Dirt; doubtlefs then this muft
be much more eafy and familiar to God,
whofe Excellency and Power can bear no
comparifon with our Abillities. Know you
not that he is higher above us, than the
Heavens are above the Earth? How far
does a Man tranfcend a Child in Wifdom
and Force? Can t one deftroy a Million
If there is fo wide a difference between the
fame *Species,* what alas muft there be between the *Creature* and the *Creator* No
Man can write, or play upon any Inftrument, without a Miracle, if he never learnt,
and to thofe that have, nothing is eafier.
The cafe is the fame. We fee Nature produces a Fly out of a Worm, without any
form ; and tho it had neither Legs, Feathers, or Colours at firft, fhe furnifhes it
with Wings, feet, and a gaudy Enamel,
nay, with Wifdom and Induftry ; nay,
farther, out of fenflefs Eggs, little vary-
ing from one another, forms Birds of various Species. Many Hundred Inftances
more may be brought to make Man mo-
dell

deſt when he diſcourſes of the Power of *Di-vinity*.   Whereupon I ſhall e'en hand down the Story to Poſterity, as I receiv'd it from my Predeceſſors ; but will moſt certainly acquaint my two Wives *Zantippe* and *Mirto*, with the ardent Love you bore your Huſ-band and ſhall not forget neither, ſweet mournful Bird, to tell them how the Gods have honour'd thee for it.   *Chærophon*, won't you do ſo too ?

Chær. Having ſo great a Precedent as *So-crates*, I ſhall to be ſure, ſince it tends to the preſerving and encreaſing of mutual Affection between Man and Wife.

R r   *Zeuxis*

Zeuxis or Antiochus.

By Capt. *Ayloffe*.

This is by way of Apology for his manner of Writing . The same thing of this Nature, has been hinted at before, when he fell foul of the Person, that call'd him Prometheus.

IN my return home, t'other day, when I had read to you something of my own, many of the Auditors saluted me, and wou'd needs see me home, but with such Eulogies and Commendations, that as I cou'd not forbear blushing at them, so I have not Forehead enough to mention 'em again, but to my very particular Acquaintance. Most of 'em seem'd charm'd with the uncommonness of my Invention, and every one instanc'd in some particular passage, that he was most feelingly delighted with ; and having nothing to expect or apprehend from me, being an utter Stranger, yet as I was a little tickled with their Encomiums, so was I nettled too ; because they seem'd only affected with the Novelty of my Works ; thus we say any Song is good because 'tis new. This made me enter into my self, and say, What ! Is there no difference between me and other Men, but that I have not trod the same beaten Path with them? Are not my words select, and justly put together? Are not my Conceptions Nervous and Nice? My Expression Vigorous, and my whole Harangue Judicious and Methodical? 'Tis this that is commendable, not Novelty like a Fashion. Give me leave *Apropos* to insert here a short account of *Zeuxis*, who very deservingly had the glorious Character of the Greatest Master that ever was in his Art, and was above trifling Vulgar Subjects to exert his Skill upon, and only undertook something Noble and New. Of all his wonderful Undertakings, the *Centaure* struck me most, tho' I saw but the Copy of it at *Athens*, for the Original was lost at Sea with many other Curiosities of *Greece* that *Sylla* took away with him. I'll give you a Description of it, (tho *Jove* is my Witness, I don't pretend to any extraordinary Talent that way) but the surprize I was in, when I saw it, has made so deep an impression in my Brains, that I will venture on it. The *Centaure* was extended on the Grass, that is, so much of it as was a Mare, the Womanish part was upright, tho leaning a little on her Elbow; her hind Legs were stretcht out, and her fore ones drawn in like a Horse going to take a Leap. It inclines a little on one side and gives its Womanish Breast to one of its Young that is in its Arms, but the other is sucking at the Mare's Teats. Above stands the Male *Centaure* as a Guard over her, tho he is vi-

sible

fible but to the Wafte, and holds out to
'em a Young Lyon that he had Caught
Notwithftanding his Smiles, his Main and
Briftle looks very terrible, and he is almoft
all over Hair. The Female is as full of
Charms as the other is of Horror ; half her
Body is compos'd of fomething like thofe
delicate *Theffalian* Mares, that were never
broke, the other of the moft exquifitely
Beautiful Woman, that Fancy can fuggeft,
only with this difadvantage, that fhe is prick
Ear'd, like Satyrs. One of the Young is
Hairy and Rough, like its Sire, the other
Smooth and Effeminate, but both of them
turn their Eyes while they Suck upon the
Young Lyon, which the Father holds up as
if it were defign'd to fcare 'em. The wonderful mixture of the Colours I leave to
the Admiration of the Ingenious Painters,
as alfo their Application, the exact Proportion, the foftnefs of the Shadows, and the
daringnefs of the Defign : I was chiefly
taken with the wonderful Skill and Dex-
terity of blending fo neatly together two
fuch different Natures, in fo much, that
none cou'd perceive where they united.
Every Body, that faw this accurate Mafter
Piece, ftood amaz'd at it · But *Zeuxis* feeing they minded only the contrivance,
and not whit he more peculiarly intended, took it away in a great Paffion
from the place where he had expos'd it to
view. But before I apply this to my purpofe, give me leave to inftance in one thing
more, concerning *Antiochus Soter*, when he
fought the *Galatians*. The number of his
Ene-

Enemies, and the good Order of their Battel quite difpirited him, and he was now refolving upon a Retreat, or a more difhonourable *Parly*, when one of his Captains gave him a new Life and Heart when the Enemies Cavalry came briskly down, and the Infantry opening to the Right and Left, for the conveniency of the Chariots, he loofed the *Elephants* amongft 'em, which before he had kept behind the Line of Battel, and they frighting both Men and Horfes, they faced about and difcompos'd their own Troops. *Antiochus* charging of 'em at this Juncture, gave 'em a very Bloody overthrow. But when the *Macedonians* came to Congratulate this mighty Victory, and made the Skies Ring again with their Shouts and *Huzza's*, Are'nt you afham'd, faid he to 'em, to be thus proud of a Victory, which is much more owing to Fortune, than your Fortitude, and wou'd have no Trophy made of that Conqueft, but only the Picture of an Elephant. But if you do not perceive my drift in thofe two Stories, I will expound my felf. The advantage I had, proceeded from what I fet the leaft by. Some are furpriz'd with the *Elephants*, as others were at the Female *Centaure*, but never took notice of what was moft worthy Admiration. This is not directed to you who are a competent Judge of what is exquifite and beautiful in a piece, but thofe, that look no farther than Novelty, without the leaft regard to any thing elfe tho never fo fine.

Hippias.

Hippias, or the *Bagnio*.

This contains a Description of some Baths, or Sweating-Houses, that were contriv'd by a great Master in Architecture.

THE Philosophers, that have confirm'd the Precepts they gave us by their own Practices, when alive, doubtless deserve our greatest Admiration, tho others indeed, that have not done so we may look upon as so many Sophisters, not real Philosophers. When a Man is Ill he sends for one, that can give him ease, not one that can give him an account of his Malady As likewise a Musician, that has both Theory and Practice, is much preferrable to him that has only one without the other. Those Commanders of Armies, that the Poets feign, such as *Agamemnon* and *Achilles*, that always fought at the Head of their Troops; and those other Heroes Recorded in History, *v.z. Pyrrhus* and *Alexander* are in far greater esteem, than the others, that knew no more than the bare Scheme of so hazardous an Art. Thus *Archimedes*, in my Opinion, who burnt the *Roman* Gallies before *Syracuse*, by wonderful ingenious Invention of his own ; and *Sostratus* who overthrew *Ptolemy*, and took the City of *Memphis* without striking a stroke, only by turning the Course of the River *Nile*, are infinitely more to be set by, than those vain Dreamers of Business that are always contriving but never execute any thing. *Thales* in like manner being neither Ingineer nor Mathematician, but only a Man of ready Thought and quick Apprehension, promis'd *Croesus* to make his Army pass dry-shod over the River *Lydia*, effected it by only turning the Current of the River. But to draw nearer our own Times, who have given us as notable and serviceable Artists as any, *Hippias* was no ways inferior to any of the Ancients, whether we take him upon Invention demonstrating, or Executing any thing he took in hand ; nor was the surpassing what was found out by the Ancients his only Master-Piece, he improv'd even their very Labours, and found out new Consequences from their Principles. To this he added an exquisite Perspicuity in the Mathematicks to a profound Judgment in the Mechanicks, in so much that he might have pass'd for the greatest Master in either of 'em. Besides, he was the most Famous Man in his time for *Geometry* and *Musick*, *Perspective*, *Catoptricks* and *Astronomy*, and plainly shew'd how very much the Ancients fell short of him. But what created the greatest wonder in me, was the last of *Hippias's* Works that I saw, and yet was nothing but the Fabrick of a *Bagnio*, which is not a

Rr 4   thing

thing very uncommon amongst us, however, the contrivance of this is incomparable. It stands upon a very high and steep Ascent, which he has made level by a Foundation supported answerable to the Weight of the whole Building, which is so jointed and cramp'd together, that it is impossible it should ever fall. The Fabrick is not too large for the Place where it stands, and has an exact proportion with the Platform. At the first coming in you have a large Court; from that you ascend by broad Steps so gradually that tho it be very steep you can hardly perceive you go upwards. Then you come to a spacious *Hall* for the conveniency of Servants and Waiters. On the left you have several Apartments for Pleasure, with neat and light Closets, which is no small advantage to a *Bagnio* Persons of a distinguish'd Character, have peculiar Apartments somewhat beyond this, and on each of the Wings are separate Conveniencies for Dressing and Undressing In the middle is another lofty and well Lighted one that has three distinct *Cold Baths* It is Lin'd with *Lacon* Stone, and has two Noble Pieces of Antiquity in Marble One representing *Health* and the other *Æsculapius*. Out of this you pass into one, whose Form is Oval, and where the Heat at first is gentle, but increases by slow degrees. From thence on the Right Hand you come into a very light Room, that is kept for *Cupping, Shaving* and *Rubbing-down*, such as come in hot from Exercises, and the double Passage which is on each Hand, is adorn'd with curious *Phrygian* Stone.   Farther on, there is one much more Magnificent and Convenient for Standing, Sitting, or Lying down in, and is no ways uneasie or disagreeable, because it is all done through with the same Stone.   Then you come to a hot Passage of *Numidian* Stone, that brings you to the last Apartment, that glitters with a bright *Vermillion* drawing near upon Purple. Here are three *Hot Baths*, and from them you may retire into the *Cold Baths* without ever passing through any of the Rooms you was in before   The whole Building (as I mention'd before) is very well Lighted, and every Apartment is a very just proportion as to the length, breadth and height.   In short all the Fronts are very bright and refulgent, as *Pindar* is pleased to direct the Entrances of Works to be. Towards the North the Architect has very Judiciously turn'd those Rooms that are to be cool, opening of those to the South for the advantage of Air and Prospect   The rest he open to the Sun   There are besides other Conveniencies for using some sort of Exercises, and laying by People's Cloaths, and all so contriv'd as to be both for Health and Conveniency   I wou'd not now, that any one should imagine, that I Trespass upon Truth, only to make an Ostentation of my Parts, for whosoever has been in it will justifie what I have asserted, and confess that nothing cou'd be more nicely manag'd for Pleasure and Use Every Room has two Passages in and out, not to insist upon the other Doors for the more convenient Communication. There are two Dyals, one going by the Sun, the other by the Water , and not to commend this admirable Piece, when one has seen it, is an equal degree of Stupidity and Ingratitude ; and that tempted me to devote these few Lines to its Glory . And if ever it happens again, that I Bath there, I question not but to hear others as much extol the Beauties of *Hippias's Bagnio,* as I have endeaou r'd to do my self.

Bacchus

BACCHUS

By Capt. Ayloffe.

This with the two subsequent Pieces are but Introductions to some Academical Harangues, especially the two first; the latter being no more than an Exordium.

BAcchus perform'd all his Exploits amongst the *Indians*, tho scoff'd at by some, and pity'd by others, who question'd not but he wou'd be trampled to Death by the *Elephants*, if possible he cou'd withstand the Force and Fury of their Arms. His Camp consisted of nothing but a parcel of Mad, Frantick, Hair-Brain'd Women, that had Cymbals and Drums instead of Bucklers: Long Poles wreath'd about with *Ivy* were their only Spears and Pikes: Their Heads had no other Helmets than a Garland of *Ivy*; *Panthers* and *Tygers* Skins were their Coats of Mail. A Troop of *Satyrs* and *Fawns* came frisking and skipping about in the Rear with Tails and Horns like Goats.

Goats. *Bacchus* in like manner had Horn but no Beard in the leaft, clad all in Purple: His Buskins were gilt, and his Treffes were interwoven with Branches of Vines Loaden with their Noble Fruit He rod in a Chariot drawn by *Tygers*, and there was nothing elfe in all his *Parade* that cou'd ftrike any Terror or Dread into the People For his Commanders, he had one an old broken Nos'd Fellow, always trembling and quaking, his Garment was yellow, and his long Ears prick'd up · His Belly as big as a Tun, and when he was not mounted on an Afs, he was always leaning on a Stick; however an experienc'd Officer, the other was a *Satyr* with huge Horns, his Thighs very Hairy, his Beard and Feet exactly refembling a Goat: In his left Hand he had a Pipe, in his Right a crooked Stick, in this pofture he ran frisking and skipping about the Field, and frighted the Women almoft out of their Wits · He was very active and violent, and when he came near 'em they ran madly after him, with their Hair about their Ears, crying *Evohe*, and acknowledg'd him for their Leader. However, this Frantick Rabble, amongft their other Actions, deftroy'd whole Herds of Cattle, and Eat the Flefh up raw The *Indians* feeing fo ridiculous an appearance, fitter for a *Mumming* than a Battel, fcorn'd to take Arms themfelves, and only *Detach'd* their Women out to engage 'em, that they might not tarnifh their own Reputation by fo unworthy a Conqueft But finding afterwards that this Army, ho contemptible fo ever they thought it at firft, had prevail'd fo far as to fet all in an uproar, for *Bacchus's Javelin* is made of Fire, which his Father had furnifh'd him with from one of his own Thunderbolts, they ran to Arms immediately, and beftriding their *Elephants*, advanc'd full of Fury and Spight to charge the Enemy. The Camps being now pretty near each other, the *Indians* form'd their Battel, their *Elephants* were in the Front of the Battel as a covering to the Troops. *Bacchus* in like manner Marefchald his Forces: The old Gundy-Guts, broken-nos'd Fellow, we mention'd before, and whofe Name was *Silenus*, Commanded the Right Wing; *Pan* the Left Wing, and he himfelf the Main Body The *Satyrs* being all Pofted as fo many Officers, the *Word* was given *Evohe* Then the *Bacchanalians* founded the Charge with their Cymbals and little Drums, and another *Satyr* Winding the Horn. *Silenus's* Afs made fuch a terrible Noife with his Braying, which being feconded by the Yelling and Schreaming of the *Bacchanalians* who at the fame time fhew'd 'em the Spear of their *Thyrfes*, and the *Snakes* that were wreath'd about 'em; that the *Indians* and their *Elephants* fled away in great Confufion before ever they came within reach of their Javelins. Thus were they utterly Routed and Conquer'd, learning at their own fad Expence, that no Man ought ever to flight and contemn an Enemy.

Now

Now you will ask me to what Intent I have made you this Recital. Why, barring the Comparison between the God and my self, I have had the same Fortune as *Bacchus* had ; the generality of Men looking upon my Dialogues as only so many Fantastical Whims and Inventions, do but turn all to Ridicule, but as they come nearer to them, they perceive the Iron wherewith they are *Shod*, from under the Vine Leaves ; and an undoubtable Magnanimity under a Ridiculous Appearance Nay, my Dialogues do more, for they do so gradually insinuate themselves, that at length they all fall a hopping and skipping, even as I do my self As for the Assembly let them please themselves, I shall oblige no Body to give me the hearing, but being in the *Indies* I am resolved to entertain you with the Rarities of the Country There goes a general Report there, that the *Machlyans* who Inhabit the Borders of the River *Indus* down to the very Sea, have a mighty pleasant Sacred Grove as you go down the River on the left hand Shore, which being covered all over with Vines and Ivy makes a charming Shade. There are three Silver Transparent Fountains in it, one Dedicated to *Pan*, t'other to *Silenus*, and the third to the *Satyrs*. Of the first of these the Younger People Drink, the Old Folks of the next, and Children of the third. The whole Country coming Yearly to them upon this account. To tell you what was the Consequence of their Drinking wou'd be Foreign

reign to my intent, the Old Men only make to my matter, who remain'd befotted and infenfible for fome time, not being capable of uttering one word: Tho fome time after they burft out into fuch a Torrent of Eloquence, that may not unworthily ftand in competition with the Storms and Thunders of *Homers* Orator, and they labour'd under this Fury till Night. Tho what is yet more remarkable, if they happen not to finifh any Difcourfe they had began, the next Year they begin again juft where they broke off, and fo finifh their firft Defign. 'Twould be fuperfluous to bring this Comparifon home , for you cannot but be fenfible how I lafh my felf in it. And if I have alledged any thing that has difturb'd you, impute it all to the Infpiration of the God , if otherwife, charge it upon the *Dofe* which for the generality diftracts the Senfes and confounds our Underftanding.

An Encomium on F L I E S.

THE *Flie* has, as much the advantage in its fize over the *Gnat* and fuch like Infects, as it wants it in competition with the *Bee*. And as it may be reckon'd among the Kingdom of Birds, fo the Beauty and Delicacy of its Wings, as far excels thofe of other Birds, as Linnen or Woollen is inferiour to Silk , it is not cover'd with Feathers like other Fowls, but has a fine

Lawn

Lawn like the *Grashopper*, and when you see it in the Sun-shine, there is as great a variety of curious Colours as in a *Pea-Cocks* Tail, or a *Pigeons* Neck. It does not fly by the strength of its Wings as Birds do, nor by skips as the *Grashopper*, but turns in a moment, the sound of its flight is not so rough as that of *Wasps* or *Drones*, but bears the same disproportion as the Trumpet to the Pipe. Its Eye is large and even with the Head, which is hard and shines like Horn, being not fastned to the Body as the *Grashopper's* is, but continu'd by a Neck that moves every way. Its Body is joyn'd together, its Legs long, tho the *Wasps* are short, several shining divisions cover the Belly like Plates of a Coat of Armour; it does not hint like *Bees* with a Sting; but has a small Trunk that does the Office of a Mouth, having at the end of it a sort of Tooth, and 'tis with this that it wounds and draws up Blood or Milk, tho without any great pain It has six Legs in all, the two foremost supplie the want of Hands, with these he Scours and Dresses himself, and feeds himself besides, with the other four it executes the same Offices as Men employ then's to. Its Original is base, being engender'd by Putrefaction; 'tis at first but a Worm, then by little and little it turns to a Bird shooting out its Legs and Wings, after it has engender'd, it produces another Worm, that in Process of time becomes a *Flie* likewise. It is in Men's Company as long as it lives, and takes the freedom to taste of all his Food, Oyl only

excepted

excepted, becaufe it is Poifon to him. And tho' its Life is but fhort, for the Fates have allowed him but a very little Line, it feems to *live* only in the Light, and is feen flying about only in that; for it refts all Night, when it neither flies, nor fings, nor moves.

I might fay, that his Prudence is not fmall, when he flies his ambufh'd Enemy the Spider: For he difcovers him in Ambufcade, and ob-ferves him, declining his Force leaft he be caught in his Net, and fall into the Mefhes of the little Beaft. I need not fay much as to his Strength or Courage; fince *Homer,* the greateft of all the Poets, when he con-fidered how he fhou'd praife the moft excel-lent of Hero's, he compares not his Strength and Vigour to a Lion, Pard, or Boar, but to the conftant and intrepid Mind and Bold-nefs of a Flye. For he fays, that he is not rafh, but Bold and Confident; for tho' you remove, and drive him away, he yet will not be gone, but hovers about feeking the Means of giving his Bite. But *Homer* is fo large in the Praife of the Flye, and is fo very fond of him, that he mentions him not once or fel-dom, but frequently, and in many places, fo much does the fpeaking of him adorn his Verfe. For here he defcribes his gregarious Flight to the Milk; and when he compares *Minerva* declining the Dart from any Mortal Part of *Menelaus,* to a Mother careful of her fleeping Child, a Fly is again brought for an Example: Befides, he adorns them with a very pretty Epithet calling them *Sweet,* and their Flock *Nations.*

But he is so Strong and of such Force, that by his Bite he inflicts a Wound, not only in a Man's Skin, but in that of an Ox and Horse. They say, that he is likewise troublesome to the Elephant, when he gets into his Wrinkles, and with his little Probescis makes an Incision in proportion to his bigness.

As for their Venereal Affairs, their Enjoyments and Marriages are far from being confin'd, but are extreamly free: Nor does the Male, like the Cock, descend almost as soon as he has mounted his Hen; but is long carri'd by his Female who bears her Husband; nay they flye in this Act, nor does the Flight destroy this aerial Conjunction.

When you pull off the Head of a Flye, the Trunk of the Body lives sometime after. but I must not pass over in silence that which is the most observable in the Nature of Flyes· And this only seems in his Book *de Anima* to have escap'd the Divine *Plato*, their *Immortality*. For if you throw Ashes on a dead Flye it will revive, and begins a new Race of Life, for it is indeed an entire new Life to him So far that it seems very plain to all Men, that he has an immortal Soul, which having wander'd aside returns, knows its own Body, enters and makes the Flye take Wing again and proves the Fable of *Hermotimus* the *Clazomenian* to be true, that is, that his Soul often leaving him, was wont to take a Progress by it self, and returning again, entred the Body and reviv'd *Hermotimus*.

Tho'

Tho' the Flye be a sort of idle lazy Creature, yet he reaps the Fruit of the Labour of others, and every where finds a full Table. For him are Goats Milk'd, and the Bees make Money for the Flyes as well as Men. For him does the Confectioners make their Sweet-meats, who tastes them before the Kings themselves, with whom they feast marching about the Table, and eats with them in all things.

He builds his Nest or Hovel, not always in one place, but taking a wandring Flight like the Journies of the *Scythians*, he makes his House and his Bed wherever Night overtakes him. But in the Dark, as I have already observ'd, he does nothing, for he will do nothing secretly, nor does he think any thing done by him base, which done in the Light wou'd not be a dishonour to him.

The Fable tells us, that the Fly was originally a very beautiful, but very loquacious Woman, a perpetual Tattler, and a Singer into the Bargain, and that she was Rival to the Moon in her Love with *Endymion*; And when she daily wak'd the drowsie Youth with Toying, Singing, and wantoning on his Body, she disoblig'd him, and the *Moon* being in a Rage at her, turn'd her into a Fly; And for this Reason she still seems to envy every Bodys Sleep, especially the tender and young, retaining in her Memory the Sleep of *Endymion*. But her Bites and thirst of Blood proceeds not from her Cruelty, but Humanity and Love. For she enjoys Beauty the way she is capable of, and crops some balmy Particles from it.

There was besides, a certain Woman among the Ancients whose name was *Musca* (i. e. a *Flie*) a very learned and beautiful Poetess; and another a celebrated Whore of *Athens*, of whom the Comic Poet says,

> To the very Heart the * *Fly* bit him.

* *Musca or Muïa signifies a Fly as well as the name of the Whore.*

By this Expression the Comic Grace was preserv'd, and the name of the Flie was not excluded the Scene: Nor did Parents disdain to give their Children this Name. For this Reason Tragedy it self has with a just Praise mentioned the Flie, to this purpose,

> That the Flie may be with dreadful slaughter fill'd,
> She flies with wondrous force upon the Body,
> And Armed Warriours fear her little Dart.

I have a great deal to say of a Flie from *Pythagoras*, were not that known to every body. There are a sort of Flies which the vulgar call Militant, others Dog-Flies, making a sharp Sound with a swift Wing: These Flies are of a very long Life, and subsist all the Winter without Food, contracting and hiding themselves, chiefly under the Roofs of Houses. And there is this very remarkable in these Flies, that both assume the part of each Sex alternately ascending one another, like the Son of *Venus* and *Mercury* who was of a double or mingled Form. I cou'd say many things more on this Head; but I will put an end to my Oration, lest I should verifie the old Proverb, making an *Elephant* of a *Flie.*

Nero

Nero, *Or the cutting of the* Isthmus.

This is a Satire on Nero, *on his Extravagant Thought of cutting away the* Isthmus *betwixt the two Seas, and his Vagaries on his Theatrical Contests with the Players. It is generally Narrative. If this Translation seem defective, the Reader must attribute it to the ill Condition of the* Greek *Copys.*

Menecrates and *Musonius.*

Menecrates. *Musonius,* Does that cutting of the *Isthmus,* which the Tyrant undertook, appear to you to proceed from a *Greek* Mind, or any greatness of Soul?

Muso. Oh! *Menecrates,* you must know that *Nero* had still greater Thoughts, than this: For he design'd to deprive the Sailers of all beyond *Malea,* by cutting through the *Isthmus* twenty Furlongs.

Menec. This was to be done, I suppose, for the benefit of the maritime as Inland Trading Towns. For if the Sea-Ports are in a flourishing Condition, the Inland Cities will be sufficiently provided by the Product of the Country. But I pray you, *Musonius,* give me an Account of every Particular, for

I have a great mind to hear the whole, unless you have otherways engag'd your Time.

Muso. I shall give you the Narration, since you seem to desire it. For I am satisfied that I shall more oblige them who are come to this pleasing Place for the sake of their Study.

The Songs of *Greece* drew *Nero* into *Achaia* as well as his Opinion of his own excellent Voice, and Performance in Singing, in which he imagin'd that he excell'd even the Muses themselves. He design'd, besides, to be Crown'd in the *Olympian* Games, famous for the Contests of Wrestlers, for he thought, that most of what was performed in the *Pythian* belong'd more to him than to *Apollo*, and that *Phœbus* durst not contend with him either in Viol or the Lute. But the *Isthmus* was not thought of by him before, nor had he any premeditated Design in it, but having viewed the Nature of the Place, he conceiv'd this Magnificent Work in his Mind, proposing to himself the King of the *Grecians*, who formerly went to the Siege of *Troy*, for his Example, who cut *Eubœa* from *Beotia*, letting in the *Euripus* betwixt them: and *Darius*, who making an Expedition against the *Scythians*, joined the *Bosphorus* with a Bridge. For perhaps he had before thought of the Exploit of *Xerxes*, which was the most Magnificent of Magnificent Works. But above all these Considerations, He imagined, that by these Means the *Greeks* wou'd be sufficiently

ficiently defended against all Foreign Invaders. For the Minds of Tyrants are often Drunk. But going into the Theatre he Sung a Hymn to *Amphitrite* and *Neptune*, and another short Song of *Melicerta* and *Leucothea*. But having a Golden Spade given into his Hands, and *Greece* being as it were committed to his Patronage and Protection, he march'd out to Digging, all the People following with Huzza's and Songs, but having Thrice, I think, struck the Earth, and given Command to those to whom the Surveyership and Guidance was committed to take Care of the Work, he return'd to *Corinth*, fancying that he had by this surpass'd all the Labours of *Hercules*. The Prisoners and Criminals that were in Chains were so ordered to cut the most difficult and Rocky parts, and the Soldiers Dug those which were most Plain and Easy. But when we had now been about Twelve Days ty'd as it were to the *Isthmus*, there arose a sort of uncertain and obscure Rumor that came from *Corinth*, that *Nero* repented his attempt of cutting the *Isthmus*. It was reported that the *Ægyptian* Geometricians had discover'd in their Measuring the Heights and Depths of each Shore that the Surface of the Sea was not of an equal Height. That having found that side towards *Lechæum* the highest, they were in pain for the Island of *Egina*. For it was much to be fear'd that if so great a Sea shou'd be let in just against the Island it wou'd be Buried in the Waves. But had *Thales* himself, tho' the Wisest of Men, and most Skill'd in Nature

S f 4

been,

been by, and perfuaded him, his Authority had not been fufficient with *Nero* to make him lay afide his Defign of cutting through the *Ifthmus*. For he was more fond and ambitious of this Exploit, than even of Singing in Publick. But the Truth of the Story was, that the Commotions of the *Weftern* Nations and the inveterate and turbulent Raifer of them (whofe name was *Vindex*) recall'd *Nero* from *Greece* and the *Ifthmus*, having made fo infipid a Dimenfion of the Seas as a Pretence. For of my own knowledge the two Shoars are of equal Height, and the two Seas Level. But it is rumour'd that the *Roman* Power and Grandeur is now in its Wain, and by Degrees declines and falls away. This you yefterday heard from the Tribune.

Men. But pray *Mufonius* inform me what fort of Voice has the Tyrant, for the Oftentation of which he is fo much in love with the Mufes, and fo fond of the *Olympic* and *Pythic* Games? For fome of thofe who come to *Lemnos* Praife it, and fome Ridicule it.

Muf. Truly, I think him neither admirable nor ridiculous for his Voice, for Nature has made him without much room for finding Fault, and therefore Indifferent. By a Guttural Preffure he makes a fort of Hollow Sound, tho' not by Nature, and by this means he makes himfelf Sing fome of our fineft Compofitions. When he is diffident of himfelf he grows alert by the true Accents of the Notes. He is the beft Performer of the

plea-

pleafantnefs and eafy modulation of the Airs, and the Accommodation of them to the Lute, the rifing, the going, the ftanding ftill, and the feveral motions on this occafion, are fuch that he feems to have no other fhame, but that he appears to be a King But when *Nero* attempts to imitate any of thefe things we have mentioned here what a general Laugh enfues, tho' under fo terrible an apprehenfion of Laughing at him.   For he nods or bows himfelf too much forward, and when he draws his Breath he raifes himfelf on his very Tiptoes like thofe who whirle a Wheel about. But being by nature of a Ruddy Complexion he grows much more Red when his Face is heated by thefe Motions.   He is but of an indifferent Breath, and that fcarce fufficient on ordinary Occafions without fo forcible an Exercife of it.

Men.   But what is the meafure of their Conduct *Mufonius*, who enter the Lifts with him and prefume to contend for the Prize? I fuppofe they pay a Compliment to his Art?

Mufo.   They do the fame Service to him in this Art as thofe do who Wreftle with him.--But *Menecrates* confider how a certain Tragedian perifh'd in the *Ifthmian* Games, for the Dangers are equal to any one who exerts his Skill and Abilities in any of the Arts, that there are Prizes for in the *Grecian* Games.

Men.

Men. What is this you hint at *Musonius?* for I am entirely ignorant of the Matter.

Muso. Prepare then to hear a thing of equal Absurdity and Insolence, and yet done openly in the Face of all *Greece.* For tho' it is an Establish'd Law of the *Isthumian* Games that there be no Prizes or Contentions in Comedy or Tragedy there, *Nero* was pleas'd to make himself Victor in Tragedy. Many there were who enter'd the List on this occasion, but among the rest there was an Actor of *Epirus,* famous for his Voice and Skill in this Art, and very much admir'd for the Perfection to which he was arriv'd, he exerted himself more than Ordinary, and declar'd his Zeal for the Wreath and that he cou'd not desist till *Nero* had given him Ten Talents for his Victory. *Nero* was highly exasperated at his Daring, and behav'd himself like a Mad-man, for the *Epirote* was sufficiently heard under the Stage in the midst of his Performance. In the midst of his Applause *Nero* sends a Notary to him, to command him to submit himself to him. But the Player fonder of Applause than Obedience goes on in the same manner, or rather exerts himself more and more; extends his Voice, and uses all the most popular Gestures to ensure his Victory. *Nero* immediately sends some of his own Players upon the Stage, as the Men who had only Right to be there at this time. For they held their Ivory Licences which were double before them like Daggers, and so went and seized the *Epirote*, and tying him to the next Pillar cut his Throat with the Edges of those Ivory Patents or Licences.

Men. By doing so wicked an Action in the Face of all *Greece* he got the Victory in Tragedy.

Muso. What do you think? This was but the Boys play to him who Murder'd his own Mother.

Men. We can't so much admire his killing the Player in the midst of Tragedy, by that means to deprive him of his Voice since he has attempted to silence the Mouth of the *Pythian* Oracle, when Sounds and Voices were usually inspir'd, that so he might also deprive *Apollo* of his Voice. Tho' *Apollo* muster'd him among the *Orestes*, and *Alcmæons*, who kill'd their Mothers too, but gain'd by the Action a sort of Reputation, as having done it to Revenge their Fathers Murthers.

Muso. But when *Nero* cou'd not tell any one whom he had Reveng'd on the Life of her who gave him Being and Empire, thought himself affronted by the God, tho' in his Answer he had flatter'd much beyond the Truth. But while we are talking, what Ship is that which approaches? It seems to be the Messenger of good News; for all their Heads are Crown'd with Wreaths like a Chorus that enters with some happy News. And behold one out of the Forecastle of the Ship holds out his Hand, bidding us to be Confident, and rejoyce crying out, if I miſtake not, that *Nero is Dead.*

Men. That he tells us ſo is now more evident by his nearneſs to the Shoar.

Muſo. The Gods be prais'd.

Men. But let us not boaſt too much our happineſs, ſince as the Proverb has it, tread lightly on the Grave.

The End of the Second Volume.

CPSIA information can be obtained at www.ICGtesting.com
Printed in the USA
LVOW110739311012

305199LV00005B/8/P